Learning Group Leadership

An Experiential Approach

Jeffrey A. Kottler

Allyn and Bacon

Boston • London • Toronto • Sydney • Tokyo • Singapore

Senior Editor: *Virginia Lanigan*
Editorial Assistant: *Jennifer Roop Connors*
Senior Editorial-Production Administrator: *Joe Sweeney*
Editorial-Production Service: *Walsh & Associates, Inc.*
Composition Buyer: *Linda Cox*
Manufacturing Buyer: *Suzanne Lareau*
Cover Administrator: *Jennifer Hart*

Library of Congress Cataloging-in-Publication Data

Kottler, Jeffrey A.
    Learning group leadership : an experiential approach / Jeffrey A. Kottler.
      p. cm.
    Includes bibliographical references and index.
    ISBN 0–205–32151–8
    1. Group relations training. 2. Social group work—Study and teaching. 3.
Leadership—Study and teaching. I. Title.
HM1086.K67 2000
302′.14—dc21

                                                  00–027289

Printed in the United States of America

10 9 8 7   06 07

CONTENTS

INTRODUCTION

Quite simply, there is no professional helping activity that is more fun, more stimulating, and more challenging than group work. No matter how much you learn, or how many books you read, classes you take, workshops you attend, supervision you receive, and groups you lead, you will still find that every experience is distinctly different from any others you have witnessed previously.

Unlike individual sessions, group work is a form of chaos in action. In any given moment that you are attending to a single event or client's needs, there are a hundred other things going on at the same time. Group members are signaling one another, smirking or frowning, shaking their heads in astonishment or perhaps confusion. Two of the participants are whispering to one another. What is that all about, you wonder, but not before something else catches your attention. Then something else. Then another distraction. By the time the group is over you will likely walk out feeling exhilarated, overwhelmed, exhausted, and confused—all at the same time. You could spend a lifetime trying to make sense of a single session and still never get a complete handle on all that transpired and what it all means.

What This Book Will Do and What It Will Not Do

Group work is a specialty area that requires a different sort of mindset than other helping procedures. In addition to everything else you have learned about helping people to change during individual or couple sessions, group work involves a whole host of additional skills, interventions, knowledge, and research. Because it is far more complex and challenging than sessions with a single person, additional training is needed. That is why you have a course in group work. And that is why you are reading this text.

Whether your goal is to run therapy or counseling groups, lead discussion groups, introduce guidance activities, use process activities in the classroom, direct meetings or task groups, or even coach a soccer team, this book contains all the basic information, theory, concepts, research, interventions, and guidelines that you will need to get started. It is not intended to provide you with *everything* you would want in order to feel completely prepared for any group situation; that is beyond the scope of any introductory course. This text will, however, help you to begin your efforts under the supervision of more experienced colleagues.

Taking an Experiential Journey

This text is a bit unusual in that it takes an *experiential* approach to the subject. What this means is that every effort has been made to help you apply what you are learning to real-life situations in class, your work, and your life. The helping professions are one of the few professional endeavors in which you have the opportunity to apply everything that you are learning in your training to your personal life. This is no less true with respect to group work. As you become more skilled and perceptive about group behavior and its management, you will find yourself developing far more confidence in any social situation. You will become more aware of what people are doing around you and what their actions mean. You will develop greater sensitivity to nuances in human behavior, even being able to "read minds" by decoding what others are thinking and feeling. You will also develop expertise in guiding others' behavior, reducing interpersonal conflicts, working toward a consensus, and helping others feel understood. While this background helps tremendously during group sessions, such skills are just as useful in your personal life.

In order to master the intricacies of group leadership, you must experience the things we are talking about. It is not nearly enough to merely read about group dynamics, hear a lecture about group stages, discuss ethical issues, watch videos of group sessions, or observe groups in action—you must *experience* the power of these ideas, first hand, in order to learn ways to lead groups. That is why a significant part of your time in this class is devoted to helping you to apply what you have read and heard about. This not only brings the theory alive, but it helps you to find out for yourself what group members experience when they talk about their reluctance to reveal themselves.

Some Legitimate Concerns

There are some legitimate apprehensions you may feel about the prospect of participating in any academic class that requires a degree of self-disclosure or reading any text that encourages you to apply what is presented to your personal life. That is why there are ethical guidelines developed to protect you from the potential harm of dual relationships in which you might be graded not on your professional development but on who you are as a person. You will be relieved to know that instructors who teach group work are extremely sensitive to these issues; that is why they will do everything they can to protect your rights and safeguard your dignity.

I have been teaching the introductory group course for twenty-five years and I quite frankly do not know any other way to help you develop as a group leader without: (1) experiencing groups as a member, (2) practicing concepts and skills in simulations and role plays, (3) personalizing the content in such a way that it becomes real for you, and (4) providing structured opportunities for you to practice leadership behaviors and receive constructive feedback for improving your skills.

There are challenges in meeting these goals for both the instructor and the student. Teaching group leadership in such a way that it truly comes alive is a difficult proposition. It is not enough for you to learn the theory unless you can apply it to actual group situations.

Test performances and essays mean little if you cannot demonstrate leadership skills where it counts most in the real world.

Your instructor must balance the need for realistic, experientially based activities with protecting your safety and rights against coercion, dual relationships, and casualties. Every effort will be made to inform you of risks involved, safeguards that are in place, and rules that protect you against harm. Ultimately, you will be given some degree of latitude in how much of yourself you choose to reveal and how much personal risk you take in venturing outside of your comfort zone. Let me remind you, however, of something that you are likely to say to your own group members again and again: Comfort is not associated with change. The more constructive risks you take, the more you venture into the unknown, the more you push yourself to try new behaviors and experiment with alternative roles, the more likely that you will experience lasting change. After all, what kind of hypocrite what you be if you asked people to do things that you were unwilling to do yourself?

Students thus have their own challenges in this class. Your ultimate goal is to learn enough about groups, the theory, research, and basic concepts, so you can actually lead them effectively. It will do you little good to recite facts, spout relevant theories, or choose correct answers on examinations if you cannot apply what you have learned to help others. That is why an experiential approach to this subject is so crucial.

Your second challenge is to reveal yourself in the class, but not so much that you have regrets or compromise yourself in ways you would rather not. Of course, it is impossible *not* to reveal yourself, even if you decide to "play" the role of someone else. In everything that you do and say, even when you pretend to be someone else, you are still being a part of yourself. In any case, you want to find a balance between presenting yourself as authentically and honestly as you can and sharing more than feels comfortable. Much will depend, of course, on how much you trust your instructor and classmates and how safe the environment feels.

You may notice a paradoxical facet of my advice to you. On the one hand, I am saying take care of yourself—don't reveal more than feels comfortable. On the other hand, I am also telling you that being uncomfortable is necessary for significant learning and change to take place. So, you might legitimately ask me, "Which is it, Kottler? Are you telling me to play it safe, or to stick my neck out?" I am telling you to do both. Ultimately, you have to decide how much you want to learn and what you are willing to do in order to reach those goals.

A Structure That Goes Beyond Basics

This text will provide you with the content you will need in order to develop a working knowledge of the field's basic theoretical foundation. This will help guide your leadership behaviors, help you to make sound ethical and clinical decisions, and more pragmatically, help you to pass any certification, licensing, or comprehensive exams. This text, moreover, will help you to go far beyond those basics.

As an experiential learning structure, each chapter will introduce important conceptual and practical information, and then help you to apply these ideas to your work and life.

There will be *reflective activities* that guide you to think about material in a particular way, considering how it might be useful in your unique situation. There will be *personal applications* that demonstrate how you can take what has been learned and adapt it to situations in your personal and professional life. There are *field studies* recommended that will gain you valuable experience observing what you have read about in the real world. Finally, there are suggested *class activities* that provide structures for you to practice new skills. The overall goal of all these assignments is to help you to personalize your learning, to make it come alive.

What You Can Expect

This text is divided into three main parts. In the first section, covering basic concepts, you are introduced to the field of group leadership. Following a first chapter that discusses the strengths and weaknesses of a group approach, as well as the types of groups you might lead, Chapter 2 puts the focus on your own group behavior throughout your lifetime. What are the roles you usually play in groups? What are your personal strengths and weaknesses as a potential group leader? What are the ways that you can develop yourself, as a person, to become a more influential and effective helper?

Chapters 3 and 4 cover the basic theory of group dynamics and group behavior in such a way that you will understand the ways people typically act. Group leadership requires a more "systemic" approach to assessment and diagnosis. This means that you must look at the *circular dynamics* that occur between people, in which every action affects, and is in turn affected by, whatever else occurs.

Chapter 5 examines the sort of individual and cultural differences that occur among people. You have probably already learned something about the importance of respecting the cultural background of each client and ensuring that differences are honored. This is a much more thorny issue in groups where peer pressure is rampant and coercion forces conformity.

Chapter 6 closes the conceptual material by reviewing the basic approaches to group leadership. Just as in individual or family interventions, there are dozens of excellent theoretical frameworks for guiding your professional actions. You must learn about these various paradigms even though you are likely to stick with only one or a few of them.

The second part, covering practical considerations, begins by considering diagnostic processes in Chapter 7. Whereas in individual sessions you concentrate on a single person's dysfunctions, personality, and presenting complaints, in a group you must do all of this *plus* attend to the larger phenomena that are unfolding. The conceptual background you developed in the early chapters will equip you with what you need in order to recognize significant patterns.

Chapters 8 and 9 are among the most practical in the text. They cover the specific skills and interventions that are needed to lead a group effectively. Chapter 10 introduces a model for leading groups with a more experienced colleague so that you might gain valuable experience under safe and constructive conditions.

The third section, covering significant issues, looks first at special populations you might work with. Chapter 11 covers groups for kids, adults, addicts, and other distinct groups. In addition, you will learn about the different ways groups are conducted in various settings from corporations and schools to private practice.

Chapters 12 and 13 review challenges, obstacles, and critical issues you will face, and Chapter 14 covers ethical issues. You will learn how to prepare yourself for these inevitable challenges in such a way that you can respond appropriately. The book ends, in Chapter 15, by looking at the ways you can apply what you have learned to the larger community. Some final advice is provided for where you can go next to continue your leadership training.

Some Final Advice

I welcome you to this wonderful world of group work. Keep an open mind as you approach the subject with a mixture of excitement and apprehension. Become reflective about your own behavior and its impact on others. Confront your excuses for avoiding action. Work to do your part to create a supportive climate and atmosphere of trust in your class. Take some constructive risks by pushing yourself to go beyond what is familiar and comfortable After all, isn't this what you intend to ask of others?

Acknowledgments

I am grateful to Virginia Lanigan, the editor of this project, for helping to shepherd this unique text into the marketplace. I appreciate the many helpful suggestions of the following reviewers who read previous drafts of this manuscript: Paul P. Schwartz, Mount St. Mary College; William V. Fassbender, The College of New Jersey; Jeanmarie Keim, The University of Memphis; Patricia A. Markos, University of Nevada, Las Vegas.

ABOUT THE AUTHOR

Jeffrey A. Kottler has authored thirty-five books in the field for therapists, counselors, teachers, and the public, including *Compassionate Therapy: Working With Difficult Clients* (1992), *On Being a Therapist* (1993), *Advanced Group Leadership* (1993), *Beyond Blame* (1994), *The Language of Tears* (1996), *What You Never Learned in Graduate School* (1997), *Travel That Can Change Your Life* (1997), *Issues and Challenges for Group Practitioners* (1997), *The Last Victim* (1998), *Exploring and Treating Acquisitive Desire* (1998), and *Nuts and Bolts of Helping* (2000).

Jeffrey is Professor of Counseling at Texas Tech University and at Heritage College in Hawaii and Washington. He has been an educator for twenty-five years and has taught the beginning group course an estimated fifty times. He has worked as a teacher, counselor, and therapist in a preschool, middle school, mental health center, crisis center, university, community college, and private practice. He has served as a Fulbright Scholar and Senior Lecturer in Peru (1980) and Iceland (2000), teaching group leadership theory and practice.

Jeffrey lives in Las Vegas, Nevada.

1   The World of Groups

There was a noticeable buzz in the room when the group leader walked in and took her customary seat. Clearly, the dozen or so adolescents in attendance were excited about the scheduled session, yet there was also a hint of apprehension in the air. The leader felt a little anxious as well: No matter how many groups she ran, or how much time she spent at the helm, she still felt uncertain about what would unfold. Would the kids be in a mood to disclose themselves in any sort of authentic and honest way? What if they wouldn't talk at all? Or worse yet: what if someone had a problem so serious that everyone else became scared off?

The leader took a deep breath and went through a mental check-off list of things to consider before she called the group to order. Remember to talk to them about confidentiality and how impossible it was to guarantee. Discuss boundaries and ground rules. Warn them about the ways that people can get hurt and that they always have the right to pass. Mention the problem of having so little time to divide equitably among all the participants. Oh yeah—most important of all—inspire them to take risks so that work can begin building cohesion and intimacy. Remember, though, pace things at a speed that keeps everyone engaged but doesn't scare anyone away.

"This group hasn't even started yet," she thought to herself with a shake of her head, "and already I feel a headache coming on."

The Challenge of Leading Groups

Welcome to the world of group leadership, a helping activity that is among the most powerful structures available to promote lasting changes in behavior. This is a therapeutic environment that is so fertile, so enriched, so stimulating and laden with learning opportunities that often people can make dramatic progress within relatively short periods of time. This potent atmosphere, however, does not come without certain risks.

1. Casualties can occur far more easily in groups than in individual sessions because the leader has considerably less control over the proceedings.
2. Peer pressure makes it more likely that participants may be coerced to do or say things for which they do not yet feel ready.

3. Confidentiality cannot be guaranteed so that personal disclosures could be compromised.

4. One member who demands disproportionate attention, or who exhibits highly manipulative or abusive behavior, can ruin the whole experience for others.

5. It is difficult to monitor closely how each participant is responding to circumstances during any given moment. Safety is more difficult to maintain. It is easier for someone to hide. Quieter members may be short-changed.

6. Members of minority groups may be forced to conform to majority values that are dominant in the group.

7. Effects often do not last once the group ends.

8. Groups are not the best setting for some people, especially those who are prone to manipulation, control, dominance, intellectualizing, or game-playing. Others who are unusually vulnerable or shy may feel too inhibited to use the structure effectively. Finally, individuals who are brain-damaged, psychotic, narcissistic, or suicidal may also not be the best candidates for a group experience.

For Reflection

Think of a time you participated in a group experience in which you, or someone else, were hurt by the experience. What happened in that encounter that most contributed to the negative effects? Write down a few notes to yourself about the steps that you plan to take in order to prevent similar casualties from occurring in groups that you lead.

In addition to any other cautions that you identify, consider the following safeguards:

1. Do not pressure anyone to do anything for which he or she does not feel ready.
2. Do not allow anyone in the group to speak or act disrespectfully toward others.
3. Check in frequently with each member to see how things going on are being interpreted and experienced.
4. Make sure that permission is secured before anyone is invited or encouraged to reveal him or herself.
5. Emphasize collective responsibility for taking care of one another.
6. Stress the importance of confidentiality and talk about how to handle transgressions.
7. Negotiate clear ground rules of appropriate behavior and enforce these boundaries consistently.
8. Do not attempt any intervention unless you have a clear, defensible rationale for what you wish to accomplish.
9. Work under the supervision or collaboration of a more experienced colleague.

The Joys of Leading Groups

I don't wish to begin our journey together by instilling in your mind a great fear for all the harm that you might inadvertently cause through your inexperience, neglect, misjudgments, or mistakes. It is a good thing to have a healthy respect, even awe, for the potential power of therapeutic groups. It is also important to keep the cautions in mind so that you proceed carefully and sensitively in your leadership efforts.

In spite of the limitations and side effects previously mentioned (or possibly because of them), groups are also ideal places for change to take place.

1. Perhaps more than ever, people hunger for intimacy and closeness with others. Groups provide a surrogate family of support and nurturance.
2. Groups provide simulated experiences for participants to practice new behaviors in safe settings and then receive constructive feedback that can be incorporated into future efforts.
3. Vicarious learning, modeling, and observational learning occur readily in groups in which members can grow as a result of witnessing others do work.
4. Participants learn leadership and helping skills at the same time that they work on their own personal issues. They are able to practice helping others.
5. Groups tend to be emotionally charged environments, sparking the kind of arousal that often leads to change if processed constructively.
6. After experimenting with new ways of thinking, feeling, or behaving in the group, participants receive feedback and suggestions for improvement.
7. Groups are often the most efficient use of available resources and tend to be cost effective.
8. Group settings provide for a diversity of viewpoints and maximum resources that may be harnessed during the process of helping people develop new alternatives.

For a Class Activity

With several partners, talk to one another about the best group experience that you ever had. Each of you should take a few minutes to describe what happened and what effects you experienced. As with any group exercise, make sure that each person gets a fair share of time and that no one person dominates the discussion.

Make a list of variables and characteristics that appear common throughout all your stories. What was it about these groups that seemed to provoke the most constructive changes? Be prepared to talk to the larger group about what you discovered are the most important ingredients of effective group experiences.

The World of Groups

Although so far we have been looking at particular kinds of groups that are designed, by their very nature, to be educational or therapeutic for participants, human beings experience group structures on a daily basis. From the moment we are born, we enter a family group that is designed to offer protection and safety and teach us the skills we need in order to survive in the world. Our species is often described as "social organisms," meaning that we are actually built to function as part of tribal units (Glantz & Pearce, 1989). At least historically, our very survival depends on the strength of our kinship bonds (Wright, 1994). Similar to ants, termites, and herd animals, humans cannot live very well on their own; we have evolved as group creatures who are dependent on cooperation, division of labor, and reciprocal favors in order to flourish (Dugatkin, 1999).

Social cooperation is certainly part of the ways that people earn a living and contribute to the gross national product. Almost all of our work is connected to the activities of others; all of our efforts are synchronized within the context of a larger group system that has its hierarchy of authority and control.

Just imagine what we would look like to aliens observing our actions from above. We commute to work in "herds," congregate together in meetings and consultations, and go out to lunch or to coffee in small units. Even when we appear to be alone, we are actually connected to others through computer or television screens, telephones, faxes, and even our fantasies.

Not only do we spend most of our lives working in groups, but we choose to spend as much discretionary time as possible in the company of others. We live with families, composed of immediate kin or perhaps chosen as roommates. Depending on cultural background, some individuals live as part of larger extended families, sometimes in the same home, but often in the vicinity. Neighborhoods become the next level of tribal affiliation, as do membership in clubs, and organizations, churches, temples, and synagogues.

Humans join hundreds of groups as part of their work, social, or leisure activities. Take inventory of your own group memberships and you will notice that you are part of various teams, committees, and clubs. You go to parties for fun. Even now, as part of your commitment to learn group leadership skills, you are part of a classroom setting, a group that exists to promote learning.

The inescapable conclusion here is that most people are group addicts. We learn best in groups, especially through direct experience in which we can (1) interact with others, (2)

For a Field Study

Look at the ways you spend a typical day. Keep a log of how much time you spend in the company of others—part of a group. Note the roles you play in these various groups. Monitor how others' behavior affects your moods, choices, and actions.

Observe others you know going about their daily business, functioning as part of many different groups. Initiate discussions with family members, classmates, and friends about the ways their lives are controlled by various groups.

observe others modeling new behaviors, (3) find support and encouragement, (4) take risks and receive constructive feedback, and (5) feel a sense of cohesion, intimacy, and strong connection to others. If you think about it, those are *exactly* the conditions that may operate ideally in this group class.

Kinds of Groups

If there are many different kinds of groups that are part of daily existence, the same is true for the variety of groups for which you may someday serve in a leadership role. Depending on your career goals, desired work setting, and preferred specialty, you may be required to lead any of the following groups.

Task Groups

Just like it sounds, some groups come together to accomplish rather specific goals. These include the work of staff meetings, task forces, committees, community organizations, and similar structures that are designed to complete mutually determined goals. They also involve the sort of informal study groups that you might organize to prepare for class projects or exams.

In task groups, while there may be attention to member needs and the process that is developing among participants, the main focus is on completing some assignment or objective that is related to the world outside of the group (Conyne, Rapin, & Rand, 1997). This could involve solving a problem, reaching a consensus, or developing a plan to be implemented.

For a Classroom Activity

Try completing some complicated, stressful, challenging assignment in which there is much diversity of opinion about the best way to proceed. For example, meet in groups of six to eight to determine a new procedure for assigning grades in the class. With a volunteer leader, take about ten or fifteen minutes to discuss various options.

Debrief one another afterwards, talking not just about your relative effectiveness in completing your assigned task, but also about how members *felt* during the experience. Did each person feel heard, acknowledged, and understood? How satisfying was the experience for each member? It is not only *what* you do that is important but *how* you do it.

Now reconvene your group to continue your discussion for another fifteen minutes. This time, however, identify two individuals to serve as co-leaders. While one leader will serve the task facilitation role attempted earlier, making sure that people stay focused on the assignment, the other leader will monitor closely the extent to which members are being heard and understood.

Discuss the differences between two group experiences.

More and more often, companies and organizations are interested in hiring group leaders or "process consultants" who can help various work groups function more effectively, not only with developing better "products," but also helping participants to feel more valued and supported.

Leaders who work with task groups tend to be skilled at not only therapeutic-type skills that are designed to help members develop trust, cohesion, and close affiliations, but also those interventions needed to keep the group productive reaching stated objectives. The balance here is between traditionally male-gendered activities that are focused on content, goals, objectivity, and measured performance, and traditionally female-gendered values that emphasize process, feelings, communication, and quality of experience. The best task group leaders borrow the strengths of each approach so that team members develop characteristics demonstrating commitment to the group goals, involvement and support of the process, a sense of pride and recognition in the contributions, and a feeling of personal satisfaction in the efforts (Kormanski & Eschbach, 1997).

Educational Groups

You are in this type of group right now. Similar to task groups, there tends to be a balance between content and process. In other words, your job in this classroom group is to learn the theory, research, and skills of group leadership, but it is also to experience the process of constructive groups. Your attitudes, thoughts, feelings, interactions, and very personal reactions to the content of the course (and this text) are just as important as the material. The objective of educational groups is to help participants meet desired learning objectives, while also addressing distinctly emotional/social needs.

Almost every helping professional leads some group in this category. Social workers, psychologists, addictions counselors, and mental health counselors run groups designed to inform participants about the dangers of alcohol and drugs. Court-ordered spouse or child abusers, as well as convicted drunk drivers, are often required to participate in groups that are structured to educate them about the consequences of their behavior. Private practitioners and other psychological educators offer courses for the public on themes related to self-esteem, assertiveness, weight loss, and eating disorders. Elementary school counselors run a whole curriculum of guidance/educational groups for younger children, covering themes of conflict, sharing, self-confidence, and values clarification. High school counselors do similar groups structured around career guidance, college planning, study skills, sexually transmitted diseases, decision making, relationship skills, and divorce adjustment. College counselors offer dozens of educational groups as well, customizing the themes to their audience. Family counselors might present short courses on effective negotiating skills, marital satisfaction, or sex education.

Regardless of the setting and specialty area, educational/guidance groups tend to be rather content-oriented with specific lesson plans and learning objectives. They rely on questionnaires, multimedia presentations, group discussions, role playing, panel presentations, mini-lectures, and other strategies that combine the presentation of information with opportunities to personalize the content (Carroll, Bates, & Johnson, 1997).

For Reflection or a Classroom Activity

Pick some topic that you know quite a bit about. It should be a subject that has an emotional component, as well as a content area.

Design a short course that you could teach to a group of people. Include a specific outline and lesson plans.

Build into your structure not only the information that you want to impart, but also how you intend to help participants to personalize and integrate the material into their lives. You might want to consider including focused discussions, reflective activities, skills practice, role plays, small group exercises, and similar structures.

If possible, present a part of your unit (5 minutes) to your class or work group. Solicit feedback from the participants on how you could improve your program.

Process Groups

If the emphasis of some educational groups is on content, another type stresses the process of learning. Imagine, for example, that a teacher is introducing a unit on the American Civil War to a group of ninth graders. The content of this presentation would, of course, be on the facts of the historical record as they are currently known: What precipitated the conflict? What were the turning points in the war? Who were the notable protagonists in the struggle? Which battles were most significant and what were their outcomes? This is the traditional introduction of content material that is deemed important.

Whether you ever work as a teacher, or become responsible for introducing some sort of content material to group members, another facet of the learning includes attention to process dimensions in addition to cognitive mastery. In the preceding example of the Civil War, for instance, the teacher might direct discussion in quite a different direction from the original lesson plan on causes of the war.

TEACHER: "Megan, I notice you seem a little bored during this talk on the causes of the Civil War."

MEGAN: "No, it's not that . . ."

TEACHER: "That's okay. Some of this material can be boring if you don't see how it means something to your life."

TIMMY: [Blurts out] "You mean like sex?"

TEACHER: "Exactly. So let's think of a way that what we've been doing really is related to what's important to you."

MEGAN: "But how could this history stuff . . . ? You know."

TEACHER: "Well, let's all think of a time when you got in a huge fight with someone over something that started out small and, over time, became a very big deal to you."

The teacher moves the discussion from one level of engagement to quite another that involves the students' own experiences, feelings, and values. One could say that this is what *all* good teaching is about, regardless of the setting and context. I'd have to agree with you.

Traditional classroom groups become process oriented when the leader takes the following steps (Kottler & Kottler, 2000):

1. The focus changes from specific information to an exploration of underlying processes that are experienced. "Let's stop for a moment and look at what has been happening these past few minutes. What have we really been talking about?"
2. The learning environment changes from a focus on correct answers to an expression of opinions, feelings, and beliefs. "I know that's why the battle started," the teacher might say, "but how do you feel about people trying to kill one another over their disputes?"
3. Participants are urged to own their personal reactions. "I know that's what the book says, but what do *you* think is going on?"
4. Small talk and rambling are reined in more than ever. Don't let the participants digress, intellectualize, or ramble. Keep them focused on their own internal processes, as well as those of the group. Anticipate that there will be some resistance to this; what you asking people to do is not only difficult and strange, but also threatening.
5. Structure discussions to be member rather than leader centered. In traditional learning environments, most communication is filtered through the teacher. If the room has been arranged in a circle, if members are directed to speak to one another, if the leader downplays authority functions and instead encourages people to talk to one another, the atmosphere becomes more open and egalitarian.
6. As the leader, attend to the dynamics and process of the group. The specifics of what this means will be discussed in the following chapters. For now, understand that you will be looking closely at the underlying meanings of behavior and the interactive patterns that emerge.

If you could listen in on the internal dialogue of a leader who is thinking in this way, you might hear the following reflections:

- "Interesting that most of the boys are hanging back and the girls are most actively involved."
- "The coalitions that have formed seem to discourage some people from talking. I've got to figure out a way to get more kids involved."
- "They seem to be staying with safe comments, afraid of revealing too much of themselves."
- "There's a lot of approval-seeking going on right now, not just toward me but toward those who are perceived as the leaders."

Experiential Groups

In the history of the group movement, the discipline developed primarily from two main sources: vocational guidance groups that were begun in schools by pioneers such as Jesse

Davis and Frank Parsons and personal growth groups that emerged in the forties from the work of Kurt Lewin, Wilfred Bion, and Carl Rogers (Gladding, 1999). It is this second force that spawned the concept of growth groups, or experiential groups, that became so popular in the sixties. Images might immediately come to mind of a bunch of hippies sitting around in an encounter group, spilling their deepest secrets, confronting one another, perhaps even ending up in a hot tub together.

Historically, growth groups were divided into three main types: training, encounter, and marathon (Berg, Landreth, & Fall, 1998). Used primarily in business and education settings, training groups were designed to develop greater interpersonal sensitivity and skills in participants. Encounter groups evolved from a training format to include growth opportunities for people in all settings. Rather than concentrating on skill development, the goal instead was to increase genuineness and authenticity. In the marathon structure, prolonged time periods (over a weekend) permitted more intense, in-depth interactions that broke down defenses and created greater intimacy.

In one sense, *all* groups are experiential in that they provide participants with direct experience—hence the title and approach of this text. That is why the group course is often taught in such a way that you can (1) study the ways that groups operate, (2) increase awareness of your own reactions to various incidents and interventions, (3) analyze and make sense of experiences in light of theory and research presented, (4) increase resources available for later learning (Wastell, 1997). In other words, you find out what works and what does not work based on your own personal observations and experiences. While this data is certainly limited, biased, and prone to "sampling error," it does provide a legitimate source of information to complement what you read, study, and hear in lectures and discussions. In fact, in one survey of social work students who received group training, the most important aspect of their course was reported to be the experiential component including both roleplays and becoming an actual group in class (Clifford, 1998).

Since the encounter group movement, experiential or growth groups have gained a degree of respectability even for mainstream settings. Many members of the clergy, for example, lead growth groups in their churches and temples in order to build greater cohesion and intimacy among congregants.

If guidance/educational groups are on one end of a continuum that concentrates on content and intellect, then experiential groups are on the other end, emphasizing affect and interpersonal engagement. They stress (1) learning through doing instead of merely talking about issues, (2) role playing and rehearsal of new skills, (3) the primacy of direct experience that comes from increased awareness and action, and (4) structured practice until new skills become part of one's normal functioning (Johnson & Johnson, 2000).

Much of the negative publicity surrounding this type of group during the encounter group era were attributed to casualties that occurred as a result of poorly trained leaders, little screening of participants, and unchecked coercion of members (Yalom, 1995). Nowadays, in *any* group, efforts are made to safeguard members through appropriate screening, informed consent (letting members know the risks involved), clear boundaries, prevention of dual relationships, and protecting the rights of individuals to pass.

Experiential types of growth groups tend to have certain characteristics that distinguish them from others. They are more focused in the present rather than the past. Members tend to be reasonably well adjusted and working on general growth issues rather than specific problems. The focus is on interaction between members, providing opportunities for feedback and practice of new behaviors. Members are invited to concentrate on self-disclosure, risk taking, and being as authentic and genuine as possible with one another.

One experiential growth group might look something like this:

LEADER: "We were talking earlier about fears of being closer to one another and how this pattern plays itself out in other relationships."

TOMAS: "Yeah. Well, it's just not part of my culture for men to be that intimate, if you know what I mean."

CAROLE: [Laughs] "Yeah, that's our loss."

TOMAS: "Hey, no call for that stuff!"

LEADER: "Tomas, talk to Carole about how you're feeling right now after that comment."

TOMAS: "It's just that she always jumps on me . . ."

LEADER: [Pointing] "Tell Carole."

TOMAS: "Why you dig at me like that? I never did anything to you before."

CAROLE: "No, you misunderstand, Tomas. I like you. I *really* like you. I'm just frustrated because you won't let me get close to you."

LEADER: "Kia, I noticed you nodding your head while Carole was talking to Tomas. Perhaps you could talk to Tomas as well about how you see him."

You can see quite readily that the emphasis in this type of group is helping participants to learn more about themselves and about the ways they interact with others. While the interaction above could easily have occurred in other types of groups we will discuss, it illustrates the main ingredients of an experiential growth group in which members work on becoming aware of issues in themselves, others, and their interactions.

Self-Help Groups

While, strictly speaking, you won't be leading this type of group, it is still important to know how they work so you can make use of their resources. This is particularly the case, considering that there are currently over a half million such groups currently operating in North America alone (Gladding, 1999).

Perhaps the most well known of all such groups are Alcoholics Anonymous and Narcotics Anonymous. Capitalizing on the same powerful factors that operate in any group—sense of belonging, mutual support, and sharing—self-help groups are blossoming in almost every community and setting. There are groups for the recently divorced, frustrated parents, cancer or HIV victims, and people trying to lose weight, to mention just a few.

Self-help groups do not have professional leaders present, although they may rotate the leadership role. In addition, they differ significantly from other therapeutic kinds of groups that you will most likely be leading. Highlighted in Table 1–1, there are several distinctions to remember (Corey, 2000).

TABLE 1–1 Distinctions Between Self-Help and Therapeutic Groups

Self-Help Groups	Therapeutic Groups
Rotated leadership among members	Professional leaders
Leader role as peer facilitator	Leader role as consultant and expert
Single issue as focus (addictions, divorce, etc.)	Multiple issues are addressed
Homogeneous membership with shared problem	Heterogeneous membership
Emphasize inspiration and support	Emphasize understanding and action
Function as surrogate family and support	Function as catalyst for change
Tend to be open-ended and ongoing	Tend to be time-limited
Accepting and supportive climate	Climate parallels real world
Often have political agenda	Attention toward changing members rather than society

If you are ever called upon to lead a self-help group, or train others to do so, you might wish to keep the following guidelines in mind (Gladding, 1999):

1. Balance the amount of structure so that everyone participates constructively but without stifling spontaneity.
2. Make sure that everyone is respectful toward one another and that people are not cut off. Likewise, distribute the time equitably.
3. Model the kinds of disclosures and behaviors that you want others to follow.
4. Offer help from your own experiences rather than from a position of authority or expert.
5. Make members accountable so that they are applying what they are learning in their outside lives.

For Personal Application

Attend a self-help group in some area of interest or need to you. This could be related to lifestyle (Weight Watchers), addictions (AA, NA), support (Alanon, loss), or even leisure and entertainment (book club).

During your visits, examine the ways that effective members make the most of the experience.

Counseling Groups

There is considerable debate in the field as to whether there are meaningful differences between counseling and therapy. With respect to group work, it is generally accepted that counseling groups tend to be relatively short-term, focused on adjustment issues, and designed for relatively normal-functioning individuals, whereas therapy groups are suited for inpatient settings or with more severely disturbed populations that require longer-term care. These distinctions become quite complex when you consider the varied professional training of group leaders, who may come from social work, psychology, nursing, counseling, family therapy, psychiatry, human services, organizational development, or education, and thus may have preferences for what they call their work. That is one reason in this text I have been using the term "group leader" (rather than group therapist or counselor) so as to be inclusive of different fields. Furthermore, regardless of whether the activity is called counseling or therapy, virtually identical processes are going on.

Counseling groups (and most therapy groups as well) create an environment that is designed to simulate the real world as much as possible. Members work on specific problems they are experiencing, often in concert with others who may be experiencing similar difficulties. Counseling groups are aimed not only at "fixing" current problems, but also preventing others in the future.

As far as what you might expect in such a group, the experiences often begin with a "check-in," in which each member briefly talks about what has transpired during the preceding week and reports on progress made related to previous sessions. Depending on the length of the sessions (40 to 50 minutes in a school, one hour in some community agencies, one and a half to three hours in other settings), several members receive specific help in the group working on their identified difficulties. Typically, members act as co-leaders, being guided by the leader as to appropriate behaviors that are most useful. Often, members identify strongly with the person receiving attention and may choose to share their own experiences or reflections related to the theme. Sometimes, a core theme may evolve in a given session and many individuals will talk about their issues related to love, rejection, failure, or a similar subject. The session usually ends with each member doing a "go-around," talking about what they are leaving with and what they intend to do during the next week to apply what they have learned.

Ideally, counseling groups are designed to be as heterogeneous as possible, with the greatest possible diversity in cultural background and experience so that more varied resources are available for members. Screening is usually done to make sure that each member is suitable for the group and will be a compatible team member. Such groups are often limited to a specified period of time—ten weeks, one semester, six months.

Peering into a counseling group in action, we join them during the fifth session, smack in the middle of the "working stage."

> MYRA: "My father doesn't listen to me at all. My mother . . . I wish she didn't listen at all, cause she's just a pain in the butt."
>
> CAL: [Laughs] "Hey, I know what you mean. My ole man . . ."
>
> LEADER: "Wait a sec, Cal. I don't think Myra was finished yet."
>
> MYRA: "That's okay. I was pretty much done. It's just that . . . I don't know . . . It's just that I was thinking about maybe leaving home."
>
> MIDGE: "Way to go, girl! Don't take any crap outta them!"
>
> LEADER: "Myra, you're getting a lot of support from Midge and Cal and others. If you look around the room you'll see almost everyone is with you right now. I guess my concern for you is what the consequences will be if you move out of the house right now. Maybe we could spend a few minutes looking at that. Anyone have some input for Myra?"

It appears as if this group is problem solving on behalf of one member who apparently is prepared to leave home without much of a plan. There is actually far more than that going on in the group. Almost all the adolescents in attendance can relate to Myra's problems with her parents. Even those who are getting along with family at home can still identify with the experience of not feeling understood and valued. While they are helping Myra sort out her problem at home, they are each looking at their own lives and what they can do to make things better. Furthermore, they are developing a level of trust and intimacy with one another that feels wonderful during these times when they often feel so alone.

For a Field Study

Interview several different people who have participated in counseling or other therapeutic/growth groups. Find out what it was about the experience that made the most difference to them. Ask them to describe in vivid detail some of the most memorable moments of the group.

Inpatient Therapy Groups

Therapy groups, whether led in outpatient or inpatient settings, are suited for those with more severe disorders. In some cases, members may have essentially the same problems as those in counseling groups (depression, anger, anxiety, physical complaints), only the severity of their symptoms is more pronounced and their duration may be more chronic.

Therapy groups are longer-term treatments than the other groups that have been presented, often lasting months, if not years. They are generally led by professionals who have more advanced training since they are often dealing with disorders that may require medication, hospitalization, or other medical interventions. In more remote settings, sometimes those with paraprofessional training are called upon to lead groups with the most disturbed populations.

Inpatient groups are an integral part of most mental health programs, whether for those patients with mental disorders, chronic addictions, or other severe emotional disturbances. The groups are often structured so as to provide daily (or at least a few times per week) support and to complement work being done during individual sessions.

Just as in other forms of group work, there are many different models employed in inpatient groups. Some approaches help participants learn coping or interpersonal skills; others attempt to create a surrogate family to work through issues from the past; still others teach problem solving strategies (Brabender & Fallon, 1993).

When working with members who are diagnosed with so-called personality disorders or psychotic symptoms, it is more important than ever to enforce firm boundaries and limits to make sure that things remain in control. While most texts advise against group therapy as the treatment of choice for those who act out in dramatic ways, the reality is that many institutions use these structures because of a staff shortage. It is possible, however, to accomplish a number of limited goals with this population, as illustrated below:

LEADER: "Who would like to tell us about something you did since our last meeting that made you feel really good?"

KIMBA: "I whacked off."

TANYA: "Gross!"

MICHAEL: "Whacka . . . Whacka . . . Whacka . . ."

LEADER: "Okay guys. Enough of that."

TANYA: "But that idiot . . ."

LEADER: "Remember our rules about no name calling and no sex talk just to shock people?"

KIMBA: "But it did feel pretty good. And that's what you asked us."

LEADER: "All right. Listen up everyone. One person talks at a time. Kimba, you volunteered first so you get to tell us about one thing you accomplished since our last session."

KIMBA: [Sulks and looks down]

LEADER: "Your feelings are hurt now. Say what you're feeling like we practiced earlier."

While this might seem like a scene out of a situation comedy, leading therapy groups with more disturbed populations does present some volatile, unpredictable, and chaotic situations. Goals are kept modest. Lots of structure is introduced. Members are held accountable for their behavior. Lots of work is done on social skills and learning more appropriate ways of communicating.

Universal Therapeutic Factors in Groups

Before you start to feel overwhelmed with all the theories and styles of group leadership, you should know that efforts have been made to look at some of the common factors that operate in groups. Among all the various formats just reviewed, there are some obvious differences in their intent, structure, process, and leadership style. Nevertheless, almost all groups contain similar ingredients (Kottler, 1994a; Yalom, 1995).

For Reflection

Before reading the next section, consider on your own what you believe are the most important elements in life-changing groups. Based on your own experiences during the times you have made the most transformative changes, as well as the observations you have made about others, which factors do you think contribute to why people change in groups?

- *Support.* Above all else, groups make it possible for people to explore the unknown. There is a feeling that even if you fall flat on your face, there will be others to break the fall and help you to recover.
- *Sense of belonging.* Most people feel very alone, especially when they are experiencing personal difficulties. Groups create a sense of cohesion and trust that make it much easier to feel safe.
- *Catharsis.* Groups create a degree of emotional intensity, a condition that is often associated with positive changes, if the arousal leads to some sort of resolution. In spite of what was once theorized, it does little good (and some harm) to stir up feelings just for the sake or expressing feelings.
- *Vicarious learning.* Unlike other helping relationships, group members learn not just from direct experience but also from observation. The leader models effective behavior. Members identify strongly with themes that others explore. Every time anyone in the group speaks, works, or is addressed, others take in what is happening, adapting the lessons for their own use.
- *Awareness.* Group experiences help participants to become more aware of their behavior and what impact it has on others. Moreover, they also become far more sensitive to nuances in others' behavior. Although such awareness is not enough, in itself, to promote lasting change, it does get people's attention in such a way that they increase motivation to grow and learn.
- *Family reenactment.* Groups provide an interpersonal context that is reminiscent of a family, complete with parental figures, sibling rivalries, and struggles for power and control. This environment makes it possible for participants to work through family issues, both from the past and present.
- *Public commitment.* There is nothing like telling a bunch of people, out loud, what you intend to do in order to increase the likelihood you will follow through with your plans. It is so much harder to back down knowing that you have committed yourself to others. Some people elect not to return to group because they are so ashamed by their failure to complete their self-declared tasks, and that should be avoided. Effective group leaders help members to set and declare realistic goals and still make it possible for them to return to group without "losing face" should they not do what they said they would.
- *Task facilitation.* Because people receive less individual attention and time in group, it is critical to help them to translate new insights into constructive plans. It is not enough to talk about problems unless members do something to act on what they have learned. That is why many groups end with a final "go-around" in which members declare aloud what they will do during the next week, and why groups begin with people reporting on what they have done. This mutual accountability is what facilitates continued completion of therapeutic tasks that bring the participants closer to their desired goals.
- *Risk taking.* There are lots of kinds of risking that take place in group, all of which get the heart pumping at high volume. Imagine what is involved in revealing out loud one of your deepest darkest secrets, something you have never told another human being. Picture the courage it takes to tell someone else in the group how much you like him

or her . . . or how irritating you find his or her behavior. Consider the level of risk involved in revealing yourself to others in the most authentic, honest, and genuine way possible. Feel your heart beating harder as you contemplate telling group members that you intend to go out during the next week and make some startling changes in the way you conduct your life. Risking is the heart of group work.

■ *Rehearsal.* One of the unique advantages of group work is that it acts as real-life laboratory for practicing new behaviors. It is possible to experiment with new behavioral options, new ways of relating to other people, and then to get feedback on the impact of this action. Roleplaying and other psychodramatic strategies also make it possible to rehearse confrontations in a reasonably safe setting and then to refine strategies in light of suggestions made by others.

■ *Confrontation and feedback.* In a high functioning group it is safe to speak the truth. Groups are one of the few places in which it is okay to be yourself and then hear how others honestly respond to you. You do not have to wonder how others react: You can ask. You do not have to second-guess what others might be thinking: You simply ask. You do not have to hold back your own thoughts, feeling, and reactions to what is going on (assuming it is communicated sensitively and respectfully): You can say what you want. This is probably the most powerful learning tool of all in groups—the gift of others' honesty.

■ *Magic.* That's right. Magic! Amazing things happen in groups, some of which defy description, much less explanation. In a matter of weeks, participants can dramatically change their lives in ways that could never have been possible in any other setting. The feeling of camaraderie and caring—yes, the feeling of love—become intrinsically healing. For the first time in people's lives, many participants feel heard and understood. They realize they are not so alone after all. They learn things about themselves that they never believed possible. The hard part, of course, is making the changes last once the group ends.

Apply This to Yourself

The previous section explores the curative factors in therapeutic groups that lead to growth and change. If you trace your own development from birth until the present moment you will find that many of these variables have been major influences in your own growth. In the next chapter, we look at your behavior in groups, with particular attention to the development of those personal qualities that would make you an optimal group leader.

Review of What You Learned

■ You cannot learn group leadership merely be reading about it; you must find ways to personalize the content and apply concepts to your daily life.

■ People can change faster, but also be hurt more readily, in group settings because of the enriched atmosphere.

- Many of the risks associated with group experiences can be minimized through protecting member rights, providing informed consent, and avoiding pressure for people to do things for which they are not yet ready.
- Although there are many different kinds of groups—task groups, self-help groups, counseling and therapy groups, and others—they all share similar dynamics, processes, and stages. Although their intent and clientele are distinctly different, you can adapt sound leadership principles to any of these settings.
- The most important part of learning to be a group leader is not what you do in class or with this text, but what you do in your own life to integrate useful concepts.

2 Your Behavior in Groups

Group leadership is not just about theory, research, strategies, and interventions, but also about the personal characteristics of the leaders. To what extent can you model what you expect of others? How much of your own charisma, compassion, and caring come through in your interactions with others? In this chapter you will examine your own behavior in groups throughout your life and understand the meaning of these characteristic roles. Being a group leader does not only involve what you do but also who you are as a person.

Personalizing the Subject

If you will ask of people that they examine their behavior in various groups in their lives, then you must be prepared to do the same. There are likely consistent patterns in the roles you have played since your earliest play groups of childhood up to the present classroom group that you are part of. Equally interesting are the different ways that people in various groups perceive you. In some groups you act in a leadership role; in others you are a follower. Some groups find you as a serious taskmaster, while others spark a silly, irreverent part of you. You feel valued in some groups but not in others. Generally, however, you have a preferred interpersonal style that you adopt consistently.

The beauty of group leadership is that there is no single style that is necessarily best. It is possible to be a quiet, reflective leader, or one who is charged with energy. You can be soft or hard, calm or dramatic, serious or fun-loving, probing or cautious, patient or proactive. Of course, ideally, it is desirable to have a number of different leadership options that you can choose from depending on (1) the kind and composition of the group, (2) what is happening in the group at any moment in time, and (3) what is precisely needed by group members in that particular situation.

When I consider my own history in groups throughout my life, I see myself as essentially a shy, insecure, and passive member. Whether in a kindergarten class, a high school social club, hanging out with friends in college, or even in a social situation today, I tend to hang back on the edge of things. I watch and observe what others are doing. I want to approach people but feel vulnerable to rejection. I long for closer intimacy and connection to others, but feel afraid of the increased exposure. I suppose that is why I became a group leader in the first place: It allows me to experience closeness to others, but at a safe distance in which I get to be the one in control.

For Reflection

What I just revealed to you about myself is somewhat risky. You want an author who is an authority, who is poised and self-confident, who seems to know what is going on and can do everything well. I think I am these things (most of the time), but still struggle with my doubts and imperfections.

Note your perceptions and reactions to me as a person. Have you lost all respect for me because I admit my vulnerabilities? Have I compromised my credibility? I suspect the opposite has occurred. When I reveal myself to you as flawed and human, it bridges the gap between us. You are likely to respect and trust me more. Funny how that happens, isn't it? The opposite of what you might expect would occur.

Consider the ways that effective and appropriate self-disclosure actually increase trust and intimacy when you feel yourself reluctant to share things about yourself in this class, or in any relationship. I am not suggesting that you spill your guts every chance you get, telling every little secret and blemish in your life. Rather, I am asking you to consider that even though you will feel some hesitance to disclose your own fears and vulnerabilities, often such actions change people's impressions for the better.

I have transcended my essential shyness and insecurity as a group leader. If you would see me in front of a class, speaking to a large audience, or leading a group, you would see someone who appears confident, poised, and fully in control of things. This is no act: I really do feel on top of things when I am in my leadership role. I have learned to overcome many of my fears so that I can perform at peak levels when called upon. Most of this progress I attained by being a member of growth, experiential, and counseling groups throughout my career and early adulthood. I learned how to get outside my comfort zone, to take risks, to push myself to do things that I fear, to ignore my apprehensions and force myself to do whatever I most avoid.

Paradoxically, whereas I function at a very high level when I am the designated leader, I still resort to old, dysfunctional patterns when I am in strange social situations. I still feel shy and insecure. You would likely see me sitting in a corner. If you approached me, I would be delighted to talk with you, but I would probably not initiate the discussion. I still feel very much like the gawky, stupid, unathletic adolescent boy who was not in the popular group in school.

Knowing these things about myself gives me quite an advantage when it comes time to examine what is happening in groups that I lead. I can so easily relate to those members who are withdrawn or shy. I monitor closely my own reactions to others in the group who are quite unlike me. Most of all, I can separate (most of the time) my own stuff from what is occurring in the group. I have a clear sense of what I have struggled with throughout my life. I know what I want to work on next. And I am good at protecting my clients from my own unresolved issues that might emerge during the intense work that I do.

For Personal Application

Just as I have reviewed my own characteristic behavioral patterns in groups, you would be well advised to do the same. Spend several hours during the next week writing in a journal about your own behavior in groups. Go back into time and snatch memorable images that stand out as representative of your typical group roles. Interview family and childhood friends to get their impressions of what you were like. Review old photographs and use them as a stimulus for deeper investigation.

Write, as well, about your own attraction to leading groups. What personal needs in you would this fulfill? Look in particular at needs for intimacy, control, and power since these are especially salient parts of group leadership.

A Lifetime of Group Skills

You arrive at this professional juncture in your life, prepared to learn group leadership skills, not without some experience in this arena. It is not as if you don't already have some background that will aid you in reading group behavior, responding in constructive ways, and even guiding others in helpful directions. I do not mean to imply that group leadership is naturally developed, because it often is not. Consistent, helpful leadership requires intensive study, much observation and participation in groups, good role models, diligent practice, and lots of supervision. Most of all, it involves the experience of group participation.

The good news is that you already have a lifetime of experience in groups, some of them quite inspirational, others downright lousy and dysfunctional. Based on your own experience (which may not be representative of others), you know what makes a group fun and satisfying, as well as what causes one to be tedious or destructive. Before I present to you what research tells us makes for the most effective type of high-functioning group, first try to figure it out for yourself.

For Reflection

Bring to mind the most satisfying, productive group that you have ever had the privilege to participate in. This was a group in which you were not only very successful in accomplishing meaningful things, getting work done, or meeting desired objectives, but it was one in which people enjoyed themselves tremendously during the process. You all learned a lot.

Construct a list of those characteristics of this group experience that made it so satisfying and effective.

For a Class Activity

In small groups, each of you take a few minutes to tell your story of the most effective group that you were ever part of. One person in your group, acting as scribe, will write down all the qualities and variables that were part of these best group experiences. After everyone has had a chance to tell his or her group story, brainstorm a list of all those factors that you believe were common among your experiences. In brainstorming exercises like this, it is best to come up with as many ideas as possible. Make your list as exhaustive as you can.

In the next step, organize all your variables of effective groups into several categories that make intuitive sense to you. Put each of your factors into one of the categories. Give the groupings names based on a word that captures the essence of these characteristics. Be prepared to share what you developed with the rest of the class.

In reviewing your own positive group experiences, you may be interested to learn that whether we are talking about productive task groups, growth groups, therapeutic groups, or even business meetings, there are some similar characteristics that distinguish them from less productive and satisfying experiences (Corey, 2000; Gladding, 1999; Hazler, Stanard, Conkey, & Granello, 1997; Kottler, 1994b; Yalom, 1995).

Following are some of the signs and symptoms that tell you a group is functioning at optimal levels. Compare these ingredients to those that match your own experience.

- *High levels of trust and safety are established.* People feel supported. They are willing to make mistakes without fear of censure or ridicule. They are inclined to take risks, saying and doing things that may involve venturing into new territory.
- *Individual and cultural differences are valued and respected.* Even with all the peer pressure, cohesion, and conformity that are common to groups, individual differences are honored. Biased or racist remarks would never be tolerated. Members are allowed to be different, their cultural, gender, and individual backgrounds welcomed.
- *Clear boundaries and rules about appropriate conduct are established.* There are few groups more frustrating than those that are chaotic, disorganized, and without structure or rules about what is acceptable and what is not. In good group experiences you know what is expected.
- *Conflict is acknowledged and worked through.* Ironically, the best groups are not those without any conflict. There is always tension and disagreement whenever more than two people get together. The danger is in ignoring or minimizing these conflicts. Solid groups are those that have developed constructive means for members to disagree with one another. Conflict is conceived as helpful when it is initiated from a position of good faith in which participants in the struggle want to resolve their differences.
- *Information and resources are shared efficiently.* You have been in groups before when everyone talks but nobody listens to one another. Effective groups are those

that have developed ways to pool their experiences. Members link their statements to what others have said. Whatever products are developed result from maximum input from all participants.

- *Everyone participates.* In every group there is a tendency for some people to hang back and others to dominate and control things. The best groups are those in which there is shared participation and responsibility. Nobody is allowed to dominate, nobody is marginalized.

- *Acting out is blocked.* Every group has members who are distracting or dysfunctional. These can include those who attempt to be manipulative, monopolizing, distracting, rambling, abusive, disrespectful, and so on. The problem is not in having such members in a group (since they provide good practice for dealing with such annoyances), but in allowing their behavior to flourish. In the best groups, *everyone* takes responsibility for confronting destructive behavior.

- *The group is efficient.* People can have a good time in a group, feel cared for and supported, but unless the group accomplishes its objectives, it has not done its job. The best groups are fun and satisfying, but also productive. All members, not just the leader, feel responsible for making certain that the planned agenda is completed.

- *Nonverbal behavior is consistent with what is communicated aloud.* There is an essential congruence between what people are saying and what they are actually thinking and feeling inside. There is an absence of covert cynicism, criticism, scorn, ridicule.

- *Continuity and follow-up from session to session are an integral part of the experience.* Groups are most productive when they do not have to start over each session, when efforts can be continued from prior meetings. All members, not just the leader, make certain that participants report on progress, assignments, and goals.

- *A healthy culture in the group has been developed.* Every group develops certain norms, or established behavioral codes, that guide how people act. Effective groups are those that have developed a positive culture that reinforces caring, productive contributions. There is an even balance of work and play. Participants feel good about being part of the experience.

- *Ideas result in some form of action.* You have been in groups before when people talk about things but nothing much ever changes. People do not act on what they claim they believe or have learned. In excellent groups, members invest time and energy outside the group to work on issues raised. The most effective groups are those in which whatever was done has lasting, significant effects on the participants' lives.

As you compare each of these characteristics to your own experiences in groups, I hope you are nodding your head in agreement, thinking to yourself: "Yes! This is exactly the sort of group I would like to be part of."

I want you to remember your own best experiences throughout your training in group leadership. You know what it feels like to be part of a group that is destructive or boring or useless. You also know how great it feels to be part of a group that is transformative. What you are learning in this course, and from this text, will only help you to supplement and strengthen your existing interpersonal skills.

A Field Study

Interview several people who know you best, including classmates, co-workers, friends, and family members. Ask them to be as honest and constructive as they can telling you about what they see as your major strengths and weaknesses as a communicator and group member. This will be a difficult assignment, doubly so because it is challenging to get people to be honest and really tell you what they think. Nevertheless, it is invaluable—make that critical—to have accurate feedback about how you are perceived by others and how they react to your behavior. You might prompt them by starting out with a few strengths and weaknesses that you already know about.

"I have an assignment for class," you might begin, "in which I need to find out as much as I can about my interpersonal strengths and weaknesses." Then explain about the class, what you are learning, and why you must have solid feedback from others who know you best and have observed you in a variety of situations.

"I already know, for instance, that I have trouble in large groups. I don't like to talk much and I don't make eye contact very often. I am also aware that I put myself down sometimes, as if I am uncomfortable with any attention. On the other hand, I think I'm pretty good at making people feel safe with me. I think I'm really a kind person, too. So, what else can you tell me that I might not already know?"

By all means, do not think of the preceding example as a script. Rather, it is an illustration of the way you might approach people to solicit useful information. When you are done with your study, you may be asked to write about what you learned in a reaction paper or to report to classmates on themes that emerged.

Group Leadership Training and Personal Growth

One of the truly amazing things about learning to be a group leader is that the more you learn about professional issues and intervention skills that will make you effective in your work, the more powerful and influential you will become as a person (Corey & Corey, 1997; Dyer & Vriend, 1980; Kottler, 1993, 1994a, 1999). Just consider some of the things you will learn in this class (and in the rest of your training):

- How to read people's behavior to make sense of their innermost desires and needs
- How to figure out what people are really saying beneath the surface
- How to determine who is working behind the scenes, and through hidden agendas, to sabotage group progress
- How to build trusting relationships in very short periods of time
- How to express yourself clearly and effectively, explaining complex phenomena in terms that are more understandable
- How to communicate persuasively in order to get people to do things they are afraid to do
- How to mediate conflicts between people

- How to confront people sensitively and effectively so that they hear what you have to say
- How to help people get along better with one another

These are only a *few* of the skills you will learn. There are actually so many more that it takes a whole book to cover the basics. Now imagine all the ways that you could apply these same skills to your personal life. Picture how much deeper, more intimate, and satisfying you could make your most significant relationships. Imagine how much better you would be at getting your needs met. Think about all the ways you could use your group leadership skills to influence people in positive directions.

Not too long ago, I was sitting in a family gathering, bored with the usual discussions about sports, politics, and what everyone's kids were doing. We always have this same conversation, and, while a comforting and familiar ritual, it never gets us past the superficial nor does it build a deeper level of closeness between us. Because I was teaching the group class (as I do every semester), I started thinking about things I might do to intervene in my family gathering in such a way that we might explore new territory together. I started with a skill you will learn later called "immediacy" in which I talked about how I was feeling at that moment about what we were doing.

"Any of you guys bored with what were doing right now?" I started things off. Of course, everyone acted like they didn't know what I was talking about, but I could tell that my brothers knew *exactly* what I was saying, even if they were a bit apprehensive about where I was going to take this. Over the course of the next several hours, I used all of my group leadership skills to encourage us to talk more from our hearts than from our predictable scripts. Every time someone introduced a topic related to the usual things we couldn't control—politics, sports, and kids—I deftly kept the focus on our relationships with one another.

The question you might legitimately ask is whether this is altogether a good thing to be using helping skills in nonprofessional settings. Indeed, the stuff you will be learning in this class is so powerful that you must be very careful how and when you use it. In fact, it is actually unethical and immoral, not to mention highly inappropriate, to use these skills for other than the most benevolent goals. What I am suggesting is that everything you learn to be a fine group leader will also make you a more compassionate, loving, and responsive human being.

Now the Bad News

Whereas the good news is that much of what you will learn is applicable to every facet of your life, this learning will not come without a certain amount of pain and discomfort. Could you really expect anything else considering that what you already know about significant change is that it involves some degree of personal sacrifice?

Although "pain" is defined operationally to mean experiences that are upsetting or distressing, Nichol (1997) traces his own development as a group leader as fraught with anguish. He first reports the pain of anger that some of his peers felt toward the leader who they felt was less than perfectly competent. They felt their own pain that emanated from their daily lives, personal issues that were triggered by group discussions. The prospect of revealing themselves and sharing personal experiences ignited a degree of painful anxiety and self-doubt. They felt pain associated with intense emotions that were sparked during the training, and then became painfully aware of themselves in new ways. It is in the process of facing and working through this pain that Nichol believes that group leaders best prepare themselves to help others in this process.

Must pain accompany your journey as well? That all depends on how you define discomfort and distress. Over the years, I have learned to embrace such experiences when I'm reasonably sure they will lead to future growth. Well, maybe that's not altogether truthful. I don't exactly feel grateful for painful learning experiences at the time; I want to run from them just like anyone else of sound mind. It is only afterwards, when I have licked my wounds, healed myself, reflected on what I've learned, and processed things with others, that I can gain some constructive perspective on what transpired.

If it is your desire to get through your training unscathed and unmarked, you can probably do so. Just avoid taking risks at all costs. Don't reveal yourself in an honest and vulnerable way. Keep your defenses at a high level of readiness. Intellectualize whenever you can. Stay as superficial as possible. Don't think about anything significant, and heaven forbid, don't personalize anything. Even so, you just might escape without suffering pain, or without feeling anything else at all. Remember, however, if that is your goal, then you will be selling the idea to your group members that they should do things that you were unable or afraid to do yourself. If you can live with yourself under those circumstances, give it a shot. I doubt very much, however, whether you can truly hide in a group class that is taught experientially. At some point, you will feel the pain of something, even if it is the fear of being discovered.

For Personal Application

What have been the greatest sources of ongoing pain in your life? Take a brief inventory of the places you hurt the most, including the following areas:

- Failures and disappointments that still linger
- Times when you were rejected or ignored
- Grief and loss over a loved one
- Situations that still make you feel very nervous and anxious
- Traumas you have suffered
- Conflicted relationships that bother you
- Periods of intense moodiness, loneliness, or sadness
- Ways you "medicate" yourself with drugs, alcohol, exercise, or escape

In reviewing the sources of pain in your life, which are the ones you might bring up to work in a group?

Practicing What You Preach

The room was packed with over two hundred counselors, psychologists, social workers, and other mental health specialists who were attending this all-day workshop on advanced group strategies. These were all professionals who led groups for a living; they were hungry for more creative and powerful interventions that might be incorporated into their groups.

I lead workshops just like I teach courses in group work—through an experiential approach that gives participants the opportunity to apply new ideas to their own lives. Frankly, I do not know a more effective way to really learn new strategies in such a way that they last over time. Besides, it is so much more fun to become actively involved in a learning process rather than sitting passively while someone lectures.

I had just introduced a method for identifying countertransference issues (personal distortions in the leader that result from unresolved problems) that might be influencing work with so-called "difficult" group members (these are the ones who do not cooperate the way we prefer). As is my custom, I randomly assigned the group leaders in groups and directed them to talk about reasons why they might be having problems with the same kinds of group members over the course of their careers. I was hoping that this exercise might get them to own their own contributions to the conflicts they were experiencing.

I began the activity by talking about my own consistent difficulties with group members who challenge my authority. I tend to overreact to these encounters, believing my very competence is being questioned. While this may sometimes be the case, more often I feel threatened to the point that I fail to remember that challenging the leader is a normal, healthy part of the group process. I overpersonalize what is occurring, exaggerate the significance of the challenge, and then exacerbate the problem by becoming defensive. Since I am well aware of this ongoing pattern, I monitor myself as closely as I can so I do not end up making things far worse than they need to be.

Self-disclosures like this, whether in groups, classes, or workshops, are most often useful when they are concise and illustrate a particular point. The idea is that by modeling what you want others to do, practicing what you preach, you make it easier for others to follow your lead (Frank, 1991; Yalom, 1995). When such modeling works best, participants feel inspired to imitate what was demonstrated by taking risks and revealing themselves in authentic ways.

I divided the audience into about twenty different groups, explained what they were to do, and then let them go. You would imagine that professional group leaders, so experienced in the benefits and joys of group membership, would be ideal participants in an exercise such as this. Indeed, as I walked around the room and observed what was going on in the various groups, I was not surprised to find many individuals disclosing at a high level and doing some solid work. Just as surprising, however, was the amount of resistance to personal disclosure: Many group members believed (or said they did) that they had no personal issues that required attention, nor could they imagine themselves talking to a bunch of strangers about their personal issues. The very idea of such a thing!

I can certainly see a number of reasons why participants in a workshop would not wish to be very open in groups. Maybe they do not feel it is safe place. Perhaps they do not want to risk jeopardizing their reputation among peers by appearing anything other than

For a Class Activity

In small groups of three or four make a list of all the good reasons why you would and would not want to disclose something very personal about yourself in this group class. Make sure your list has an equal number of items on each side.

Now that you understand what some of the major concerns of participants might be, imagine that each of you will be the leader of a subgroup of classmates. Your job will be to help them experience what a group is like so they will be better prepared to address the resistance and reluctance of their own clients. Plan several strategies together for how you might (1) relieve some of the apprehension that is felt, (2) protect the safety of participants, and (3) encourage deep-level disclosure.

perfectly in control. It is also possible that they do not want to stir things up without adequate time to complete the process. I am sure you can relate to their concerns as you might struggle with a similar dilemma about how much of yourself to reveal to your classmates and instructor.

What struck me about the resistance of some group leaders to participating in an experiential group was the inconsistency and hypocrisy evident in the assumption that "Groups are for everyone else, but not for me!" I wondered how it is possible to operate in good faith when you are not willing to do what you ask of others. Furthermore, how do we face our clients, urge them to take risks, disclose their innermost thoughts and feelings, push themselves to do what is most difficult, when we are not willing to do the same?

Being a group leader actually affords you the opportunity to constantly work on your own personal functioning so that you may live your life with the degree of passion, commitment, and courage that you want for those you help. I love this about our work, although it also terrifies me. There are so many times, every week, that I confront a situation I would rather avoid. Just when I am about to escape, or run away, I think to myself: "Now, what would my clients or students say if they saw me in this situation? They would expect me to

Field Experience

If you have not yet participated in a therapeutic or growth group, make plans to do so as soon as you can. Join a group at the local counseling center or a community agency, or a support group in some area of interest. As I review my own training as a group leader, with all the courses I took at the undergraduate, masters, and doctoral level, all the workshops I attended, all the books I read, all the supervision I received, all the experience I logged as a co-leader, I still believe that I learned the most as a member of a group for a year. It was as a client in a group that I was able to find out, firsthand, what worked best and what did not. I could try out various helping strategies under the supervision of the leaders and receive instant feedback. So can you.

practice in my life what I tell them to do." I start to feel so much like a hypocrite that I cannot help but force myself to face what I fear the most.

When I am at parties or other social situations, where I would prefer to hide in the corner, I picture what my students and group members would say if they saw me cowering. That image is enough to give me the impetus I need to take risks and experiment with new ways of behaving. I would describe myself as a fearless risk-taker because, as a professional group leader, I do not feel like I have a choice. It comes with the job.

The Personal Qualities of Group Leaders

It should now be apparent that being an effective group leader is not just about what you can do but about who you are. Knowledge, skills, a bag of tricks that you can draw from—these are all important. But so is who you are as a person. What do you bring to groups that would motivate people? What personal qualities do you model that others would be wise to imitate? What do you demonstrate in your life that will act as an inspiration for others to follow? Which personal characteristics do you have that you feel most proud of?

I find these questions so important to answer. If it is true that who you are is as important as what you do as a group leader (see Borgers & Koening, 1983; Dye & Norsworthy, 1997; Edelwich & Brodsky, 1992; Kottler, 1994a; Kottler & Markos, 1997; Shapiro, Peltz, & Bernadette-Shapiro, 1998), then the interesting question is what you are doing to develop yourself as a person as well as a professional. Your training program will likely spend lots of time filling you up with content, teaching you skills, techniques, methodologies, having you memorize ideas, master theories, analyze cases, write papers, and take examinations. What program are you following, however, to develop yourself as a more powerful, inspirational human being, someone who leads by example?

Following is a list of characteristics most often associated with effective group leaders, whether they operate in the arena of therapeutic groups, the business world, politics, or the media. As you review each of these personal qualities, assess the ways that you demonstrate this characteristic in your own style.

Trustworthiness

The first and foremost goal of any group leader is to create an atmosphere in which members feel safe enough to reveal themselves in authentic ways. "Trust is created (when it can be created at all) by deeds, not words" (Edelwich & Brodsky, 1992, p. 36). This means presenting yourself to others as utterly truthful, maintaining integrity, and doing everything you say you will do. For many group leaders who live and work in small communities, it is not enough to exhibit dependability and trustworthiness only while the group is in session; wherever you go, people are watching to see if you are one of those "crazy shrinks" who does not practice what he or she preaches. People watch your children for signs of instability. They scrutinize every move you make and wonder if it is evidence that you really are not what you pretend to be. Obviously, this puts tremendous pressure on you to "walk the walk." Part of the walk, however, is accepting yourself as imperfect, fallible, and prone to mistakes.

Self-Acceptance

Often a turning point in every group is the moment in which the group leader is caught doing or saying something that is less than perfect. An error in judgment, an insensitive remark, a miscalculation or lapse—any of these brings a gasp to the mouths of members who put you high on a pedestal, beyond mortal beings.

Whenever I make my first dramatic mistake, I shrug it off and move on. At least I try to. Inside my head, of course, I am berating myself for such a stupid lapse; on the outside, I am trying to show that I accept myself as imperfect (which I really do not do very well). In any case, rarely am I forgiven for my errors, at least initially. Group members prefer the illusion that their leader is beyond mere mortal flaws. They desperately want to believe that we are omnipotent and omniscient so that we might be perfectly prepared to protect them from harm.

In my last group, I made some irreverent remark that I thought was funny. I knew I was in trouble when very few members laughed, and those who did had this sickly expression on their faces. I immediately apologized but I could see it was too late. Now they saw me as human, too. This time, like almost every time, it took several weeks for us to work through this turning point. In the process of showing that I accept myself as imperfect, the group members came to see themselves in a more forgiving light.

Charisma

This comes in many different kinds of passion and enthusiasm. Depending on your personality and interpersonal style, you can be either loud or soft, dramatic or understated. The

For Reflection or a Class Activity

Write in your journal, or talk to classmates in a small group, about which personal qualities that you might develop into a base for charismatic leadership. It is important to be extremely honest with yourself at this juncture. If there is no way that you can ever imagine yourself as the "Elvis" or "Madonna" type of leader, strutting yourself in the most dramatic way, then look at other personal strengths you have that could be harnessed in such a way to communicate your passion and commitment to others.

Since one of the overriding beliefs of group leadership is that people *can* change who they are, become quite different people if they so choose, talk (to yourself or classmates) about the kind of person you would someday like to become. One student expressed this as follows:

You probably look at me now and see a pretty shy and quiet girl. And I know I look so young that I appear as a girl, not a woman. That's okay, though. People tend to underestimate me. But I know I have within me the capacity to be much more assertive and forceful. You haven't seen me when I'm with my brothers, but believe me when I tell you that I don't take any crap from them at all! I want to be tougher. I want to be taken more seriously. I don't want to be seen any more like this innocent girl. I intend to be a wise, worldly woman. Just watch me!

key, however, is to radiate power to the extent that people are inclined to listen to you. You must be persuasive and influential. You must command attention.

Some time ago, social learning theorists like Bandura (1969) discovered there were many ways that models could stimulate sufficient interest in people that they would likely be influenced by a group leader's behavior. Being perceived as an expert certainly works well, but so does appearing to others as nurturing, prestigious, attractive, or even physically imposing. The common denominator is that in order for people to be persuaded by what you have to say, or disposed to imitate what you do, they must be interested in you. Whether you call this charisma, power, passion, enthusiasm, or attractiveness, you must use your personal attributes to best advantage.

Sense of Humor

Group work can be very grim and depressing business. After all, many of the participants are depressed, suicidal, anxious, addicted, hopeless, and abusive. And these are just the groups in the business world. Just kidding!

Humor and playfulness are an integral part of the group experience, used for a variety of purposes to reduce tension, loosen people up, deal with forbidden subjects, build shared experiences, express creativity, and spice things up (Kottler, 1994a). Of course, humor can also be abused, especially if members are scapegoated or ridiculed (Gladding, 1997), or if its tone is overly hostile, mocking, aggressive, or defensive (Bloch, Browning, & McGrath, 1983).

In this context, we are not talking about the use of humor as a technique or intervention in group as much as we are exploring the quality of humor as a personal characteristic in the group leader. You could certainly make a case that there are many excellent group leaders who would never be described as humorous or playful, and this characteristic may very well reflect my own biases as a group member who gets bored very easily (and is an ex-class clown). Nevertheless, playful group leaders do have an advantage over their chronically serious brethren by having at their disposal the means to change the tone of a group as needed. Besides, leading groups can at times be so stressful, draining, and futile that you must have some way to build in comic relief.

Flexibility

This is probably the most important characteristic of all for a group leader. You certainly should go into every group with a plan, an agenda, a set of goals for what you hope might happen. More often than not, however, things will not unfold as expected. In the preceding week, for example, you talked about a theme related to fears of mediocrity. A number of participants spent time interacting around the messages they received when younger that they would never amount to much. Almost everyone got involved sharing examples from their lives in which parents or teachers betrayed them. As an assignment for the next session, almost everyone in the group declared a personal goal they intended to work on related to doing something in which they felt they were excellent. The session ended with people excited about future possibilities.

Now you have your plan for the upcoming session. Check in with the participants on how their homework proceeded. Follow up on Mischa who said she wanted some time. Make sure that Nathan gets some attention because he was so quiet last time. Then return to the mediocrity theme to complete what was begun.

It is a brilliant plan, you think. And you should have just enough time to get through everything on your agenda. Then, the group members arrive, take their seats, and before you can even open your mouth, Cassandra starts sobbing out of control because her mother was hospitalized after a serious car wreck. So much for your plan.

Flexibility is not only important in the way you structure group sessions, but also as a personal trait. Being flexible means being a creative problem solver. It means being able to respond *instantly* to the most subtle nuances in human behavior. One moment you are about to intervene to stop a member from rambling, and out of the corner of your eye (or maybe it was a tiny sound), you sense that an opportunity has opened for a chronically silent member to be cued.

One of the reasons leading groups is so exhausting is because every second, not just every minute, the atmosphere and circumstances of a group change. You have to track continuously not only what the person-in-focus is saying but also how everyone else in the group is reacting, both internally and externally. As if that is not daunting enough, consider that the whole is even greater than the individual parts—meaning that the interactive behavior among participants, their meaningful looks, whispers, nonverbal behavior, connections and interactions with one another, must also be attended to.

I do not mean to frighten you unnecessarily if you are telling yourself at this point that maybe you no longer want to do this sort of work if it is so difficult. Once you have completed this course, studied hard, practiced diligently, you will be able to do this stuff (awkwardly at first) under the supervision of a more experienced co-leader. One thing that will make things go much easier for you is if you develop greater flexibility so you can go with the flow of what is occurring. Go ahead and make your plans, if that makes you feel better, but be prepared to throw away your agenda so that you can track and respond—moment by moment—to whatever arises.

For Reflection

Consider the ways that you are overstructured and rigid in your life. Think of a recent time in which you were unusually reluctant to give up your commitment to a particular way of doing things, even though there may have been several other better courses of action. What would it have taken in order for you to stop the direction you were heading, consider other options, and perhaps take a different path?

What are some ways that you could develop greater flexibility in the ways your respond to situations in your life?

Honesty

Be who you want your group members to be. If you value sincerity, authenticity, and genuineness in your groups (and in the world), then demonstrate these qualities in your own behavior—and not just while you are working. Remember: Group members will watch you very closely to see if you are able to deliver what you promise. Furthermore, they will check up on you as much as possible to find out if you are really the compassionate, caring person that you appear to be. After all, would you trust a leader just because he or she said you should?

In so many groups, participants are hardly volunteers. Many have been referred by the courts, are mandated to attend by authorities, or are being blackmailed by relatives ("Either you go or I'm walking out"). Other members have long-standing trust issues (or rather *mis*trust issues) and tend to be very suspicious of anyone like yourself who seems so helpful.

You are likely to be tested. Group members will watch for the slightest inconsistency between what you say and do, or what you say now versus what you have said before. If you walk through life with a commitment toward honesty and authenticity, you are much more likely to earn the respect and trust of people who have some very good reasons for being cautious.

Compassion

There are other words I could use here to describe the essential caring that must be communicated to group members—loving, respectful, empathic, nonjudgmental, warm, kind, supportive—but what they all mean is that you are someone who is really invested in others' welfare.

Hopefully, you are doing this work in the first place because you want to make a difference in people's lives and you recognize that group work is the most ideal environment to make these changes possible. In your search for techniques and interventions and skills that will make you optimally effective, do not underestimate the power of your own compassion. While it is often not enough to simply care for people (if this were true then we would not need professionals), the relationships you develop with group members are at least as important as anything else you do. Relationships are, in fact, the core of all professional helping efforts (see Brammer & MacDonald, 1999; Bugental, 1990; Derlega, Hendrick, Winstead, & Berg, 1991; Kahn, 1997; Kottler, 2000; Rogers, 1980).

Clear-Headedness

Group members depend on you to be fair, honorable, equitable, free of biases, prejudices, and other oppressive attitudes. They also need you to be somewhat logical and analytic, a steady hand at the helm of the group, navigating through both calm and stormy waters. In addition, being clear-headed means being based in reality, aware of yourself and others.

I have mentioned earlier how countertransference issues, those distorted reactions that leaders have toward particular members, must be resolved fully or people may be harmed. As you look around most any group, you are likely to have strong reactions to everyone present. Some participants will seem attractive to you; others may elicit strong negative reactions. Although some of your personal feelings may certainly be the logical response to provocative behavior, at other times you may indeed be overreacting based on your own distortions and failure to address your own unresolved issues.

Many of the dangers associated with exaggerated personal reactions can be checked when you are working with a co-leader (Edelwich & Brodsky, 1992). Unfortunately, that option is not always available because of strained resources and overscheduled caseloads. As much as it might be nice to depend on an experienced colleague or supervisor to keep you continuously clear-headed, rarely will you receive all the feedback and help that you need. That is why experiencing group and individual counseling are so useful for beginning practitioners: Not only are you able to reduce personal conflict and stress during a difficult time of transition, but you are also able to know what it is like to be in the client's chair.

For Reflection, a Class Activity, and a Field Study

For Reflection: Make a list of all the excuses you have for not seeking the guidance of a counselor or therapist at this time in your life. Make sure to include the old standbys: (1) You can't afford it, (2) you don't have time, (3) if you did have the money and time, you don't really need the help, and (4) it would be too embarrassing if others found out. This, of course, is *exactly* what your clients will say!

If you were going to consult with a professional (for the experience if nothing else), what are some of the personal issues that you could work on? Keep in mind the sort of problems and struggles that people are likely to bring to your groups and what that might trigger for you.

For a Class Activity: Talk to a group of peers about the ways you might profit from a counseling/therapy experience. Share with one another some of your buttons that might be pushed inadvertently by group members. Common areas to explore might include: fear of intimacy, fear of failure, perfectionism, recurrent conflicts, addictions, poor self-esteem, childhood trauma, grief reactions, chronic depression or anxiety, family difficulties, loneliness, career confusion. In other words, we all suffer from the same kinds of things that bring people to our offices.

For a Field Study: Now the hard part. Make an appointment to attend a few sessions in a group or individual counseling experience. Pay attention to all the ideas you have been reading and learning about to see how they arise in your own experience.

Guidelines for Group Membership and Participation

You have probably noticed that I hold a very strong belief that in order to be an effective group leader, you must first know how to function optimally as a member. You must know what it's like to sit in the client's chair, to know what works and what doesn't, to feel the dread and reluctance when you are pressured to reveal more about yourself than you feel comfortable. Of course, you are actually living that role as we speak: You are now a member of a class group devoted to learning leadership skills.

One of your first jobs as a group leader is to teach members how to get the most from the experience. They don't know the rules, nor what is expected. They will do their best to cooperate, but many of their assumptions about what you are looking for may not be valid. For instance, some members will talk too much because they think they are pleasing you. Others will stir up conflicts because they once saw that on television. It is your first objective to provide members with ground rules and guidance for how to behave in the group and how to get the most from the experience.

Some leaders distribute handouts that review ground rules and suggestions for how to behave. Others handle this orientation during screening interviews or the first group meeting. Still others devote the first session to helping members create their own rules, knowing that people are far more committed to obeying norms that they have had a role in creating.

If not all ground rules are established ahead of time, sometimes they can be defined as things proceed:

> **LEADER:**   "Caroline, I see you couldn't get here on time again."
>
> **CAROLINE:**   "Sorry about that. It's just . . ."
>
> **LEADER:**   "I didn't mean to make you feel defensive. I just wanted to bring up the issue here in the group to see how people wanted to handle late-arriving members. What do you all want to do in the future?
>
> **KIM:**   "It's no big deal to me."
>
> **SAM:**   "Well, it is to me. I was in the middle of something when Caroline came in late today. I don't like to be interrupted like that."
>
> **KIM:**   "That's your problem then."
>
> **LEADER:**   "Wait a minute, Kim. Let's allow others to have their say. Is it okay for people to come late? Or leave early? If so, how do you want to handle this?"

Obviously, you can't have a very high-functioning group without basic rules for timely arrival and respect for boundaries. From your own experiences in group situations, you know how distracting it can be if people come and leave when they want. One way or another, you must indoctrinate members into the most healthy norms possible for group behavior.

For a Group Activity

Meet in groups of six and pretend that this is your first session. Create a list of ground rules and guidelines for members that would ensure that the experience would be safe and productive.

Compare your rules to those of others in your class to reach a consensus.

Several authors (Berg, Landreth, & Fall, 1998; Trotzer, 1999) have gone to the trouble to develop written guidelines for members. Such a list might include the following:

1. Speak only for yourself in the group. Use "I" rather than "we."
2. Blaming, whining, and complaining about people outside the group are discouraged.
3. Racist, sexist, or otherwise disrespectful language will not be tolerated.
4. All members take responsibility for making sure they get their own needs met in the group.
5. Nobody will be coerced or pressured into doing something for which he or she does not feel ready.
6. What is said in this group is considered privileged information. Everyone is responsible for maintaining confidentiality.
7. Time must be equitably distributed among all members.
8. Any member who is late more than three times or misses more than three sessions will be asked to leave the group.

These are just a few examples of what might be included in a list of guidelines. In order to develop the most useful and comprehensive list possible, you will not only wish to consult numerous published sources, but also draw on your own experiences as a group member. Whether you know it or not, you are already an expert on being a group member, even if you haven't functioned as optimally as you would like. You know what makes you bored, frightens you, and drives you crazy. You also have some idea of what others respond best to. This limited sample of experience is hardly enough, but it is a great start.

Learning to be a skilled and competent group leader results not only from serious study and supervised practice, but also from your personal experiences—both good and bad—in the role of consumer. Next, we broaden your perspective, moving from your own behavior to that of a larger perspective of how group dynamics typically unfold.

Review of What You Learned

- Group leadership involves far more than what you do—it also involves who you are as a person.
- There are certain personal qualities that are associated with effective leaders. You do not need to be born with these characteristics—you can develop them through hard work and commitment.
- High-functioning groups, whether designed around content or process, have similar structures that balance attention to agendas, as well as participant reactions.
- Group leaders must be as committed to their own growth as they are the development of their clients.
- Much of what you learn as a group leader will help you function as a more powerful and effective human being.

3 Thinking About Dynamics and Systems

In this chapter you learn to think in new ways about human behavior, attending not only to the individual but also to the larger systemic and interactive dynamics between people. Working in groups requires a whole different set of perceptual filters by which to make sense of what is going on. You will look at the bigger picture of how each person's actions fit within a larger context of his or her world, as well as the group. You will not only diagnose individual difficulties but also assess interpersonal patterns, group stages, systemic functioning, coalitional alliances, and other dynamics that are important to understand.

Linear and Circular Causality

The funny thing about leading groups is that you are attending not only to group members as individuals, but also to the interactive effects of how each person's behavior influences, and is in turn affected by, everyone else's actions. Look at your own classroom as one example.

The instructor does and says things that have a huge impact on what happens in the room. It would appear as if you and your classmates react in a linear way to the stimulus of a statement like: "Okay, count off by fives and organize yourselves into small groups." Some students groan. Others eagerly comply, excited that they do not have to sit quietly for the period. You might feel both apprehensive and interested about what is about to occur next.

According to one model, favored by traditional behavioral theorists over the years, human reactions occur either as a stimulus-response, "classical conditioning" (à la Ivan Pavlov) process or as a response-stimulus, "operant" (à la B. F. Skinner) mode. In the former, the instructor's directions elicit an automatic response in class members that has been conditioned over time; in the latter case, a particular response—the instructor's observation that the energy level is low in the room—is conditioned by a stimulus designed to alter current conditions. In both examples, behavior is viewed as linear in nature: One action affects the other in a direct line.

Even contemporary behaviorists now see this as a gross simplification of what happens during complex human interactions (Spiegler & Guevremont,1998). There are not only internal cognitive and affective processes going on within each person that influence how the world is perceived, but behavior in groups follows a much more circular rather than linear path. In explaining what often happens in family therapy, Goldenberg and Goldenberg (1999) describe *circular causality* as the influence among group members moving in all directions at the same time: "Such a reverberating effect in turn impacts the first person, and so forth, in a continuous series of circular loops or recurring chains of influence" (p. 11).

For a Class Activity

In groups of three, identify one critical incident or dramatic moment that recently occurred in class in which many people were affected by what transpired. Go back and try to recreate what might have led up to the culminating event, as well as its aftermath. Rather than relying on linear causality, employ a model of circular causality in which you examine how each person's behavior was both a trigger, as well as an effect, on others' actions.

As one example, linear causality might lead one to say that a student asked a "dumb" question, eliciting groans from classmates, frustration in the instructor, and then shame and regret in that student for opening his mouth. If you look at that same incident from a circular perspective, you identify that many more complex processes were occurring. The student asked the question in the first place because he read a look in the instructor's eye that seemed to invite such an inquiry. The instructor *was* actually trying to encourage more student participation because he interpreted that this particular student was bored when he was really confused, and so the student checked out for a while. Once you bring in the contributory influences and effects of others in the room, you have quite a complex situation, far more so than you ever imagined.

Whether in trying to make sense of what is going on in a classroom, or what started a fight between a group of people, it is virtually impossible to identify who caused what. All group behavior occurs within a context that includes the individual's perception of reality, as well as the interactions taking place, both consciously and unconsciously, between all people present.

Systems Theory

The concept of circular causality is only one of many ideas spawned from what has become known as "systems theory." Developed by biologist Ludwig von Bertalanffy (1968), this approach to understanding behavior was designed to make sense of the way that all living creatures organize themselves and act in predictable patterns. Being a biologist, and also fond of physics metaphors, many of the terms he introduced to describe the way groups of people behave sound more appropriate for a science class: homeostasis, morphogenesis, and feedback loops.

Until group leaders had a framework in which to look at systemic behavior, that is, the interactive patterns and subsystems of a group, there was a tendency to treat group work like doing individual counseling or therapy, but with an audience present (there are approaches to group work that still essentially work that way). Largely, it has been the family therapy movement that has borrowed systemic thinking as a means by which to assess the ways that groups of relatives organize themselves over time, creating stable patterns (homeostasis) that are inclined to return to familiar states (equilibrium).

For Personal Application

Think of a time in your family when someone created a problem or conflict in order to "help" everyone one else resume a familiar, stable pattern. For instance, your parents were having a disagreement, and you or your siblings distracted them by acting out. Consider the ways that your family of origin organized itself consistently into the same, familiar ordered system. Whenever things would become destabilized or chaotic, what roles did you and others play to bring things back to equilibrium?

Most family therapists, who are also group specialists, favor a whole glossary of terms that are used to describe the way family systems tend to operate (Fennel & Weinhold, 1997; Goldenberg & Goldenberg, 1999). Many of these ideas are quite useful in understanding behavior in all groups, not just family systems. As one more example of this, a group member claims that another participant hurt him deeply by confronting him about his tendency to ramble. The confronting group member defends herself by saying that the rambler drives her crazy with his tendency to talk too much. Each believes the other is causing them to act the way they did, even though each is actually both the cause *and* the effect of the other's behavior. I simplified this interaction considerably, of course. Remember that they are both part of a larger group in which there are also other members covertly involved in this interaction, rooting for one person or the other depending on their loyalties.

Group *coalitions*, or *subsystems*, are also important phenomena to observe and identify. All groups organize themselves into smaller units, each with its own set of rules or *norms* that regulate behavior (remember: homeostasis is the key in this model). Each of these smaller coalitional groups have certain *boundaries* between them that control who can say what to whom. In a family, this phenomenon might be readily observed as a father-mother subsystem, another between two of the three siblings, and another composed of the mother, her mother, and the third child. You can therefore appreciate that these coalitions are organized around mutual needs, loyalties, and control of power. When these subsystems are dysfunctional and destructive, such as when a parent is aligned with a child against his spouse, or a child is in coalition with a grandparent against her parents, the therapist's job is initiate realignments in the structure and power, creating a new set of subsystems that are more functional.

In groups, as well, you will observe that members will align themselves with allies according to shared values and what is in their best interests. You will notice this most dramatically when members form a coalition against *you* as the leader, a common dynamic that can be therapeutic if handled constructively.

Not only can you apply family systems ideas to look at the *structure* of a group, but also its *patterns of communication*. A number of group theorists (Agazarian & Peters, 1981; Donigian & Malnati, 1997; Durkin, 1981) have adapted systems thinking to all group

For a Class Activity

Groups are powerful means for solving problems and completing tasks, given the right atmosphere and structure. The type of leadership and members who participate also play a significant role in group productivity.

This activity has two main goals:

1. To practice the art of compromise and consensus seeking
2. To witness group dynamics in action

The first step involves taking about 10 minutes to make a list of what you consider to be the ideal characteristics of a good group member.

Get together in groups of about eight members. Two of you will serve as observers of group dynamics. Your job is to watch how the group shares information, makes decisions, and works towards consensus. You will take notes on what you observe and lead a discussion afterwards about what transpired, sharing your perceptions as well as eliciting reactions from participants.

All of you in your assigned group must come to agreement about what the best qualities are of excellent team members. You have 20 minutes to identify what you consider to be the ten most important member attributes. During this process it would be helpful to view differences of opinion as helpful rather than harmful in your consensus seeking. Just make sure that you budget your time so you are able to complete the task in the allotted 20 minutes.

Under the leadership of the observers, take another 10 minutes afterwards to talk about the dynamics of your groups, especially with regard to: (a) how you organized yourselves, (b) how you shared ideas, (c) how you achieved consensus, and (d) what sort of climate emerged.

settings in which you can observe and label the characteristic ways that members relate to one another. In fact, you can step back from any group you are part of and ask yourself a number of questions about the systemic functioning:

- *What roles are various individuals playing in the group?* Who is placating whom? Who has the power in the group?
- *Which coalitions have formed?* Who is aligned with whom? Which alliances have formed temporarily and permanently? Which members are in conflict with one another?
- *How do members communicate with one another?* Are the lines of communication clear and direct? Where do members direct their attention when they speak?
- *What norms have developed in the group that regulate behavior?* Which rules were established by the leader versus which ones emerged covertly by members? What are the *metarules* (the rules about rules) in the group? These are the ones like: Make sure you don't say anything about bald people or it will piss the leader off.

- *How is information exchanged among group members?* How did people share what they know with one another? Who was excluded or ignored? Which data were accepted and rejected? What critical information was neglected? How was the information synthesized?
- *How do decisions get made in the group?* Who gets time and how is that negotiated among members? Other than the leader's direction, how is it decided who talks and what is discussed?
- *How are conflicts resolved?* Who doesn't like whom? What are the ways that members try to sabotage or undermine one another or the leader? How do members show their disagreement with what is going on?

This is just a sample of questions that could emerge from systemic thinking applied to groups. So far, we have been looking at group systems as they are contained within a closed unit. Of course, each individual, and each group system, is part of an interconnected series of other, larger systems. An individual's behavior in a group is influenced not only by what others are doing in that system, but also by significant others in the outside world, as well as from the person's family of origin.

For Personal Application

Pick a group system that you would like to understand better. This could be your own family, a social group, or perhaps the class. Apply the principles introduced in this chapter to analyze the structural and communicational patterns of this system. You might find it helpful to use a *sociogram* (a tool used by social psychologists and sociologists) to plot out the various subsystems in your group. Use a graphical drawing to display the coalitions, communication patterns, control and power issues, and boundaries in place. You can either make up your own method for plotting and illustrating patterns, or consult standard manuals that teach family systems specialists how to diagram structural and communication patterns (see Imber-Black, 1988; McGoldrick & Gerson, 1999).

In addition to illustrating the group dynamics that you observe, answer the questions listed above to sort out the roles played by various members, who controls power, what the norms (and unstated rules) are, and what your final assessment is about the relative strengths and weaknesses of this group system.

Family of Origin Issues

Assume that the way people act in your group is representative of how they tend to act in any group throughout their lives. Of course, there would be exceptions to this, but generally speaking, people "will create the same interpersonal universe they have always inhabited" (Yalom, 1995, p. 28). This means that people will create a "social microcosm," an extended reality of what they are used to in their outside world. They will negotiate with others in the group for comfort zones that are familiar. They will engage in the same dysfunctional patterns that get them in trouble elsewhere. And they will respond to people not just as they really are, but how they imagine them to be.

This phenomenon in which people's unresolved issues with members of their original family play themselves out in a group presents some difficult challenges and some wonderful therapeutic opportunities. Under the right circumstances and leadership, the group environment can be used to produce a "corrective emotional experience" (Frank & Ascher, 1951). This sort of critical incident occurs once it is recognized that someone is experiencing a strong emotional reaction to someone or something occurring in the group, often way out of proportion to what would be expected. Through member support and feedback, reality testing, and then the increased awareness and recognition of entrenched patterns, an individual can use the group to work though destructive patterns. Such an interaction would look something like this:

> **DOROTHY:** "When I was your age, I never . . ."
>
> **NEVIN:** "What is this crap about when you were my age? You were NEVER my age! I'm so sick of hearing people like you judge me when you don't even . . ."
>
> **LEADER:** "Hey, Nevin, calm down. I can see you're upset with what Dorothy said but you need . . ."
>
> **NEVIN:** "You're another one! Always telling me what I *need* to do. You know what? Ya'll can just kiss my ass. I've had just about enough of this."
>
> **MONTY:** "Nevin, man, hey, the guy's just trying to help. *Tranquilo*, buddy. He don't mean nothing. He's just trying to help."
>
> **NEVIN:** "Stay out of it. This ain't your business either. This is between me and the old broad. She's been on my back since this group started."
>
> **LEADER:** "Okay, Nevin, let's stop for a minute and look at what's going on. Even though I know this is uncomfortable for Dorothy and Monty, I can see that your feelings are hurt too. I think this is important stuff. In all the time we've been together, Nevin, this is the first time you've really spoken from your heart."
>
> **NEVIN:** "Damn right!"
>
> **LEADER:** "And while I applaud your courage to finally say out loud what you've been feeling—including confronting me, too—I can't help but think there's something else going on here as well."
>
> **NEVIN:** "Whaddya mean?"
>
> **LEADER:** "Anyone want to help Nevin with the question?"

You can see how the leader is trying to get other group members involved in sorting out why Nevin reacted so strongly to Dorothy's offer of help, and then reacted rather strongly to his friend Monty's support. The leader has a hypothesis that what is going on right now has little to do with the present members but is actually a reenactment of previous interactions that Nevin has experienced before. With further exploration and prompting, it is discovered that Dorothy reminds Nevin of his fifth-grade teacher, the one who beat him with a set of extra long rosary beads for no reason that he could ever understand. Furthermore, the whole group reminded him of situations he had faced over and over again in his life—a bunch of do-gooder white folks pretending to care but secretly harboring racist beliefs.

It turned out that this interaction was a very familiar one to Nevin. This time, however, events unfolded considerably different from in the past. Once it was recognized what was occurring, the dynamic could be labeled, and alternative responses could be developed.

Reviewing the process that was just described, there will be times when you are sitting in groups and notice that people seem to be reacting not to what is actually occurring but to some perception they have that is more influenced by their past experiences rather than present circumstances. When you notice such a phenomenon, ask yourself the following questions:

- What is this emotional outburst really about?
- What is this person seeing, feeling, and experiencing that I am missing?
- What is it about this person's cultural, ethnic, and gender background that would explain his or her unique experience?
- How does this fit with what else I know about this person?
- To what extent is this person distorting or exaggerating what is going on?
- How are others in the group reacting to what his happening?
- What does my intuition tell me is going on?
- What can I do to help this person become more aware of his or her behavior and find connections to the past?
- What do I need to do to work this through toward closure in the group?
- What object lessons can be generalized from this single episode to other group members' experiences?

For Personal Application

Think of a time recently when you were especially puzzled by the way someone reacted in a group or social situation. The person's behavior struck you as so inappropriate or strange that you could not fathom what was going on. You may have felt annoyed, frustrated, or even angry by this incident.

Attempt to review this incident again, but this time leave your own frame of reference and view the incident from the perspective of this person you did not understand. Try to use pure empathy and compassion to get inside the other person's skin and imagine what it must be like to experience the world through this other's senses and background. Take into consideration the person's unique cultural, religious, family, educational, and historical background. As much as you can, try to be this person, seeing the world through his or her eyes.

Of course, you can never really know another's experience, but using your empathic skills, intuition, and some logical hypothesis based on limited information available, reconstruct the meaning of this outburst in light of this person's background. Remember, this person likely felt misunderstood, so make sure that you describe this situation the way he or she would.

Now, talk to yourself (or to others) about how you could use this methodology, as a group leader or in your personal life, whenever you confront behavior that appears incomprehensible to you.

Interaction Patterns

In groups you will be observing not just how members speak to one another, but also how they behave. This includes their facial expressions, nonverbal behavior, and anything else that provides clues about internal states. It would come as no surprise to you to learn that people do not always say out loud what they are thinking, nor do they tell the truth all the time, nor do they sometimes even know what they are feeling inside. During those times when group members know what they want to say, and intend to be utterly honest in their disclosures, they still can't communicate as fully as they would like. With words, much gets lost in the translation.

As a group leader, you will not only be listening very closely to what participants say, but you will be observing very carefully how they are behaving. Listen inside the mind of a group leader during a typical moment in a session when she is processing the interaction patterns she observes:

Cynthia is saying that she is upset by what happened in her life this week, but she looks like she is almost proud of the attention she is getting. And notice the way her eyes keep flitting over toward Kevin, as if she is looking for his sympathy. But he is ignoring her, turning his body toward Carlos: I wonder if they know some secret about Cynthia?

Trina, over there, on the other side, is not even listening to Cynthia; she seems to have something else on her mind altogether. It looks to me like she is waiting for a pause so that she can say something. That certainly isn't the case with Mai today. Look, she has her chair pulled back, as if she wants to be closer to the door. Candy looks worried about her, too; she keeps trying to get Mai's attention but Mai is ignoring her, ignoring everyone, as if she is in her own world.

The whole energy of the group seems restrained today, as if there is some collective conspiracy not to get into too much. I wonder who has been talking to one another outside the group this week? I've got to get a more accurate picture of what is going on behind the scenes. . . .

Hey, what's that? Is it my imagination or is Megan finally going to say something. Look, her foot is fidgeting and she's playing with her hair. I know she needs an invitation to talk, but I wonder if this might be the moment in which she will jump in all on her own. Should I cue her or not? Wait. I have a better idea. Paul appears to see the same thing I do. He is looking at me, as if to tell me that I should do something to invite Megan to say something. That's what I always do, though.

This time I think I'll let Paul do the work. Maybe it will help wean Megan of the notion that she needs to be invited to talk before she can say something. I know this is the way she has been treated her whole life. Her family never lets her talk at home, so why should she be any different here? But she can be different, starting right now! The first thing I've got to do, though, is switch direction from Cynthia (who is rambling now anyway) to cue Paul so he will bring out Megan.

The remarkable thing about this whole internal dialogue is that in the one minute this took place (Yes, that was only one minute in the mind of a group leader! Are you exhausted yet?), all these assumptions, hypotheses, and observations were based completely on nonverbal behavior. It is certainly possible that if you train yourself to notice nuances in behavior, to watch behavioral cues, to decode underlying meanings that are just beneath the surface, you will mine a rich source of data that can be used to make accurate assessments about what is happening and make informed choices about which interventions to choose.

For a Field Study

One of the best ways to learn about group dynamics and leadership is to familiarize yourself with the journals in the field that are devoted to group work. Spend some time in the library perusing the literature so that you can identify those sources that will be most valuable to you in the future. Many times you will find yourself confused and hungry for information about a particular problem.

There are hundreds of such journals that include articles about group leadership. Following are some of the specialized group sources you will wish to consult:

Group
Group Analysis
Group Dynamics: Theory, Research, and Practice
Group and Organization Management
International Journal of Group Psychotherapy
Journal of Child and Adolescent Group Therapy
Journal of Group Psychotherapy, Psychodrama, and Sociometry
Journal of Social and Personal Relationships
Journal For Specialists in Group Work
Leadership Quarterly
Small Group Behavior
Small Group Research
Social Work in Groups

What to Look For

All groups organize themselves in particular ways, with or without designated leaders. You could spend a whole lifetime trying to familiarize yourself with all the literature and research that has been accumulated on this subject. At some time, you may wish to review a basic text on group dynamics (see Cathcart, Samovar, & Henman, 1996; Forsyth, 1999; Stewart, Manz, & Sims, 1998) that reviews the science of group behavior, including such topics as interpersonal attraction, conflict, performance, decision making, problem solving, power, influence, team building, and so on. Here is a review of some basic ideas.

Proxemics

People adjust their physical distance from one another according to the degree of attraction or tension they feel. There have been studies done that actually measure the number of inches that people stand from one another when they talk and how that is correlated with physical attraction. Obviously, friends stand closer than strangers, women are more comfortable than men with intimate space, and when you like someone you are inclined to approach that person more closely.

In a group, you will want to watch the ways that members seat themselves—who they prefer to sit next to and who they position themselves opposite from. Watch not only for where people choose to sit, and how close they sit to one another, but also body positioning and other clues that may reveal inner states.

The structure of how and where people sit has major significance for how you decide to arrange the room. You would be amazed at how often leaders fail to organize the room in such a way that is conducive to open communication, shared responsibility for the meeting, and constructive interaction. In a typical classroom, for example, chairs are arranged so they all face the front. Besides the instructor, the only other thing you can see are the backs of classmates' heads. This works well if you believe that all learning emanates from the mouth of the instructor, that nothing valuable happens as a result of group interaction (it also is the most efficient use of space when resources are limited). If your goal, however, is to encourage group members to interact with one another, then a far better arrangement is one in which people sit in a circle. In any groups that you lead, make certain that you arrange the room in such a way that the seating is most conducive to the structure and atmosphere you wish to create.

Nonverbal Behavior

When observing members in your group, you will want to monitor not only their body positioning but also other nonverbal states. In a previous section, we looked at the interactive patterns among members; you will also want to examine behavioral cues that let you know what people are thinking and feeling. You notice, for instance, that one group member is smiling a lot, but this expression is incongruent with the serious nature of what he is saying. Another participant sits quietly, seemingly without a care in the world, but every time a particular subject comes up, you notice she moves her leg up and down in a nervous jiggle.

For Reflection

Professional poker players watch one another carefully for "tells" that give away clues about how an opponent is feeling at any given moment—nervousness, jubilant expression, caution, frustration. By watching nonverbal behavior, they hope to identify when someone is bluffing or not by identifying consistent patterns.

Look around your class to identify the "tells" of classmates, as well as the instructor. How do particular individuals act when they are excited or frightened? How can you tell when your instructor is disappointed or frustrated? How can you determine when he or she is greatly satisfied with what is happening?

One of the most difficult challenges of leading groups, distinguishing it from individual sessions, is that you must monitor the way a dozen or more different individuals are reacting to what is happening in any moment. That job becomes so much easier if you teach the group members to monitor their own behavior, as well as that of the others, so that you do not have to be continuously responsible for knowing what is going on every second.

Silences

It is not just what people say that matters, but also what they do not say, and how they choose not to say it. It is impossible not to speak; sometimes the "loudest" members of the group will be screaming through their dramatic withdrawal. I recall one recent group in which during the go-around, one member, with arms crossed and chair pulled back, announced that he had nothing to say. This was very unusual behavior because it had become a norm that everyone would briefly check in to start the group. If someone really did not want any attention, all he or she would need to do is make up some report, or give a perfunctory statement like, "Well, not much going on this week. I'm doing well and feeling fine."

When pressed by other members, and me, as to what was going on, the man insisted that nothing was happening; he just had nothing to say. Throughout the rest of the session, he sat with his arms crossed, scowling and looking bored. He never said another word to the group (and dropped out the next session), but he completely dominated the meeting with his dramatic silence.

Silence is often a very normal, natural, useful part of any group session. It gives members time to think, reflect on things, formulate or process ideas, take a breath, or just relax a little between intense intervals. It is rather important during groups to establish norms that it is okay to be quiet for a while; otherwise, people will continuously chatter even when they have nothing to say.

Beginning group leaders fear silence among their most dreaded critical incidents. What you actually do in such situations depends very much on what you believe the silence means. If it is productive time for reflection, then you might let it go for a while. But if people are confused, looking for direction, feeling unduly anxious or uncomfortable, you might need to do something. My favorite thing to do, by the way, in this or any other situation, is to cue other members to do the work rather than having to take the lead myself.

For a Field Study

Try out this method on your own. Next time you are in a group situation in which you become aware that you are having a strong reaction (boredom, anxiety, frustration, anger, amusement), look at others carefully until you find someone you are pretty certain is feeling the same way that you are. As you are probably well aware, some people show what they are feeling so easily you can read them instantly.

Cue this person to speak out loud what you sense is being felt by you and others. Validate this person's experience by sharing your own reactions as well.

I might notice, for instance, that I am feeling bored in the group. I interpret the silence to mean that there is a marked lack of motivation and energy on that day. The increasing quiet times do not appear to be useful; they are making the session seem interminable. Rather than confronting this situation myself, and risking the usual strong reactions to leader behavior, instead I scan the group and notice someone else who appears to feel the same way I do. That is my signal to cue that member to do the work for me: "Arthur, I notice that you are looking bored by what's been happening in the group today. When Kara was speaking earlier, you seemed particularly distracted. Maybe you could talk about what's going on for you today?"

The important thing to remember about silence is that it can be extraordinarily useful, a waste of valuable time, or even destructive. Are members being resistant or defensive? Are they punishing you or others through withdrawal? Perhaps members do not understand what you want. Maybe they are afraid of saying the wrong thing—this could be evidence that trust levels are not yet sufficient to do what you expect. You have to read what exactly the silence means and then respond accordingly.

For a Field Study

Find a place where you can watch unobtrusively a group of people interact with one another. This can be at a playground, a party, a dinner, or even in a class. Pretend you are an expert in interpersonal behavior whose job it is to make inferences and predictions about how people are likely to act in the future. Like any respectable anthropologist or social scientist, make field notes about what you observe. Try to uncover clues as to what people are really saying to one another and what they really feel and think inside.

Try to identify sources of tension and conflict. Figure out who is most attracted to whom. What are people feeling and thinking but not saying out loud?

Member Roles

People adopt particular roles in groups depending on (1) what they have done in the past, (2) the composition of the group, and (3) what gets triggered by the unique dynamics of the situation. These characteristic roles can be seen as basically facilitative or obstructive to the process and goals of the groups (Capuzzi & Gross, 1998). When someone takes the lead in supporting others, as well as offering encouragement, this role is often helpful. Yet another variation of this theme can be dysfunctional when an overly supportive member continuously rescues people when things get intense because of his or her own fears of intimacy.

Another common dynamic has to do with "scapegoating," in which some members disown or project unacceptable parts of themselves onto others. When it appears as if one designated person is the only one to exhibit strong feelings of guilt, anger, or shame, this person is actually serving as the "lightning rod" for others uncomfortable feelings (Smith & Berg, 1995). This could easily happen, for example, when tension is high and one member takes the risk of talking about what is going on. This person can end up the scapegoat, not only for that interaction, but for others in the future.

Just as often that one member is repeatedly attacked as a scapegoat for the group's disowned feelings, another might very well become designated the "holy cow" (Schoenwolf, 1998). This person is idealized in the group as a sacred object, or the favorite child, just as so often happens in a family. These are just a few of the dynamics that often develop with respect to designated roles.

A number of writers have catalogued the typical roles that people play in groups. Within families, Satir (1972) identified four different roles that block good communication among members. The *placater* appears to be accommodating and cooperative ("I'll do whatever you want"), but actually sabotages things by refusing to say what is really thought and felt. The *blamer* plays the opposite role ("This is all your fault"), using criticism and aggressive tactics to put others on the defensive. The *irrelevant* member is distracting and annoying ("That reminds me of a story") to the point where it is difficult to work cooperatively. Finally, the *super-reasonable* member appears at first to be very helpful ("Logically, this all comes down to basic needs"), but actually prevents any deep level intimacy from occurring.

These typical dysfunctional roles in families occur with regularity in all groups, in addition to others that have been identified (Hansen, Warner, & Smith, 1980; Vander Kolk, 1985). The *aggressor* keeps everyone off balance by trying to control others. The *monopolist* attempts control by filibuster: talking so often that nobody else has a chance to contribute. For the *rescuer*, who keeps things from getting too deep, or the *withdrawn* member who says nothing at all, the object is to hide as long as possible.

For a Class Activity or a Field Study

Find a group of about six members, either among classmates or friends. Explain that this is a fantasy exercise, but in order for it to work, you all have to pretend that it is real, that you are all really in this predicament. Unless everyone is prepared to take the task seriously, you will not experience a meaningful demonstration of group dynamics and roles.

You are all traveling together via a small cruise ship that encounters an unexpected storm. The ship sinks and you are the only survivors who have washed ashore on a deserted island. You have an unlimited supply of fresh water but limited food supplies on the island, enough to last all of you just a few weeks.

After just having rested and recovered, you meet together to decide your fate and make some preliminary decisions about how you will live, how you will govern yourselves, and what you will do to survive.

The particular content of your group discussions are relatively unimportant. This is merely a vehicle by which you can observe and experience various group roles and dynamics that you have read about.

After spending about 20 or 30 minutes in your survival simulation, debrief one another afterwards by talking about how you functioned together, the roles each of you played in the group, aspects of your behavior that were both effective and dysfunctional. Talk about what you learned from this exercise and what you can use from it in your life.

In addition to the various dysfunctional roles, there are also constructive roles that members play in order to further process and task goals (Gladding, 1999). The *facilitator* works as a host to make people feel welcome and comfortable. The *gatekeeper* keeps people on task, making sure that established norms are honored. The *compromiser* acts as a mediator during conflicts. The *energizer* motivates people during times of boredom or when some action is needed. *Information seekers* work to collect relevant data and help members to share information. The *evaluator* lets the group know how things are going, encouraging adjustments for greater efficiency.

This is a brief sampling of roles that you will see, and have experienced and played in the past. The important point is to recognize that all groups naturally (and with prodding from the leader) create a division of labor. The point has been made by evolutionary biologists (Dugatkin, 1999; Wright, 1994) that one of the attributes that makes us so successful as a species is our tendency to specialize in various functions within groups. One person in a tribe hunts, while another skins and cleans, another cooks, and another cleans up. In groups as well, members will organize themselves into different roles that are needed for things to proceed in an orderly manner (unless the goal is to keep others from getting too close).

Regardless of the roles played by various group members, or those that you feel are important for participants to adopt in order to be facilitative, your job as leader is to teach everyone to serve several important functions for one another, and for themselves, in order to get the most from the experience. These can include, but are not limited, to the following roles suggested by Berg, Landreth, and Fall (1998):

1. Group members will each be valued, and in turn, be encouraged to value one another. If nothing else is accomplished, or no specific goals are identified, at the very least all members should be helped to feel validated and supported.
2. Group members will feel that they are understood. The leader will model appropriate listening and responding behavior, but beyond these fundamental skills, an essential value develops in the group that everyone should play a role in helping others to feel they have been heard.
3. Group members will work collaboratively, sharing in decision making and owning responsibility for the outcome. You must make it clear that this is *their* group, not yours. Your job is to act as the facilitator, but their job is to make sure that the group meets their own needs.

For Review: High- and Low-Functioning Groups

When you put together what you now understand, you will see an image emerging of groups that work well, and others that do not. The following are characteristics of the best groups (Johnson & Johnson, 2000).

1. Participants know what is expected of them. Their individual goals are consistent with those of the group.
2. Healthy norms are established that permit a balance between structure and spontaneity.

3. Dysfunctional group roles are kept in check, while power is centered among those who work toward collaboration and completion of tasks.
4. There is a high degree of trust, safety, and cohesion in the group.
5. Information and experiences are shared readily among participants.
6. The style of leadership is described as democratic, with shared responsibility, rather than authoritarian or laissez faire (passive).
7. Conflict and disagreement are viewed as constructive. They are worked through rather than ignored.
8. There is a high level of honesty and openness in the group so that constructive feedback is shared.
9. Communication flows in multiple directions. There is an equitable distribution of power, control, and contributions.
10. There is consistent, observable growth and change among the members, not just in the group, but in their lives.

Keep in mind that the dynamics described in this chapter represent general principles, especially as applied to groups among mainstream, North American populations. You have learned previously that members of various minority and cultural groups may behave according to different norms. For example, dimensions of power and prestige develop in different ways among group members of some cultural groups over others (Kelsey, 1998). What this means is that with all the concepts contained in this chapter and book about group dynamics and processes, you must make adjustments according to the unique background of the people you help.

4 Stages of Group Development

Jeffrey A. Kottler and Jerry Parr

There is a lot of apprehension associated with leading groups. This is especially the case related to making sense of what is going on at any moment in time, as well as predicting what might happen next. What you need is a roadmap to follow, a rough plan of the territory, so to speak. Such a conception would allow you to understand current behavior in light of its evolutionary sequence. It would also permit you to make some reasonable assumptions about where things are heading and what you might do to push things along in desired directions.

Every group follows a similar path in which participants struggle to know and trust one another, reach some sort of accommodation, complete their work with different degrees of effectiveness, and then disband. This same developmental sequence has been applied to so many other facets of human behavior, including Sigmund Freud's stages of psychosexual development, Erik Erikson's stages of psychosocial development, Jean Piaget's stages of cognitive development, Lawrence Kohlberg's stages of moral development, even Elizabeth Kubler-Ross's stages in the grieving process.

What You Should Know About Developmental Theory

Certainly you have had some experience with developmental stage theory previously. Consider the ways that so many of your relationships have evolved over time. First, you meet someone and become superficially acquainted. You engage in small talk and test one another to see if you share mutual interests and values. If this appears mutually satisfying, you spend more time together, taking things to the next level in which you reveal more of yourself. If you stick with it long enough, trust develops, as well as deeper intimacy.

You probably didn't set out to develop a relationship according to formal rules; they just developed naturally over time. These "norms" were negotiated as to how you would behave with one another and how decisions would be made. You may, for example, join together in a business partnership. Romantic relationships may bloom into marriage with children, careers, and community roots. Finally, all relationships end, sometimes due to fierce conflict, as in divorce, sometimes because of circumstances where one moves far away from the other, and sometimes due to death.

Whether we are talking about the stages of relationships, or physical maturation, emotional development, family evolution, or most any other facet of growth, developmental theories proceed according to certain principles that operate in groups as well:

1. Development occurs in an orderly progression of stages.
2. Generally, the sequence of stages cannot be skipped.
3. If you know what stage people are currently operating within, you can predict where they are going next.
4. Developmental evolution can be encouraged and facilitated by helping people move to the next level.

For Personal Application

Learning to be a group leader involves going through a series of progressive stages that began when you first decided to seek additional training. For instance, most counseling and therapy practitioners go through stages that look something like this (Kottler & Blau, 1989):

Training	*What if I don't have what it takes?*
Hero Worship	*If only I could be like you.*
Enchantment	*I can't believe I get paid for this!*
Golden Years	*Hey, I'm really good at this!*
Mid-Career Doubt	*What if I'm not really doing anything?*
Pre-Rustout	*Another day, another dollar.*
Revitalization	*What in me is getting in the way?*
Mentorship	You want to be like ME?

Make up names for what you think are the sequential transitions that might take place as a group leader grows in experience and expertise. What stage are you in now?

In the previous chapter, it was mentioned that groups may be thought of as a dynamic social system, analogous to any other living system that exists in the world. This particular conception has formed the basis for much of what we understand about the ways that families evolve, as well as groups.

Metaphorically, then, groups are formed and pass through periods of "childhood" when they learn how to get needs met, then through "adolescence" when authority is tested. Later, groups mature into "adulthood" when work is accomplished and contributions are made. Finally, groups, like families, settle into quiet reflection and poignant reckoning of what has been gained and what must eventually end.

Group dynamics, member and leader behaviors, and focal issues change over the life of a group. Knowing about the general parameters of group stages provides leaders with a compass that helps them steer the group in the best direction. It helps leaders to keep their bearings when the group enters uncharted, stormy waters. It enables leaders to sequence their interventions in a timely and effective manner. Finally, it provides valuable benchmarks that can support leaders' intuition about group processes.

In the previous chapter we have examined the ways that groups, as living systems, seek some sort of balance and equilibrium on the one hand, yet also move toward increasing levels of complexity that make room for interpersonal and individual growth (Csikszentmihalyi, 1990). This tug of war between safety and risk-taking threads throughout the group's life, assuming different forms and levels of intensity as the group develops.

For Personal Application

Work with a partner to flesh out your own ambivalence and conflict regarding safety versus risk-taking in this group class. Arrange yourselves so you have some privacy and bring an extra chair, if one is available (if not, you will take turns vacating the other chair).

With prodding from your partner, you will imagine that each chair contains the part of you that wants to take greater risks in the class, reveal more of yourself, versus the part of you that would rather play it safe and protect yourself. Stage a dialogue between the two different parts of yourself, changing chairs as you switch roles.

Such an enactment might look something like this, to get you started . . .

RISKY SELF: "I guess I'd like to show more of myself in class, but . . ."

SAFE SELF: "You're damn right, BUT! I mean, what's the point? These people will judge you. And it won't be pretty."

RISKY SELF: "I know that's possible. Some people will, but then some won't."

SAFE SELF: "What about the instructor, though?"

After you have completed the exercise, give your partner a chance to try it out. When you are both finished, talk to one another about what themes emerged for you and what you resolve to do based on this awareness.

Donigian and Malnati (1997) draw upon Whitaker and Liebermann (1964) to address the intrinsic conflict in groups. Essentially, they contend that members are motivated to express wishes, desires, and needs that will move them forward, but inner fears of rejection, humiliation, and punishment argue against the expression of these motives. This inner clash or conflict creates anxiety, a signal to either find a workable solution, or to fall back on failed but familiar defensive maneuvers. The purpose of group work, from this prospective, is to activate group processes that trigger self-exploration of conflicted issues so that members can acquire more adaptive solutions to interpersonal living. Growth occurs when fears are faced, thus enabling motives and needs to surface in a context where more adaptive solutions can be tried and supported.

These dynamics apply equally to the group as a whole, as well as the individual members and leader. Developmental stages provide a useful framework for viewing these dynamics at work over the life of a group.

So Many Group Stages

If only there was just one model of group stages. Alas, like so many other aspects of this profession, there are many! Some authors (Corey & Corey, 1997; Gladding, 1999; Jacobs, Masson, & Harvill, 1998; Napier & Gershenfeld, 1993; Tuckman, 1965; Vander Kolk, 1985) conceive of group stages as unfolding along a sequential path, similar to developmental theories in other domains. This model fits particularly well with relatively short-term groups.

Donigian and Malnati (1997) discuss an alternate perspective that views longer term groups as moving through a cyclical rather than linear process. It is helpful to keep in mind that these stages would also vary according to the type of group, experiential and therapy groups evolving in slightly different form than task groups (Wheelan, 1994). Regardless of the type of group or the length of time it meets, there are many similarities in the processes that characterize group stages.

Perhaps a caveat to any generalizations about the ways that groups are supposed to evolve is that believing in stage theory may create its own reality (Becvar, Canfield, & Becvar, 1997). Thus, some theorists (called "postmodern" or "social contructionist") caution against prejudging how groups might develop because such filters might lead you to see something that is in your own mind rather than actually in the group.

With this reminder, group stages have been described as including somewhere from three to ten distinct stages, with five being the most popular (Kormanski, 1988). Table 4–1 summarizes how several writers have labeled and characterized group stages.

TABLE 4–1   Summary of Group Stages

Authors	Number of Stages	Labels/Description
Bennis & Shepard (1956)	Two	Authority and structure; intimacy and interdependence
Schutz (1958)	Five	Inclusion; control; openness; mutual trust; and letting go
Tuckman (1965)	Five	Forming; norming; storming; performing; and adjourning
Fisher (1970)	Four	Orientation; conflict; emergence; and reinforcement
La Coursiere (1980)	Five	Orientation; dissatisfaction; resolution; production; and termination
Vander Kolk (1985)	Four	Beginning; conflict and dominance; cohesiveness and productivity; and completion
Wheelan (1994)	Five	Dependency and inclusion; counterdependency and fight; trust and structure; work; and termination
Yalom (1995)	Three	Orientation and search for meaning; conflict, dominance, and rebellion; and cohesiveness
Corey & Corey (1997)	Four	Initial; transition; working; and ending
Donigian & Malnati (1997)	Five	Orientation; conflict and confrontation; cohesiveness; work; and termination

Stages of Group Evolution

When you examine all of these different descriptions of group stages, it is clear that some solid themes emerge. We have simplified considerably the stages of group development and synthesized the features we like best into four distinct segments that will make immediate, intuitive sense. This will make it easy to remember when you are in the midst of panic, trying to figure out which stage you are in and which one comes next.

Stage I: Induction

Members first enter a group needing considerable orientation. This is a type of *induction stage* wherein members lean heavily on the leader for guidance and direction. Members are asking themselves questions like: "What the heck is going on here? Who are these people? How am I supposed to act? Is this the right place for me? What do they want from me? How much am I willing to share?"

Most often, members are prepared for participation in the group through some induction or screening procedures that inform about rules, rights, consent, policies, and goals. They may be asked to fill out background questionnaires, write an autobiography, or disclose in an interview about personal history (more about this will be discussed in later chapters).

Emotionally, this first stage is one of tentativeness and guardedness because safety is in question. Closely related to safety, members wonder if they will be accepted and valued by other group members and the leader. They feel insecure and disoriented. They also may feel doubts about whether the group will measure up to their expectations and fantasies.

You can expect a high degree of defensiveness and resistance. This is not only normal but a healthy way to deal with an environment that may be dangerous. Trust is thus one of the biggest issues.

The work of this stage is to find constructive ways to be with one another. Members don't know the rules. They don't know how to be good group participants. It is your job to teach them. This is where you set the stage, explain what is expected, what roles will be played, and provide the initial structure that is needed to move to the next level of minimal cohesion and intimacy. It is also important to provide reassurance during those times when a member departs from what you had in mind.

In one recent group class, a student was talking at length about his plans for the future even though the instructor had been guiding participants to talk about the present. The interaction developed in this way:

> **KIRK:**   "So if I could just find a way to relocate, I think that it would . . ."
>
> **LEADER:**   "Excuse me, Kirk?"
>
> **KIRK:**   "Uh, yeah?"
>
> **LEADER:**   "I couldn't help but notice that you were speaking primarily about the future rather than how you are feeling and thinking in the present."
>
> **KIRK:**   "Oh gosh! I'm SO sorry. I heard what you asked us to do, but I guess I got carried away. I suppose the future is just weighing heavily on me right now so that's what I wanted to talk about."

LEADER: "You're absolutely right. And you didn't do anything wrong. When you're being a member in this group, your job is to go after what it is you need most. You are allowed to be selfish, even encouraged to meet your needs. It is MY job to make sure that we follow a particular agenda or balance the participation."

KIRK: "But I feel so stupid . . ."

LEADER: "I actually appreciate that you were being so proactive in letting us know what you wanted to talk about. And we will get back to that again shortly. For now, though, let's finish talking about what you are experiencing right now, even in response to this interaction."

During this dialogue, the instructor was trying to do two thing simultaneously: first, to teach Kirk and other members about norms related to following instructions, and second, to demonstrate that even when you violate those rules, you will not be censured but rather gently guided back on track. Both messages are critical because during this early stage, members need to be reassured that a structure will be enforced and yet departures from this agenda will not signal that you will be ridiculed or censured.

How do you know when a group is ready to move from the induction stage to the next one? Look for evidence of the following:

- Ground rules have been internalized, accepted, and are followed consistently.
- At least moderate levels of trust have been established.
- The group is perceived as moderately safe by most everyone.
- Facilitative communication patterns have become established in which members appear respectful and caring, yet open.

For a Class Activity

In small groups, make a list of all the norms that have been established in your class. Review how you were inducted into your assigned (or self-adopted) roles. How is it that you learned the appropriate ways to be viewed as an able student and constructive group member? What are some of the unstated, subtle, or "secret" rules of the class that are not talked about overtly?

Stage II: Experimental Engagement

Groups usually graduate to the *experimental engagement stage* by the second to the fourth meeting, though this can vary considerably. This is the time when members naturally want to stretch themselves, the leaders, and the group itself to new levels. Members want to test the group to determine how it responds to bids for power and to deeper levels of self-disclosure. They have their eye on the leaders, wondering if they can maintain the group's safety while allowing for more direct challenges. Members may send out test balloons by disclosing something more dear to their being but more controversial in meaning.

The following statements are examples of what members often say at this stage:

- "We don't seem to be getting anywhere; shouldn't we have an agenda?"
- "I'm not sure I want to bare my soul any more because some of you have barely opened up."
- "I sense that it is wrong to be deeply religious here. I feel judged about my faith in God."
- "This group doesn't seem real to me—the real world is dog eat dog."
- "We don't seem to talk about real issues. I was hoping we would discuss how to deal with a mean boss."

There is typically great variability in members' readiness levels to become engaged with one another. Some participants are impatient, more than willing to get involved as deeply as possible. Others feel suspicious, cautious, even hostile. They may have become disenchanted because the leader fails to offer the structure and wisdom they had expected. Still other members are satisfied to dance to any tune, so long as they feel safe.

The best descriptor of behavior in this stage would be "tentative," as all actions become experimental, testing the waters to see if it is safe. Tension, jealousy, conflict, power struggles, and coalitional battles are common in this stage as members fight for influence and personal agendas. Some members are experiencing rather strong "transference reactions" (those that represent distortions) toward the leader, just as you may also be feeling your own personal feelings toward certain members.

Direct confrontation is usually avoided during this stage, but that does not mean there is not a high degree of conflict. Compared to the alternative, when members pretend that everything is perfect, disagreement and tension at this stage are not a bad state of affairs and can often provoke constructive engagement. The greatest problems you may face occur with certain members beginning to act out.

Many, if not most groups, never get beyond this stage. They remain in a state of superficial, cautious, minimal engagement with one another. They get some work done, but the quantity and quality is limited, if not mediocre. Members never feel very safe, but tell themselves that this tension is acceptable, especially considering that the risks don't feel worth any additional gains.

The following tasks face group members during the experimental engagement stage:

- Members find the courage to surface their lingering concerns about safety.
- Members test the leader's ability to manage member-to-member conflicts.
- Members establish a means of feeling empowered and valued.
- Members test the leader's ability to receive confrontation nondefensively.
- Members move toward higher levels of emotional expression.
- Members begin to gain insight into their interpersonal issues.
- Members learn how to utilize conflict as an instigator of interpersonal and personal growth.

Your job during this stage is to manage your own anxiety level in the face of increasing group tension. People are watching you very carefully to see how you handle yourself and deal with conflicts that emerge. More than anything else, you model ways of supporting and confronting that you want others to adopt.

When is it time to move to the next stage? Actually, the progression will happen so slowly that you will barely know that you are there until you have arrived. You will notice that people feel closer to one another after a critical incident. Trust and risk-taking have increased. More and more, members spend as much time taking care of one another as they do their own interests.

For Personal Application

If you think about it, most of the groups you have experienced in your life, at work, in class, at social gatherings and organized activities, remain in this stage of tentative, safe, experimental engagement. What if you wanted to initiate a movement to the next level of cohesion, intimacy, and productivity?

Think of one group in your life that feels unsatisfying, or at least less productive and joyful than you would prefer. This could be within a family coalition, roommates, neighbors, friends, social organization, or a class. It could be a long-term group you are part of that has remained superficial, or it could be a group that is just beginning.

Bring to this group your awareness of the stage in which you have been operating and what this means for your relationships. Initiate a discussion among members about what it would take to move to the next level.

Stage III: Cohesive Engagement

If groups grow beyond this stage—many do not and some should not—a *cohesive engagement stage* is entered. This is what is ordinarily described as the "working stage," which means that sufficient trust and accommodation has been reached such that productive activities take place.

Whether your groups ever reach this stage depends on several prerequisite conditions (Berman & Weinberg, 1998):

- First of all, it takes time: the longer the group meets, the more likely that things will reach an advanced stage of engagement.
- Homogeneous group composition leads to cohesive functioning more quickly.
- A stable setting for the group helps members to feel safe.
- An atmosphere in the group should be conducive to individual self-expression.
- Taking on the leader, and resolving this rebellion successfully, can be very constructive in moving toward mature group development.
- A democratic rather than authoritarian leadership style is preferred for preventing dependency and destructive coalitions.

In this stage people know what is expected. They know how to behave most constructively. Furthermore, the leader no longer has to do all the work. Because the members

For Personal Reflection

Think of a time in which you were part of a group that stalled in the early stages. To what extent were the conditions just described absent or present?

As you look back on this experience, what could have been done to make the conditions more favorable to cohesive engagement?

have learned appropriate facilitative behavior, the leader plays mostly a supporting role in this stage, cueing members as needed, monitoring safety and progress, but pretty much allowing things to proceed according to the needs of the participants.

What "cohesive" means is that members are sensitive and responsive to one another's needs, often without being told. They feel an emotional attachment to one another, as well as a high degree of trust. Self-disclosures occur at very intimate, revealing levels. Members take risks in their behavior. Not everyone will feel this way, of course. You will still encounter bumps, distractions, and challenges along the way, but you will no longer be responsible for managing these difficulties alone. In a group that has attained cohesive engagement, most participants monitor their own behavior.

In a sense, the group has become a high-functioning family—in some cases, the healthy family that members have never experienced before. People are caring and compassionate towards one another, but they are also very honest and direct. If work is truly taking place, then people also feel free to disagree and confront one another.

Other things you will notice during this stage is that participants spend more time centered in the present. They talk to one another about how they feel about one another. They ask spontaneously about previous homework assignments. They bring in material from previous sessions.

Here are some statements that illustrate what might be said by members at this stage:

- "Jill, I have been reviewing what I said to you last week. I want to add something very important that I failed to mention: I appreciate your courage to be confrontive, even though it scares me when directed my way."
- "I thought of a name for our group—The Magnificent Eight—because we all seem to rally behind the underdog."
- "Ralph, I have wondered all week, did you ask her out?"
- "I want to take up where we left off last week, Kim, if we might."
- "Paul, could you personalize that? I get the idea but not your part in it."

Leaders wrestle with several temptations during this stage. The members have reached a level of autonomy that can beguile leaders into believing that their input is no longer needed. Members may collude in this belief for what has been termed a "flight to health." Some leaders may abdicate their role and attempt to become a member. Others may miss the limelight and resort to structured exercises, which are rarely needed or useful at this point. Experienced leaders monitor the group's dynamics, gently urging members to go deeper, however slightly. The following statements illustrate what leaders might say at this stage:

- "Barbara, you have shared much, but I have yet to hear the music in your story. Your feelings, please."
- "Fred, you haven't answered Gloria. Would you try again or tell her what keeps you from doing so?"
- "Maria, I think your observations are important. Who here are you addressing?"
- "Patsy, when ready, put words to your tears."
- "I'm enjoying our lighthearted mood, but I am wondering if that is all you want from today."
- "Mike, you have sought input from Barbara, Sandy, and Jill each week, but never from Troy, Jerry, or Arturo. Any hunches about this?"

Members are thus challenged with several tasks during this stage to develop more intimate connections with others, to take greater risks in what they say and do, to go deeper in what they reveal about themselves, and to take more responsibility for their own changes, as well as the direction the group takes next.

Stage IV: Disengagement

Groups enter their final stage as the end draws near, usually when only a few sessions remain. As a way of previewing this stage, we have been struck by how many students say that what they will miss most with graduation is belonging to "their" interpersonal growth group, a regular feature of our training program. Our response is often to reassure them that groups exist in most cities and that wherever their career takes them, they can join another group. The look in their eyes expresses their doubt that this will come to pass, and indeed, upon reflection, we realize how rare it is for any of us to feel a part of a group that feels truly safe and secure, yet encourages us to be as honest, genuine, and open as possible.

Most groups exist not only for the pure pleasure, support, caring, and entertainment they provide, but also for the changes they promote in the outside world. Ultimately, the true test of a group's functioning is not how well members are getting along when they are together, but how they are performing in their lives. The questions you must ask members at this stage, and encourage them to ask one another, include: To what extent have you reached your stated goals? In what specific ways have you changed as a result of this experience? Where are you now in relation to where you would like to be? What is left to do before the group ends?

This final stage may be the trickiest of all. It raises issues of grief and loss, the process of letting go and moving on. Given that members have experienced such a high level of caring and support, there is tremendous ambivalence often felt at the prospect of ending the group. On the one hand, members are excited about their freedom, yet they are also feeling sad to say goodbye.

One of the greatest challenges you will face is helping members to continue their progress after the group ends. It is not unreasonable to fear that people will have setbacks, or even regress back to dysfunctional patterns. That is why it is so critical at this stage to help participants to express their fears, work through their apprehensions, and plan for inevitable challenges they will face.

A part of this last stage is really a final chapter called "follow-up" in which, at some point in the future, you may call for a reunion, or at the very least, engage in some sort of post-group checkup to see how members are progressing. This not only keeps people accountable for their behavior after the group ends, but also allows you to monitor their progress and recommend additional treatment if needed.

For Personal Reflection

Applying the various stages of group development to your classroom, where do you believe your class is currently operating? Identify evidence to support this assumption by thinking about specific behaviors that are representative of this stage.

If you were the instructor and wanted to move things to the next level, how would you do so?

Group Stages in Action

So far, this stage business sounds pretty theoretical, so let's apply the concepts to an actual group that was experiencing a kind of "civil war." The group was composed of eight students, half of each gender, who were participating in an experience to satisfy the requirements of the group leadership course. Although things had not been proceeding in an altogether smooth transition, the critical incident occurred during the fifth meeting.

Halfway through the session, a woman interrupted one of her counterparts and angrily charged her with wanton, seductive, and compulsive pursuit of the attention of the male group members. Two other women quickly joined the fray, angrily adding similar accusations. Sensing immanent bloodshed, the male group members avoided the conflict as they inspected the floor for minute traces of some unidentified substance. The group leader, as well, was caught in the grips of inaction, fearful of doing anything to make matters worse.

Eventually, the group leader intervened by directing the confrontive members to focus on their own behavior rather than that of others. As their stories unfolded, it was clear that they wanted desperately to feel more comfortable with their own sexuality. As is often the case, the preemptive attack was not only about the one woman's behavior, but what it sparked in the accusers.

Once she regained her sense of balance, the confronted member revealed that she was all too aware that she depended on her femininity to gain attention and approval. She also shared that she hated this about herself and wanted to change.

When the group leader debriefed the incident with his supervisor, he was first asked why he had failed to see the growing tension between these members. Surely, this conflict had been brewing for some time?

One reason, he admitted reluctantly, was because the confronted member was indeed strikingly attractive and seductive. She wore very provocative clothes over a voluptuous figure. The leader had been so uncomfortable with his own attraction toward this woman that he completely denied what was going on. He neither recognized what was inappropriate about the woman's behavior, nor did he realize how others were reacting. Typical of this experimental engagement stage, one member's behavior became the focus, the scapegoat, of others' strong feelings.

Like so many critical incidents in a group, this one became a catalyst for members to become more cohesive and less competitive. The confronted member changed dramatically after this session, not only in appearance but also in behavior. The group came to value her wit and perceptiveness, abilities she yearned to express. Similarly, two of the confronting members unveiled a vivaciousness that seemed to energize the entire group.

The transition from experimental to cohesive engagement, also referred to as moving from "storming" to "norming," often occurs as a result of some incident that brings people closer. Finally recognizing what might have been happening, the group leader was first able to support and protect the confronted group member. Yet it was critical that he not collude in denial of an issue so rich in meaning for all members. It was essential that the here-and-now exchanges become a normative feature of the group's culture.

What to Look for over Time

It is highly likely, in any debriefing or supervision session you have, that some discussion will take place about the stage in which the group is presently located. Generally, the following patterns will be observed as the group develops:

- Communication becomes less leader-centered and more member-centered.
- Self-disclosures change from being impersonal and in the past to those that are more present-oriented and personally revealing.
- Instead of being minimized, or avoided altogether, conflicts are acknowledged and worked through.
- Norms change from being imposed (via ground rules) to being developed specifically for the group's culture.
- Boundaries between members move from being rigid toward more flexibility.
- Individual and cultural differences become increasingly respected and cherished rather than feared and resented.
- Rather than fearing honest feedback, members become hungrier for direct input.

Consistent with an approach taken by Corey, Corey, and Haynes (2000), beginning group leaders would be well advised to develop their skills in:

1. Identifying the major characteristics of each stage.
2. Recognizing the needed therapeutic tasks for each of the stages.
3. Applying specific interventions that are best for each stage.

As an example, imagine that in a group you are leading that has just gotten started (third session) and members appear reluctant to confront one another even about the most obvious transgressions. When a person rambles, people make faces but don't say a word of protest. When someone feels hurt, he suffers silently. Some members come late but their behavior is ignored.

Before you decide how to handle matters, you must first assess accurately how these dynamics represent the current stage of development in which trust and cohesion are minimal. You wouldn't want to force things before participants are ready or they may shut down even further, perhaps even flee. Neither can you ignore the covert avoidance of honest interaction that is typical of a group that has yet to really get going. What you would do at this is time, therefore, is very different from how you might handle this situation once the group is in the working stage.

For a Class Activity

Meet with several partners to discuss alternative intervention options for how you might address the avoidance of direct communication in the illustrative example. Based on what you know about this group's current stage of development, what might you do next?

Review of What You Learned

- Group stages are naturally occurring phenomena. Like any other living system, they are progressive and sequential.
- Knowledge about stages helps the leader to assess what might be happening and predict future patterns.
- Stages follow different progressions in some groups, so use the theory as a rough guide rather than ultimate blueprint.
- There is an ongoing struggle in every group between playing it safe versus taking risks. Your job is to shepherd the process along from early stages of reluctance to greater sharing and experimentation.
- Groups have a beginning, middle, and an end, each stage of which has its own developmental obstacles and challenges. Over time, you are helping people to develop sufficient safety, trust, and intimacy so that individual and group goals may be accomplished.

CHAPTER

5   Group Work with Marginalized Groups

Jeffrey A. Kottler and Aretha Marbley

Surely you have been exposed at some point in your study to the challenges of helping people who come from diverse cultural backgrounds, especially those who have been marginalized. We are speaking here not only of diversity in the strict sense of ethnicity, but culture broadly defined to include others who have experienced oppression and discrimination.

Group leaders have been particularly concerned with developing structures that can be adapted to the unique needs of specific populations, as well creating an atmosphere in heterogeneous groups that makes it possible for everyone to feel welcome. As you are no doubt aware, members of minority groups are more likely to avoid therapeutic experiences, whether in individual or group work, and they are more likely to drop out prematurely (Garrett & Myers, 1996; Pedersen, 1996, 1997; Ponterotto, Casas, Suzuki, & Alexander, 1995; Sue, Ivey, & Pedersen, 1996). Furthermore, when such individuals do participate in counseling, therapy, or group work, they are far more likely to leave with unsuccessful outcomes (Essandoh, 1996; Sue & Zane, 1987).

It is clear that in the past group leaders have not been particularly responsive, or effective, in addressing the needs of those who have been marginalized. We are speaking here of members of oppressed minorities (i.e., Native American, Latino, African American, Asian American), those with disabilities (physically, mentally, and emotionally handicapped), those who have been without voice or power (the poor, disadvantaged), those who have experienced discrimination based on sexual orientation, gender, age, religion, or other human characteristics.

If you hope to serve those people who need your help the most, you must devote considerable time, energy, and commitment to learning ways to adapt your leadership skills to fit the unique needs of each cultural group. This is not an easy challenge. Obviously, anyone who has felt marginalized in the past may very well be cynical, pessimistic, and suspicious regarding what it is that you hope to offer.

For a Field Study

You must make yourself an expert in all the various cultural groups with whom you expect to work. Start out by identifying three or four of the most prominent cultural groups that are likely to show strong representation in the groups you will lead and those you know little about.

Interview several members of each of these groups to find out what their concerns would be participating in a group you would lead. Ask them to educate you about the main cultural values that would be imperative for you to understand in order to help them. Find out the reasons why they would feel reluctant to participate in a group that is not led by a member of their culture. What could you do to create a climate that would be optimal for them?

Once you have gathered this information on your own, next consult the literature on the subject. You will be relieved to know that there has been considerable research done on this subject, specifying the unique ways that groups should be adapted from particular cultures. Classified by ethnicity, there are specialized group structures for populations such as Native American (Colmant & Merta, 1999; Dufrene & Coleman, 1992), indigenous New Zealander (Silvester, 1997), Chinese (Kelsey, 1998), Orthodox Jewish (Bilu & Witzum, 1993), Asian American (Leong, 1992), Latin American (Gloria, 1999; McWhirter, McWhirter, & McWhirter, 1988), and African American (Brinson & Lee, 1997; Lee, 1982; Pack-Brown, Whittington-Clark, & Parker, 1998; Williams, Frame, & Green, 1999). In addition, methods have been developed for use with such groups as nontraditional women (Dazzo, 1998; Kees, 1999), incarcerated fathers (Berg, Landreth, & Fall, 1998), and immigrants and refugees (Nakkab & Hernandez, 1998).

Your job, in this field study, is to gain a working knowledge of the cultural backgrounds that you are most likely to see in your work on a daily basis. Each week or month, you can make it a priority to learn about another cultural group that is beyond your experience.

Until You Have Walked in My Shoes:
The Marginalized Experience

This chapter will focus on factors that are unique to marginalized groups by utilizing examples from participants in group experiences. These narratives will highlight some of the special challenges you will face. We will also discuss some of the concerns that culturally diverse clients wrestle with when they participate in groups, as well as some of the common mistakes that leaders make. It is our intent to help you understand what it feels like to experience racism, prejudices, and oppression that impact current perceptions and behavior. This will allow you to create more culturally sensitive and responsive interventions, regardless of the people you are helping.

Marginalized groups in North America (and elsewhere) often feel like they have yet to grasp the fully promised freedom, justice, and equality enjoyed by white, able-bodied, heterosexual men. Anecdotes of massive injustices and historical accounts of intolerance in

North America against marginalized groups and many other accounts can be found in so many sources, including the practice of group work (see Pack-Brown, Whittington-Clark, & Parker, 1998). The experiences of injustice, hatred, discrimination, racism, and intolerance are all real to marginalized clients; the resulting feelings of oppression and fear leak into other relationships, including (especially) those in groups.

For a Class Activity

In small groups, tell a story about a time in which you have been, or felt, marginalized or oppressed. This was an instance in which you were treated disrespectfully, or even abusively, because of your gender, religion, race, sexual orientation, disability, or some other factor.

After each person has mentioned a particular oppressive incident, talk about what it would feel like for you to be in a group with members, or even the leader, who resemble others who have hurt you.

Imagine being in a room with a group of people who appear to be neither physically, spiritually, culturally, or emotionally similar to you. They talk differently. They even think differently than you do. These are people you have learned to distrust over the course of your life. You have heard stories from friends and family about what they will do to you if you let your guard down. You have been warned repeatedly that although they may pretend to like you, secretly they despise you and think you are inferior. At the very least, these are people who don't understand your culture or experience.

Now, imagine that you are asked to share or disclose your most intimate thoughts and feelings with these people. You are expected to be vulnerable, to say what you really think and feel, even though you have some very good evidence that this may be incredibly stupid, self-destructive behavior. The following scenarios are from group members from diverse ethnic and racial backgrounds who decided to trust the group process and yet had negative experiences. Each story is told in the person's own words.

Scenario One: Understanding the Blood

The first thing I noticed was that they had a nurse and someone who wasn't licensed leading the group. This really upset me, but it was one of things that was, like, "Oh." I was surprised that they did a fairly good job.

There were about six different families in the group. We were there because of problems we were having with our stepdaughter. What got me was—and it didn't dawn on me until I left—that the problem was a cultural one. Because what was happening was that people were saying to me that she, my stepdaughter, was my daughter and that I should treat her as my daughter.

Her mother and stepfather were sitting in the room, too. I told them she already has a mother. I will do what I can, but she is not my child by blood. I am Indian and that is important to us. I could tell that they just didn't understand the concept of bloodline. This was frustrating that the other people, and the leaders, didn't understand what I was talking about, but my husband did. After that, I just didn't trust the atmosphere that much.

They asked the child if I ever hugged her or anything like that. But, I'm not a hugging, touching person. I am just not that way. They asked my stepdaughter about that but it wasn't an issue for her. It was a issue for them. They made me feel like something was wrong with me.

This was very frustrating. It was a very negative experience. It made me not want to go to groups ever again.

For Personal Application

Think of a time in which you were in a group or social situation in which people tried to pressure you to be or act a particular way that was in direct conflict with your values and beliefs. If a leader had been present, what would you have liked him or her to do on your behalf to protect your rights and help you to feel understood?

In this first example, the Native American participant never felt accepted in the group; she never felt like she belonged there. Moreover, she felt judged harshly by others, convinced that there was nothing she could do to change their minds. This was clearly unfortunate because she desperately needed help in her relationship with her stepdaughter.

Scenario Two: "You Got to Stand Up"

The group didn't work for me because of the way I was brought up in a Mexican American family. My mom did basically everything for my dad and the household. When I got married, though, my wife wanted more equal kind of stuff. But, I wanted her to have my supper ready when I came home from work, wash and iron my clothes, and things like that. She was saying, "Hey, I work too."

I don't remember if it was the leader or a group member who said, "You got to stand up! If you are not getting what you want out of this relationship, then get out of it." So, I went home and told my wife, "If you are not going to do those kind of things, then we can go our separate ways." I told her that I was going to move out and then I packed my things. I wasn't gone for no more than twenty-four hours. She came by and talked to me and we cried together and we talked about it.

I started thinking, "Why am I doing this? What's wrong with changing my ways? Why do I have to be like my dad was?" So I asked her for forgiveness, and we got together, and we started doing things together. Now we do a lot of stuff together and I do my share of the chores.

That group almost ruined things for me. They wanted to support me and all but they didn't take the time to get to really know my situation or where I was coming from.

For Reflection

If we would interview the group leader, or other members, we might hear a very different version of this story. Perhaps this man was not really told to go home and lay down the law to his wife—*maybe that's just what he heard*. The critical error may not have been with this ill-advised suggestion, but rather the leader's failure to check out what this participant heard and understood, and what he was going to do. Of course, we are giving the leader the benefit of the doubt.

Assume that a situation such as this would arise in a group that you were leading, what steps would you take to make sure that miscommunications and cultural misunderstandings are minimized?

Again, a member from a minority group felt misunderstood by others. In this case, he genuinely felt the concern from others, but the help they offered was misguided because neither the leader nor the members had the appropriate background to understand the context of his situation.

Scenario Three: Group Class

I was required to be in a group as part of my training. When I first entered the room, I felt a sinking feeling grip the bottom of my stomach, closely followed by a deep feeling of something akin to dread. I felt painfully uncomfortable. I felt trapped. As I looked at all the white faces, I felt like I was in an enemy camp.

I slowly pulled out a chair and joined the others sitting in a circle: one African American clustered with twelve Euro-American group members. Our ultimate purpose, as explained by Mac [the leader], was to learn how to become effective group leaders. Mac was a sixtyish, long-legged, physically fit white gentleman who was as always casually and neatly dressed. Both his nonverbals and verbals epitomized the Rogerian therapist: active listening and reflecting, sitting squarely, open, leaning forward, and very attentive and relaxed. His voice was soft and his eyes were warm.

Mac, charming, suave, and soft-spoken, had spent previous class sessions discussing theory, techniques, and the characteristics of an effective group leader. This group was to be experiential and we were to find out what it was like to be members in the sort of groups we would some day be leading.

In spite of the best of intentions, this group was a nightmare to me. I felt attacked and that my thoughts and feelings weren't understood, respected, or validated. I don't recall the exact context or details of the group, but even after so many years I am still plagued by that awful, depressing, horrible group training experience and that overwhelming feeling of powerlessness.

This group member describes with vivid power the kind of casualty that can result from groups—even with well-meaning and highly skilled leaders. As long as one or more participants feel like an alien in the midst of others who appear to share a common bond, feelings of alienation will often result. As can be observed in this example, sometimes the negative effects are so enduring that the person becomes reluctant to ever join another group.

For a Class Activity

The previous narrative is, of course, your own worst nightmare. Whether as a group leader trying to prevent casualties or a participant trying to protect your own safety, you are extremely concerned with people being hurt as a result of incompetence, neglect, or insensitivity.

Although the details of the preceding story are sketchy, it is clear she felt powerless. She also mentions feeling like an alien, being the only black member of an otherwise white group. Her differentness never seems to have been transcended.

Talk in class, or small groups, about what this story triggers for you.

Scenario Four: A Blind Date

I would like to relate an incident that happened in a group situation which I found to be very demeaning. I knew from the beginning that the facilitator was not comfortable with me being in the group. I knew it was because I was blind. I tried to be positive. Yet, I was virtually ignored.

Throughout that first group session, I felt isolated and unwelcome. I was not encouraged to participate in exercises that were part of the group session. The hurt, the anger, and feeling of isolation are still with me today.

Thank God, I left the group after the first session. I left feeling that my time had been wasted and my efforts to continue with the group had been thwarted. Normally, I would have assertively confronted the facilitator on a one-to-one basis at a later time. However, this time I didn't have the energy or the desire. I felt that the facilitator's perceptions were more than I wanted to deal with.

For Reflection

Imagine that this blind person, accompanied with her apprehensions, fears, and her own preconceptions, joins a group you are leading. What steps might you take to help her feel welcome?

Scenario Five: Sexism in the Leader's Chair

My group experience as co-leader with a male partner was absolutely traumatic. As a single parent in school I was also juggling work and home, often rushing to go from one thing to another. I showed up huffing and puffing for group, often right as things began.

Throughout the group, I noticed often the male co-leader dominating the conversation and behaving as if he knew it all. He would cut me off and interrupt constantly. I often felt that he was attempting to dominate the group and I did not think we were working well as a team. It seemed that his domineering behavior got worse as the group progressed.

Once, as I was entering the door, I heard the male co-leader tell a group member to "shut the door on her." I immediately opened the door as it was shut and nothing was said to me during that session. I didn't say anything in group because I didn't want to argue publicly, thus causing the appearance of lack of cohesiveness in group leadership.

At the end of the group experience that semester, one of the female group members pulled me aside and told me that she felt it only fair that I be told that during the previous meeting the male co-leader and the male professor had conspired. They had plans to ask me in front of everyone what I had given to the group process. In her mind, she felt they were sexist and controlling, unwilling or unable to relinquish typically male patterns of dominance. I had to agree with her.

This example has lots of complicated issues. First of all, it demonstrates the ways that cultural conflicts and misunderstandings occur between leaders as well as members. Second, it shows the way tension between leaders gets played out in the group, with other members taking sides and becoming triangulated in the conflict. Third, it illustrates the ways that gender roles related to power and control can become toxic and hurtful.

We don't wish to leave you with the impression that all members of minorities or marginalized cultures have unsatisfactory group experiences. Quite the opposite is true: When efforts are made to help people to feel included, to respect their differences, to help them feel heard and understood, groups are perfect places for positive changes to occur. The problem has been, at least historically, that leaders have not be well informed and prepared to work with diverse cultures.

Start with Yourself

You are, of course, a member of a variety of cultures related to your ethnicity, religion, gender, sexual orientation, even your family background. Whether you identify strongly with one culture or another, you will be perceived by others as a member of various groups.

You bring your own biases and prejudices to any group, based on your previous experiences. You form first impressions of people based on their physical or behavioral characteristics. This is nothing necessarily about which to feel ashamed. It is actually adaptive behavior for humans and other animals to form instant assessments of others as to whether they might represent danger. We tend to view "others-like-us" as safe, and "those-not-like-us" as being a potential danger. These initial impressions are often changed quickly in light of new information, but it does not change the fact that we are all prone to make impulsive judgments toward strangers based on previous experiences with those who resemble them.

Whether you are black or white, whether you were born on this continent or not, whether your native language is English or something else, whether you are a member of the majority or marginalized culture, you still have some strong attitudes and values that you bring to the group. These include what you think is good for people and what they should do to get the most out of life.

For Personal Application

All of us have a rather long list of values and beliefs about what we think is good for people. Personally, I think people are much better off if they are involved in a romantic relationship, if they have lots of friends, if they know how to enjoy their own company, if they are resourceful, if they have lots of choices, if they are educated, and so on.

Write down a list of those strong preferences you have about what is good for almost all people.

Consider how these beliefs are embedded in your own cultural values and might clash with those who come from very different cultural groups.

Much of our discussion thus far has been on the effects of a leader who is a member of the majority culture working with others who have been marginalized. It is just as important for minority leaders to become aware of how their own internalized oppression can have equally detrimental effects on those members who are part of the majority. Ignorance about one's biases and prejudices, as well as internalized oppression, salient or invisible, can easily thwart any of your efforts to be helpful in groups (Abernethy, 1998; Chen, Chai, & Gunn, 1998; Gainer, 1992; Kelsey, 1998).

Group Work with Marginalized Clients

The big question for you, as a beginning group leader, is how do you adapt what you have learned (and are learning) about general principles of group dynamics, development, and growth to the specific needs of each participant? Every member brings a unique cultural heritage that shapes his or her perceptions, values, and behavior. Those from marginalized cultures have also suffered their share of abuse from group leaders in positions of power and control.

Caution

The first principle to keep in mind is to remind yourself that people from marginalized groups are more likely to be suspicious and tentative in their participation. We offer this cautionary advice with a degree of hesitance, since any generalizations we make are, in themselves, contributing to stereotypical views. One of the truths about human diversity in general is that the variations within any given culture are often greater than those between cultures. What this means is that there are often greater differences in basic values within groups of African Americans or Native Americans or Mexican Americans or lesbian paraplegics then there are between these groups.

Keeping this warning in mind, it is safe to recommend that you proceed carefully, sensitively, and cautiously when dealing with any person who has suffered discrimination or oppression previously. If it turns out such caution is unnecessary, you can always accelerate your efforts.

Remember, as well, that it is an absolute myth that you must be so careful that you tread lightly in discussions of cultural or racial differences. An open forum for talking about such diversity can actually promote even greater closeness and cohesion (DeLucia-Waack, 1996).

Labeling

How you identify a person is an important part of both his or her culture and identity. This is especially true with those who have experienced oppression. It is important for clinicians to be aware of the politically correct reference to groups, but most importantly, to be sensitive to how the person wants to be identified. When in doubt, always ask. Spend some time in the group discussing the issues openly so everyone understands what is preferred. Such an interaction might sound something like this:

> LEADER: "I noticed that you just referred to yourself as Indian, rather than Native American. I wonder if you wouldn't mind saying more about what that means to you?"
>
> SALLY: "In my family we are proud of being American Indians. Native Americans is just a name that whites have given to us. But I am part Paiute, part Ute, and I have Irish blood too."
>
> LEADER: "So what you are saying is that you would feel more comfortable if we talked about your *Indian* heritage. If you feel ready to do so, tell us more about your background that you think would be important for us to know about you."

The leader is showing as much respect and courtesy as possible while demonstrating interest in her cultural background. Permission is secured for eliciting more information. Requests are worded tentatively, giving Sally a way to decline if she would prefer. The leader is also modeling the way the group will explore and honor the cultures of each member.

For Personal Application

Everyone has an identified culture (or many cultures) that include their core values and beliefs. These can include your ethnic background, your ancestral blood, your geographical location, your religion, your profession, your sexual orientation, gender, or recreational pursuits. It is not only a matter of being an African American, a Jew, a gay, or Italian American, but also being a marathon runner, a rural Nevadan, a feminist, or an engineer. In each case, you may identify strongly with the values, interests, and beliefs of this group.

If you were going to educate a group about the basic things members need to know about you in order to understand your background and help you, which would be your strongest cultural identifications? Within those cultures, what are the basic ideas that you think others should know in order to understand your origins?

If time permits, talk to classmates in a small or large group about what they would most need to understand. For example, I (Jeffrey) might say that being Jewish, it is important to know how much education and achievement are valued. Also that I hold this ingrained fear that some time in the near future, there will be another Holocaust, another systematic attempt to kill everyone of my religion, just as there has been every century previously.

After you have each had a chance to share your cultural backgrounds, talk about what you learned from the experience.

Self-Disclosure

As you are probably well aware, members of different cultures treat personal disclosures in varied ways. It is even a completely foreign concept among some people to tell those outside their family anything personal. This disclosure may be viewed as a form of weakness or betrayal.

Anything that has been said previously about the importance of trust in a group to encourage sharing and risking goes double when there are marginalized members present.

Level of Acculturation

Obviously, not everyone who says they are Latino, Filipino, Baptist, or feminist means the same thing. Since there are degrees of commitment and attachment to particular cultures, you would want to be careful to make assumptions without first checking things out. When someone says he is Jewish, is he Reform, Conservative, Orthodox, or nonpracticing? When someone says she is Catholic, does this mean she honors all proclamations of the Pope, attending Church every week, or does she attend only Easter Mass? When someone says he is Cuban American, does he speak Spanish in the home? When someone says she is Asian American, which one of the hundreds of cultures is she a member? How long ago did her family immigrate? How important is it for her to be Chinese or Korean or Cambodian?

We are speaking here about two concepts that you will likely learn about in more specialized study of multicultural issues. *Acculturation* pertains to the process by which an immigrant adopts the attitudes and values of the new culture. *Cultural identity* refers to the particular point at which a person of any ethnic background embraces core values and beliefs. Assessing these two factors in minority group members is especially critical considering that they are often related to dropout rates, attitudes toward the group, and the kinds of problems that will be presented (Sue, Ivey, & Pedersen, 1996).

One of the valuable roles that groups can play is helping minority members deal with the acculturation process, learning ways they can preserve their own heritage at the same time they adopt the language and customs of their new home (Nakkab & Hernandez, 1998).

The group becomes a sort of surrogate family, but one with diverse perspectives about preferred strategies.

For a Field Study

Identify several types of groups that you might like to lead with relatively homogeneous groups that have been marginalized. Read articles written by group leaders who have specialized in work with these populations. You might, for instance, consult sample descriptions of group programs for nontraditional women (Dazzo, 1998), Asians experiencing career confusion (Pope, 1999), or others mentioned earlier in the chapter. This is a good way to get some preliminary background on the populations you intend to work with.

Second, go to original sources. Talk to members of the target culture. Find out what their previous experiences in groups have been like, what they liked best and least. If they had negative outcomes, what could have been done differently? What advice do they have for you in reaching out to this population?

Finally, interview group leaders who already work with your identified populations. Pick their brains about the mistakes they have made and the things they have learned over the years.

Power

Because of many marginalized clients' experiences of oppression, the process of empowerment is important when leading marginalized groups (Sandu & Brown, 1996). According to McWhirter (1994), empowerment means that powerless people are made aware of the debilitating power dynamics in their lives and are helped to regain and exercise control. Certainly you can appreciate that a group is an ideal setting in which to deal with these issues, given that so many interactions are really about dominance and control as members attempt to get their needs met and influence others according to their preferred way of thinking.

Validation

Groups are ideal settings to validate the experiences of marginalized groups that led them to distrust institutionalized systems, such as mental health services, in the first place. Most, if not all, marginalized populations (including women) focus on the group or tribe or self-in-relation, not the individual, as the most salient element of existence. This is in direct conflict with the predominant Western values that so control our existence—autonomy, independence, privacy, competition, individual power, and control.

Yet groups are actually a perfect place to practice those values that are so much a part of minority cultures. In order for a group to operate effectively, cooperation is stressed over competition, trust and intimacy over privacy, relationships over self-sufficiency, interdependence over autonomy. Groups function as a tribal system, very similar to those of an indigenous culture, or those most familiar to Latino, Asian, or African origins.

In group work, we return to the roots of human culture, stressing the importance of collective rather than individual actions. To the extent that we can build a climate that respects the cultural diversity of all members, that is so inclusive that nobody feels marginalized, we begin to heal the rifts and conflicts that have been so much a part of our larger society.

Review of What You Learned

- Be careful of making gross generalizations about people based on their apparent or even espoused cultural identity. There are wide individual differences.
- Drop-out rates and unsatisfactory outcomes are more frequent for marginalized group members unless special efforts are made to help them feel validated and understood.
- Your own cultural identity, including values and biases, impact the way you lead a group.
- Culturally diverse groups provide more opportunities for all members to confront issues related to powerlessness and oppression.
- Help each participant to inform all others about important cultural beliefs that provide a context for understanding current concerns.

CHAPTER

6 Theories of Group Intervention

If there was ever a time when an experiential approach to the subject was needed, surely it would be in this chapter on theory applied to groups. Never in so short a space will you be exposed to so many new terms and confusing ideas that either seem so alike you can't tell much difference between them or seem so different that you can't imagine how it's possible that you could lead groups in such opposite ways. I will give you a hint, though: These different theories of group work are far more alike than you can imagine, and also more different than they seem. Confused already? Not surprising, considering the complex nature of this subject.

Naturally, there are whole books devoted just to the theories of group work (see Brabender & Fallon, 1993; Corey, 2000; Gladding, 1999). You are also probably aware that there are complete semester or year-long classes devoted exclusively to theories related to counseling, family therapy, consultation, or intervention. Perhaps you can therefore appreciate that if you ever hope to learn even the most rudimentary overview of these various theories, you must find a way to personalize and integrate them into your life.

The goal of this chapter is not to help you master the various approaches to group work; there will be plenty of time for that later. As a beginner, your job is to familiarize yourself with the very basic ideas, at least to the point where you can recognize many of them even if you will not be able to distinguish them clearly. Another preliminary goal would be to search through these conceptual options to identify those that seem most appealing to you, most compatible with your values and style, and most applicable to the setting in which you hope to practice.

Keep in mind that the theories we will review are not limited to group settings; most of them were originally designed for individual sessions and were later adapted for group leadership. Once you have narrowed down the work settings in which you hope to practice, as well as the styles that seem most appealing, you will be able to concentrate further study on those few approaches that seem most suitable. You will most likely not limit your exploration to how a theory is applied to group settings only, but also how it is employed with families, individuals, or even organizations.

Obviously one chapter is an absurdly limited space to cover all of the theoretical approaches to group leadership. It is anticipated, however, that you will integrate what you learn here with other theory courses or study that you will undertake.

For Reflection

Review in your own mind what you already know about theories of helping. You might, for example, recall the names of certain approaches that have historical significance—Freudian or psychoanalytic, for instance. Consider what you already understand about the ways that these theories are organized. For example, you might remember that a "behavioral" approach helps people to set specific goals or that a "humanistic" approach concentrates on the quality of relationships. If you have had little background or training in theory thus far, then make your own guesses about how they are probably constructed.

Now, before you read about theories of group leadership, make some inferences and predictions about how various approaches you already know about would be adapted for groups.

Theories and Group Leadership

You already have your own ideas about the best way to help people in groups. You might not have a well-articulated theory, or one grounded in systematic research and field-tested across multiple populations, but you do have some notions about the best ways to use groups for constructive purposes.

You have been watching people for most of your life, observing how they behave at family gatherings and meetings. You have some rough notions about how to enliven up a party, how to restrain someone at a dinner who is being distracting, or how to help people who are meeting for the first time to feel comfortable. Although it may seem to you that these techniques represent a mere collection of "best practices," tested and tried through

For Group Discussion

In small groups, reflect on the behavior of your instructor so far with respect to the theory or theories that you believe are guiding his or her behavior in leading your class group. He or she has probably already given you clues (or made explicit statements) about which theories he or she favors, but keep in mind that what people espouse is not necessarily what they are doing in practice.

Make a list of all the statements, disclosures, and evidence that support a particular theory that your instructor may be following. For instance, she seems to like demonstrations and roleplays a lot, or he believes the past is important in understanding the present, or she says that people learn leadership through direct experience and immediate feedback. Don't worry about giving a name to the theory (you may have not learned that yet). Just try to identify consistent patterns that you have observed.

Exchange your analysis with other small groups to note the different perceptions.

experience, you may be surprised to realize that you already have a well-developed conceptual paradigm that guides your behavior. You have preferred explanations to account for why people act the ways they do. You have hypotheses that lead you to behave in ways in certain group situations that you believe will produce desired outcomes. In some cases, you may have even spent the time organizing what you know and understand into a coherent framework. This is not unlike the theories that you will study—each represents an attempt on the part of an individual, or team, to make sense of why people act the ways they do in groups and what can be done to organize things in such a way that growth and change is maximized.

A theory helps you to organize what it is you know, not to mention providing a structure for explaining or predicting behavior (Patterson, 1986). Rather than a single entity that remains constant over time, your theories constantly evolve with new experiences (Peterson & Nisenholz, 1999).

For a Field Study

Interview several experienced group leaders to find out about which theories they subscribe to in their work. Ask them about the journey they followed to arrive at their particular set of operating assumptions. Ask them to describe their process of theory development starting from the moment they began their training until the present time. What advice do they have for you, just starting out in the field, about the best way for you to learn and apply the theories you are reading about?

Keep in mind that although we will be looking at different approaches to group work that appear to follow unique lines of inquiry and apply radically divergent methodologies, they all actually share the same basic operating principles. Even if the theories in their raw form strike you as so at odds with one another (one may say that you should remain only in the present while another will insist you dig into the past), most group leaders tend toward a degree of pragmatism in their style (Kottler, 1994a). This means that regardless of their espoused theories, they do what works according to what a given situation demands.

This reason this chapter follows others that were about group dynamics, stages, and processes, is because in spite of their ideological differences, most group practitioners share similar ideas about the ways that groups organize themselves. For example, in their treatise on the psychoanalytic group approach (to be covered shortly), Rutan and Stone (1993) describe the use of leader interventions like confronting inappropriate behaviors and clarifying member statements that almost all professionals employ. Likewise with each of the theories presented, you will find facets that belong with other perspectives as well.

Why Bother with Theories?

If it is true (Do not take my word for it: Ask group leaders in the field) that most group practitioners do not practice theories in their pure form, and if the approaches are often diluted, adapted, and integrated into others, why do you need to bother to learn this stuff at all?

For Reflection or Group Discussion

How about answering the question to yourself or with classmates? Why is it important for you to spend time learning about various approaches to group work if you are most likely going to end up using an integrated approach that combines the best features of each?

As a result of your thoughtful reflection and discussion of the matter, it is likely you realize that a theoretical grounding in the major approaches gives you some options about ways you can proceed in any situation. Once you understand the history of the field, the ways that various ideas and leadership styles evolved, then you can make some informed choices about which approaches might be best for which clients and contexts. Moreover, before you can integrate the best parts of theories into an organized framework you can follow, you must first be aware of which options are available.

As a beginning group leader, you would be well-advised to stick with the basics presented in the earlier chapters, plus the selection of one theoretical model for you to follow, at least initially. As for which theory you should select, that will depend on:

1. *Your professional identity.* Some professions are more closely identified with particular models. Social workers leading hospital inpatient groups would choose a different approach than would family therapists doing couple enrichment groups.
2. *The needs of your clients.* Elementary school kids, chronic pain sufferers, or drug abusers would respond better to some approaches over others.

For a Class Activity

In general, study groups are excellent structures by which to master complex ideas. Each participant takes responsibility for providing expertise in a particular area. Peer support provides needed encouragement. All members are able to pitch in to help understand complex ideas. Most of all, it makes learning fun!

If you have not already done so, it would be a good idea to team up with several classmates in order to learn the theory basics contained in this chapter. There just is not enough time in class, or space in this text, to cover all the material that you will need to know. I am *not* talking about stuff you should know for any exam—far more importantly, you must understand these theories in order to function effectively in your leadership efforts.

Even if time is limited and you are overloaded with other commitments, it would still be worthwhile to form a study group for a short duration in order to talk about the theories in this chapter. Even if you could only meet a few times, you could still talk to one another about points of confusion, areas of interest, and personal applications. Ideally, each of you could take responsibility for summarizing a few of the theories, directing others to additional sources for further study.

3. *The guidance of your instructor and supervisors.* Your teachers and mentors will help you narrow the choices to those that they think are most appropriate for your situation. They will offer you a good starting point to build upon.
4. *Your own felt sense.* Pay attention to which theories seem most attractive to you and which ones seem less interesting. Each theory has its own philosophy, values, goals, and strategies that will strike you as more or less compatible with your own beliefs.

In the next sections, you will be introduced to the basic concepts of several major theoretical approaches to group leadership. Concentrate on the "broad strokes" rather than the finer details that you can pick up through more intensive study.

The Psychoanalytic Approach

Like most of the theories you will read about, the psychoanalytic or psychodynamic (so named because of its attention to intrapsychic or internal struggles) approach evolved originally as a form of individual therapy. We are covering this theory first because it has had such a powerful influence (for better and worse) on all other approaches.

Review of Basic Assumptions

You will recall that Sigmund Freud and his followers developed a theory that helped people to investigate past experiences that continue to exert influence over present behavior. For example, if someone appears inappropriately hostile to a teacher, it might be theorized that some sort of "transference" is going on in which injustices by previous authority figures of the past are clouding current perceptions. Perhaps you can imagine how easily a dynamic like this would play itself out in a group in which people are constantly responding to one another not as they really are, but how they imagine them to be.

For Reflection or a Class Activity

Record the names of your classmates in a column down the side of a page. Next to each of their names, write down how each person reminds you of someone else who looks, acts, or talks a bit like that others you have known. If you find yourself drawing a blank for someone, then just skip that person; alternately, you can just take a wild guess and list someone who bears a passing similarity in some trait.

During private reflection, or discussion with others, explore the challenges of developing relationships with people when there is so much distortion going on. What are some ways that you can see people more clearly as they present themselves, rather than as you imagine them to be through your perceptual filters?

You have probably had some exposure to other Freudian ideas that are important in therapeutic relationships. In this type of group, attention is directed toward deeper processes, exploring underlying needs and desires rather than surface expressed goals and presented symptoms (Livingston, 1999). There is also an interest in uncovering core issues of abandonment, emptiness, intimacy, and achievement that are grounded in early experiences (Altfeld, 1999).

The unconscious plays a big part in this theory. In other words, people are motivated not only by conscious intentions but also by forces beyond their awareness. This means that group members will do and say things that, at first, appear to make little sense in light of their stated desires. A woman proclaims, for instance, that what she wants more than anything is a lasting, intimate relationships with a partner. It has been apparent to everyone, however, then when she is presented with viable opportunities to make this goal come true, she inadvertently sabotages things and chases the person away. Unconscious influences may be operating here in which, beneath her awareness, she is so terrified of intimacy that she is actually seeking to protect herself.

In the previous example, we see a manifestation of something psychodynamic theorists call *defense mechanisms*. According to this approach, core threats are kept at bay through the use of characteristic strategies that act as buffers to ward off perceived attacks. You will see the following defenses in action many times in groups (or any social situation).

- *Denial.* A group member has been told repeatedly that every time there is conflict in the group, he works to diffuse it, acting as a rescuer. He vehemently denies that this is his intent, claiming that he is just trying to help others. What you know about his past, however, is that he came from a home in which there was a high degree of conflict that he found so intolerable he ran away as a teenager.
- *Projection.* "You seem so angry today. Must have had a tough day, huh?" Actually, the person who is being addressed is quite puzzled since she did not at all have a difficult day; on the contrary, it is a pretty good one. Furthermore, she does not feel so much angry as she does misunderstood. After exploring the situation further, we find that the first speaker is the one who is feeling upset about something that happened at work and he projected those unacceptable feelings unto someone else.
- *Rationalization.* "It's really no big deal. I decided a while ago that I wouldn't even want to go to college. I don't know why we are even talking about this." It hurts too much, of course, to admit to failure. An alternative defense that employs a type of intellectualizing denial is one in which the person seeks to disown the hurt by explaining things away.
- *Reaction formation.* You happen to know for a fact that one group member absolutely despises everything that another member stands for in terms of lifestyle and basic values. Yet in the group, you notice that he goes to extreme lengths to appear overly conciliatory and cooperative with this person. As in the previous defenses, a person may push down threatening feelings by overcompensating in opposite ways than would be expected.

Given more space, we could review other defenses, as well as other important psychodynamic concepts. You can get a taste for how this sort of group would operate from the following principles:

1. The focus of attention would be on past experiences that impact current behavior.
2. Under the leader's guidance, members would seek to increase awareness of their characteristic defenses and unconscious motives.

3. Dreams and other unconscious material would be used to access feelings and experiences beyond awareness.

4. Groups would be of relatively long duration, helping members to develop the degree of safety and support that would be required to explore long-standing patterns.

5. Intrapsychic (internal) and interpersonal tension play a large role in the group as members attempt to sort out their reactions to past experiences and one another's behavior.

6. Insight plays a huge role in these groups. The focus is much more on understanding oneself, and one's interactions with others, than with translating this awareness into action.

What Do You Do with This Stuff?

Assuming that you see some validity to these ideas, you might wonder how to actually use them in practice. As with most groups, the leader's job is create a safe and supportive climate that makes it possible to explore frightening ideas and experiment with risky behavior. Since these types of groups aspire to go deeper than most others, cohesion is even more important.

Psychodynamic groups are often designed as relatively long term—more than a few months and sometimes for a duration of years. As you can imagine, it takes quite a while to develop the level of trust that it would take for people to be willing to explore their deepest, repressed issues. Also, because these groups are after characterological changes rather than only symptomatic relief, considerable time is needed to produce this sort of transformation.

The group leader presents him- or herself as "neutral" and objective as possible so as to maximize transference opportunities that could be worked through when members "project" their authority issues onto the leader. Needless to say, it is also critical for the leader to monitor "countertransference" reactions (those personal reactions directed toward members) that might distort or impede therapeutic work.

Interpretation is used a lot in group—of individual as well as group behavior—in order to bring repressed material into awareness. It was observed in one group, for instance, that rather lengthy silences occurred after one member, Kathryn, confronted another, Toby, about behavior that she found irritating. Rather than responding, Toby withdrew (his normal defense). Other group members brought this to his attention as characteristic of what he always did as a child when his parents censured him. Couldn't it be possible, they wondered, that he was responding to Kathryn the way he had to his mother?

To complicate matters further, Kathryn had her own issues brought into play. Her reaction to Toby seemed way out of proportion to his alleged transgression. Group members went to work on her as well, until the point where the leader intervened and offered: "It seems to me that many of you are working very hard to keep the focus on this disagreement between Toby and Kathryn as a way to keep any attention being directed towards yourselves. Mandy, is this not the exact scenario you described used to happen at your dinner table all the time? You mentioned how you would keep everyone from getting into your stuff by keeping the focus on others."

These interpretations, by members and the leader, are typical of a group that sees as its primary mission to increase awareness of self and others by addressing unresolved past issues. While traditionally, such a group structure has taken many months or years in order to operate effectively, more recently psychodynamic group structures have been developed that are designed to work more efficiently (Kleinberg, 1999; Rutan & Stone, 1993; Strupp, 1992).

Other Psychodynamic Groups

It could be said that almost all other theories are offshoots of psychoanalytic thinking since it really was the first therapeutic approach. There are several distinct models, however, that are now becoming far more popular than traditional psychoanalytic groups because of their greater responsiveness to contemporary life.

Object Relations.   Originally designed for work with severe personality disorders, theorists such as Heinz Kohut (1971) and Otto Kernberg (1975) developed a model that group leaders are now using to create group structures that stress patterns of early interaction experiences that manifest themselves in other social situations. Since severely disturbed individuals present fairly primitive, chaotic, manipulative patterns, groups are designed to maintain strict boundaries, consistent norms, and a "holding environment" that is conducive to feeling safe. These kinds of groups are not for beginners, by any stretch of the imagination.

Adlerian.   Given more space, this group model is at least as deserving as others for more detailed treatment. It is not strictly a psychodynamic approach even though its inventor, Alfred Adler, was once a disciple of Freud's—the one, in fact, who most adapted the theory for group situations. While Freud looked primarily at the biological basis for human behavior, Adler examined social roots.

Similar to other approaches we will cover later, the Adlerian group is viewed as a psychoeducational environment in which members examine the ways their early family experiences are affecting their current relationships. In contrast to the psychoanalytic approach, however, this model is concerned far more with the present rather than the past, with action over insight alone, with being integrative rather than exclusive in its selection of techniques, and with feeling a sense of belonging in the group (Dinkmeyer, 1975; Dinkmeyer, Dinkmeyer, & Sperry, 1987; Dreikurs, 1969; Dushman & Sutherland, 1997).

Psychodrama.   This is not so much a theory of group leadership as much as it is a psychoanalytically derived method of accessing deep material. Freud, you may recall, placed great emphasis on the value of "catharsis," the release of emotional energy that takes place when people are given the opportunity to resolve long-standing issues. Rather than merely talking about traumas or themes, J. L. Moreno (1964) devised the strategy of helping people to act out their stories.

Psychodrama, roleplaying, and other enactment strategies are designed to help members to work through issues and problems by acting out the scenarios in which confrontations or critical incidents take place. Almost all group approaches now make use of this technique to help members practice or rehearse new behaviors, as well as to uncover new material to work on in group.

As with all the approaches included in this section, psychodrama works with present conflicts and problems as manifestations of unresolved issues from the past. The theory goes that once these core struggles are resolved, present symptoms will resolve themselves.

For Reflection

Decide for yourself whether you believe present conflicts and problems often result from past, unresolved issues. Think of an ongoing problem that you have faced through-out most of your life. A good place to look is at issues related to intimacy, acceptance, approval, and competence.

What might be the origins for how this theme developed in your life? What are your earliest memories associated with this issue? What were some of the messages you got growing up that have shaped the way you now see yourself?

Write about the connections you have made, linking present behavior to past experiences. Talk to others about what you now realize.

The Person-Centered Approach

Among all his contributions to therapy and counseling, Carl Rogers was first and foremost a group specialist. He believed that group settings, with their climate of support, cohesiveness, acceptance, and caring, were the perfect environment for change to take place (Rogers, 1970). If a group leader could create a place of safety for participants in which an atmosphere of genuineness and empathy prevailed, he believed that members would grow and learn at their maximum potential.

Certainly you have heard about (or can remember) the encounter group movement of the sixties. The idea was that groups could be structured for almost everyone in which they could encounter one another in honest and authentic ways. Unfortunately, because little was known at the time about how to prevent casualties and little training was available for leaders, many people were wounded by these experiences. Nowadays, person-centered groups are designed according to the same guidelines as any other professional group experience that fosters growth while protecting people from coercion and harm.

Basic Principles

Person-centered groups are probably more familiar to you than you could imagine since they have been depicted in films and television as the classic group experience in which people sit around a circle and share their feelings with one another. In reality, this limited and obsolete vision is only part of this model.

1. *Feelings are where are the action is.* The previous group models we examined place a great emphasis on the intellect and reasoning powers. The person-centered approach, by contrast, sees the understanding and expression of feelings as the most

legitimate focus of work. If an individual was to say, "My best friend ignored me," the psychoanalytic group would explore the deeper meaning in this statement with regard to past issues, fears of abandonment, family of origin issues, and so on. In a person-centered group, members would instead help the person to explore more deeply his sense of hurt, anger, betrayal, and confusion. They would help him to feel heard and understood. They would validate those feelings, resonate with his experience, perhaps join him in his struggle by sharing similar examples from their own lives. Most importantly, they would let him know he is not alone.

2. *Relationships are everything.* It is through the relationships among members that growth, learning, and healing take place. The content about which people speak, the issues they raise, and the subjects they discuss are far less important than the bonding that takes place among members. The leader models this type of connection as much as possible by demonstrating in his or her own relationships with participants the same qualities that he or she would like to see others develop. Person-centered leaders are thus warm and accessible as opposed to the more objective, detached posture of the psychoanalytic leader. They present themselves as authentic, transparent, honest, and genuine as possible, hoping that these qualities will become contagious in the group.

For a Class Activity

This is among the most challenging and risky of all experiential activities in this book. It is not for the timid, nor is it for anyone who does not feel ready for such an intense, authentic encounter with others. Keep in mind, however, that you do not want to ask others to do anything that you are not willing to try yourself. If you are not yet willing to "volunteer" to be open and honest with others, consider what it would take for you to arrive at that point.

Arrange yourselves in small groups with your chairs pressed together as close as you can. Take a few minutes and make eye contact with everyone in the group. Do not speak. Resist the urge to laugh. Do not whisper. Keep your attention focused completely on the eyes of each member in your group.

As you make contact with each person, note how you feel inside. Pay attention to the various reactions you have to each person, the complexity of sensations and awarenesses. Tune into the dialogue inside your head as well, but concentrate mostly on your primary feelings.

After everyone has had a chance to connect with eyes alone, begin speaking to one another about your feelings and reactions. You must follow these rules: (1) Preface what you say with the stem, "I feel . . ." or "I am aware of . . ."; (2) do not talk about what is happening, only what you are experiencing in the moment; (3) be respectful, caring, and sensitive in what you communicate; (4) be real and genuine.

After several minutes of this encounter, talk about what it was like for you. Mention the things you found most uncomfortable as well as the parts you enjoyed. Talk about how you can incorporate this "way of being" into your life.

3. *Growth is as important as remediation.* Although many other models concentrate their efforts on fixing problems and alleviating symptoms, the person-centered theory is growth oriented. It seeks to help anyone, regardless of present functioning, to reach greater potential.

4. *It is all about trust.* The conditions of high-functioning groups are designed to encourage a degree of openness and honesty that are not possible in other settings. Imagine there is a place where you can say whatever you want without fear of being judged or criticized.

5. *Being real.* The hallmark of a person-centered group is the attention to immediacy. This means being aware of what you are feeling in the present moment and being willing to express those genuine feelings aloud. Obviously, it takes a lot of courage and trust to do such a thing.

6. *Active listening and responding.* The person-centered approach to helping is most known for its skills geared to reflect others' feelings. The group leader models this behavior as much as possible, letting group members know they are being heard and understood at the deepest possible level. It sounds something like this.

SUEANNE: "I can't seem to figure out what's wrong exactly. It's all kinda muddled in my head, like it's . . . I don't know."

LEADER: "You're feeling so confused about everything you've been saying that it's hard to sort out what is most important. It is also really scary for you that you don't feel in control."

SIMON: "Yeah! That's it for me too, Sueanne. I mean, as I was listening to you talk and all, I was feeling confused, too. Not about what you were saying so much, but about something that has been going on in my life as well that I don't understand."

LEADER: "Simon, you're feeling relieved in a way to know that you aren't the only one who is so confused. And Sueanne, I can see by your face that something that Simon said really hit home with you. I wonder if you could talk to him about what is happening for you right now."

You can see quite easily how this person-centered leader is trying to keep members in the present, focused on their feelings, and facilitating their deep communication to one another. The leader is using active listening, or reflection of feeling, to encourage this process.

7. *Facilitation.* Rogers believed that anything worth learning cannot be taught. Whether in the role of therapist, counselor, teacher, or parent, he felt strongly that our job is to help people to teach themselves. As such, the leader role is seen as "nondirective," which really means "subtle" rather than controlling.

Rogers (1967) believed that growth oriented groups proceed along a series of developmental stages (such as those reviewed in Chapter 4) that include the following progress:

- milling around and small talk leads to . . .
- resistance to intrusions leads to . . .

- expression of feelings about the past and present leads to . . .
- sharing of personal issues leads to . . .
- immediacy of feelings toward self and others leads to . . .
- intimacy, acceptance of self and others leads to . . .
- reduction of games, defensiveness, and facades leads to . . .
- feedback and confrontation leads to . . .
- deep encounters with one another leads to . . .
- behavior change inside and outside the group.

You may have your doubts that such behavior in the group necessarily leads to permanent change outside the group, and this skepticism is a reasonable caution. What makes a person-centered group (or any group, for that matter) most effective is when the leader does make sure that participants generalize what they are learning to their lives in the outside world.

The Existential Approach

The person-centered group, like the Gestalt group that follows this section, is considered to be part of the larger family of existential theories. What this means is that these models are primarily concerned with helping people find meaning in their lives. Of course, in one sense every group is existential to the extent that it helps its members explore issues related to personal responsibility, isolation, meaninglessness, and death (Johnson, 1997; Saiger, 1996).

Basic Philosophy

Perhaps more than any other theorist, Viktor Frankl (1963) embodied existential philosophy when he wrote about the survival strategies employed in Nazi concentration camps. Here was a group environment so toxic, so filled with hopelessness, that people literally died of despair; they simply gave up. Frankl tried to create some meaning in his experience, some reason to live, even if it was to tell the world about what he witnessed. He constructed a form of therapy that attempted a similar path—to help people find meaning in their suffering.

Borrowing from the work of existential philosophers, and building on the early work of existential therapists, Bugental (1978, 1990) and Yalom (1980, 1995) have been among the most responsible for translating existential ideas to the practice of group work. Many of the core group texts in the field (including this one) are existentially based as well, helping students to develop an appreciation for complex issues related to finding personal meaning.

Uses of the Existential Approach

Some people will come to you with specific symptoms or problems in need of attention, whether in the form of addictions or other dysfunctional behaviors. Others will present issues that do not lend themselves to easy resolution or may not even have complaints that you can do much about. Imagine, for instance, individuals who have a terminal or chronic disease.

An existential focus to a group seems especially appropriate when the members can profit from making sense of their existence rather than necessarily initiating specific courses of action. Like the person-centered or psychoanalytic approach, this is an insight theory, one that follows the premise that people should be challenged to reflect on their lives, where they have been, where they are headed, and mostly, where they are now.

When participants can profit from greater self-awareness, when they are struggling to find some purpose to their lives, when they must create some meaning from their suffering, perhaps unable to change conditions outside of their control (disease, poverty, oppression, age), existential issues come to the forefront. This is as much true for the leader as it is for the participants, since this is an approach that requires a high degree of authenticity and humanness on the part of the helper. "My willingness to remain open to my own struggles," writes Jerry Corey in describing his existential orientation, "determines the degree to which I can be a significant and positive influence for others in the group" (Corey, 2000, p. 266).

What Such a Group Looks Like

Groups become existential when members explore core issues of personal meaning. Most anything can push things down such a path—loss of control, restriction of personal freedom, reluctance to accept responsibility, feelings of isolation, or the recent death of a close friend.

ARON: "I don't know. It's just so hard to accept the idea that he's gone. And it was all so sudden. It could happen to any of us at any time."

NED: [Laughs] "Not me. I'm going to live forever!"

CAROLE: "Hey, if you're talking immortality, don't forget to include me, too."

LEADER: "I notice that it's hard to stay with Aron and his grief, not to mention the issues he's raised. Anyone notice something interesting that just happened?"

PAM: "Sure. As soon as Aron reminded us that we could all die at any moment, Ned and Carole started joking around, trying to diffuse the subject because it's so scary."

LEADER: "What about that, guys?"

[Silence in the group for a minute that seems much longer.]

ARON: "I don't mean to bum ya'll out or anything by talking about this stuff; it's just that I'm kind of blown away. This friend of mine had so much to look forward to, and then . . . Wham! . . . snatched just like that. It's really got me thinking about my own priorities. I'm wondering about whether I want to keep doing the things I'm doing with my life."

LEADER: "How about the rest of you? What has this stirred up in you?"

When groups take an existential turn, members become reflective and deeply personal. They talk about the directions their lives have taken and what they can do to make different choices.

For Personal Application

Imagine that you have just been told you have a terminal illness with only a few months left to live. What would you do differently with the time you have left? What unfinished business do you need to complete before you die? What choices would you make to live your life more fully, to experience more love and excitement and tranquility? What would you do to extract every precious moment from your limited time left on this planet?

In fact, you *do* have a terminal illness. And you *are* dying this moment just as your heart and body slowly wear out. You may not die in a few months, or even a few years, but each second is taking you closer and closer to your own mortality. What do your resolve to do in light of this realization?

Talk to others about your resolutions, committing yourself to more intense engagement with your own existence.

The Gestalt Approach

Like the person-centered approach, Gestalt therapy was born for groups. Similar to the existential approach, Gestalt groups are concerned with issues related to freedom and responsibility, especially in the present moment. Yet, whereas in the previous theories members talk about their concerns, Gestalt groups are intensely action-oriented.

Fritz Perls, the founder of the Gestalt approach, was vigorously anti-intellectual. Like most therapists of his day, he was trained as a psychoanalyst. Like so many of his brethren, he found this theory to be restrictive and not at all suited to his personality and style. Perls enjoyed being dramatic and provocative. He was not as concerned with the past as with the present. An existentialist at heart, he cared deeply about the ways that people attempted to escape the present.

Gestalt Principles

Gestalt means a sense of wholeness, an integration of the various parts of self. According to this theory, people become fragmented in contemporary life, pulled in so many different directions that they lose their sense of being grounded. They escape the present with forms of self-medication. They avoid responsibility for their lives. They become cut off from their essential wants and needs. They feel disconnected from the community of others.

Gestalt practitioners follow several basic procedures:

1. They keep the focus of the group in the present.
2. Instead of delving into why people do the things they do (most people don't know and this keeps them in the past), attention is directed to "how" and "what" questions.
3. Self-awareness is paramount. This is the most experiential of all groups in that participants are urged to become actively involved in interactions and "experiments" and then report on what they sense and feel (but not think).

4. Enactments and roleplaying help members to become more aware of their inconsistencies and unfinished business.

5. Certain language patterns that reflect avoidance of responsibility are confronted. Members are asked to substitute "I won't" for "I can't," "I choose to" instead of "I should," and "I" instead of "you." In each case, the emphasis is on personal responsibility.

Gestalt Techniques

More than other group approaches, Gestalt therapy comes loaded with a bag of tricks, filled with clever and powerful exercises designed to help members experience themselves and others more fully. Various exercises are introduced that help group members explore their fantasies, speak to their opposite selves, act spontaneously, increase awareness, work through dreams, and develop greater intimacy. Since it is somewhat incongruent to talk about Gestalt theory instead of experience it first hand (remember: its essence is primary experience), the best way to learn about it is to try it out for yourself.

For a Class Activity or Field Study

One favorite Gestalt method is called the "hot seat," so named because it turns up the heat for those who are willing to risk being completely honest with themselves and others. This is also an exercise useful for those who are first learning to use open-ended questions—those that require elaboration about deeply personal issues.

The rules are deceptively simple. Each group member takes turns, on a volunteer basis, to answer any question that others might ask. The intent is to build intimacy and cohesion rather rapidly by moving beyond small talk to the most personal aspects of human experience. The other group members construct questions that are designed to facilitate deep exploration. I like to put it this way: Imagine that you can ask this person only one question, and based on the answer you hear, you must give a twenty minute talk on the essence of what this person is like.

Whether at a family gathering, social situation, or in any group, you can imagine how quickly intimacy and trust would develop. Try it for yourself. Here are a few of my favorite questions to get you started:

1. What are you most proud of in your life?
2. What are you most ashamed of?
3. When was the last time you cried? Describe what happened and how you felt afterwards.
4. When was the last time you felt out of control?
5. What is something that nobody in the world knows about you?
6. Which question are you most afraid I might ask? (Answer it.)

The object of this exercise is not to be intrusive or nosy. It is designed to help you practice getting to know someone in an efficient period of time, and it helps the volunteers to work on issues related to self-acceptance.

Most students either love the Gestalt approach or hate it; it is hard to feel neutral about a method that is so provocative, so dedicated to stirring things up in order to work them through. It is likely that even if you do not find the theory suitable for the type of work you intend to do, you will still use a lot of its techniques in whichever groups you lead.

The Cognitive Behavioral Approach

Now, here is a change of pace. For the first time we are looking at a theory that is far more action-oriented, more logical and analytic, more focused on problem solving, and more geared toward teaching specific, adaptive skills. This may very well appeal to those group leaders who will be doing relatively short-term groups in a psychoeducational format, such as the kind favored by school counselors and substance abuse therapists.

Whereas several of the previous theories have valued feelings and experience as the most legitimate source for group attention, this approach works on underlying thinking patterns. Basically, the belief is that people experience emotional suffering not because of what happens to them, but because of how they choose to interpret those events. It is their thinking patterns that determine how they feel.

Underlying Assumptions

Rather than speaking about one approach, this section refers to a family of theories that share similar underlying assumptions. Whether it is called rational emotive behavior groups (Ellis, 1992; McDuff & Dryden, 1998) or cognitive behavioral groups (Beck & Haaga, 1992; Brok, 1997; Toner, Segal, Emmott, Myran, Ali, DiGasbarro, & Stuckless, 1998), the intent is essentially the same: Teach group members to become more aware of their dysfunctional thinking and how to substitute alternative strategies that produce more desirable outcomes.

In this approach, it is believed that if people think differently, then they will feel and behave differently. If, for instance, a group member thinks to himself, "I've been disrespected by this guy in the group," he will likely feel angry and upset. If, on the other hand, he thinks, "I've been misunderstood," then he will only feel mildly annoyed. The goal of this approach is to help people choose the way they would like to feel, a powerful enticement.

Basic Structure. Cognitively oriented groups are often structured around a teaching model in which participants learn sound principles of working through emotional struggles and then applying the concepts to specific problems in their lives. The leader acts as a tutor who, after introducing basic ideas, coaches group members to help one another dispute their irrational beliefs and reason through alternative ways of thinking about their situations.

Irrational Beliefs. According to this theory, people get in trouble when they adopt certain thinking patterns that are not considered part of reality. They represent distortions, exaggerations, and faulty logic. Here are several the most common ones:

1. *Life is not fair.* This is irrational because clearly the world is not a fair place where everyone gets exactly what he or she deserves.

2. *This is terrible*. People tend to exaggerate what they have experienced, believing it is truly awful, rather than annoying or disappointing, that they did not get what they wanted or expected.

3. *I can't stand it*. A corollary to the previous irrational belief, this one represents that one's situation is far worse than it really is. It may seem so bad that you cannot stand it, but actually, you can tolerate anything except death.

4. *I must do well*. People also make absolute demands of themselves (and others) that cannot possibly be attained. Nobody can do as well as he or she expects in every situation.

Disputing Beliefs. Cognitive groups tend to be fairly confrontive settings in which members are challenged by the leader and others to examine what they are saying to themselves inside their heads and then to learn other alternative interpretations of their situation. This process can unfold in a somewhat unstructured manner in which members bring up issues and then learn the method as it is applied to the situation, or they can follow a far more structured program. Some cognitive behavioral groups proceed according to a series of "lesson plans" in which the first few sessions are devoted to exploring the presenting problems, the next three sessions to learning how to identify and challenge the dysfunctional or irrational thoughts, the next sessions to systematic problem solving, and the final few sessions to other applications and generalization of learning (Scott & Stradling, 1998). Throughout this process, members have specific written homework assignments to complete.

Listen in on a Group

What would it sound like to listen in on a group that places such emphasis on teaching thinking and problem-solving strategies? In the following dialogue that takes place during the fourth session, after members have already learned the basic ideas, one person is struggling to digest the notion that she is creating her own problem.

CHRIS: "I tell you, he really *does* make me so angry."

LEADER: "Yeah? How does he do that? How does he get inside *your* head and trigger your emotions? I thought only *you* had the power to do that."

CHRIS: "Oh, you know what I mean. It's just that he can be so mean . . ."

DON: "So because he acts cruel, that means you have to get all bent out of shape over it?"

LEADER: "And it is just your perception that he is mean. I don't imagine that he would agree with you."

CHRIS: "No, he'd say he is just trying to help me."

MORGAN: [to Leader] "Is this the time when I ask her to look at what she's telling herself about his behavior?"

LEADER: "Go for it."

If this sounds like you are really just doing individual therapy in a group setting in which everyone takes turn getting help, that is often what occurs. Since this is an educational model, the focus is more on meeting individual member goals rather than facilitating group dynamics and processes. Of course, cohesion and trust are still important, but only to the extent that they create a climate useful for the learning.

The Reality Therapy Approach

This is another action-focused model of group work that helps people to be more reality based in their perceptions and behavior. Originated by William Glasser (1965, 1985), and further developed for group work in a variety of settings (see Wubbolding, 1990, Fuller & Fuller, 1999, and Henry & Cashwell, 1998 as examples), this approach bears a similarity to the cognitive models we have just reviewed. It is educationally based and seeks to persuade people to choose different ways of behaving in order to meet their self-declared goals. In fact, the whole theory is all about making choices, which is why Glasser (1998) now refers to his approach as "choice theory."

Some Basic Premises

There are a few basic questions that are asked of people in reality therapy, whether in groups or individual sessions:

1. What are you doing?
2. What are the consequences of this behavior?
3. Is this getting what you want?
4. What would you like to do differently?
5. What is stopping you from doing what you claim you want?
6. What will you do in the future?

For Personal Reflection

Identify one area of your life right now in which you are experiencing difficulty as a direct or indirect result of the strategy you have currently adopted. Ask yourself the reality therapy questions and answer them. What will you do differently?

Gets right to the point, doesn't it? Group members are challenged to examine the choices they make every day, with every decision they make, and every action they take. They are forced to look at what works in their lives, and what does not work. Finally, they are encouraged to make a plan for being more effective in meeting their needs.

The leader takes a highly directive, active, and confrontive role in the process, teaching group members to challenge one another, asking the difficult question: Is what you are doing getting you what you want? Since the answer is inevitably in the negative, the group is used as a brainstorming session to consider other options and what their likely consequences would be. Needless to say, this type of group becomes problem-centered and is especially well suited to participants such as addicts, offenders, and delinquents who have not been acting very responsibly.

As with some of the other approaches we have examined (cognitive, person-centered, Gestalt, existential) the emphasis is on the present rather than the past. Also similar to Gestalt and cognitive groups, the atmosphere tends to be very confrontive. No excuses are accepted for failure to do what you said you would do. That is not to say that anyone is blamed or shamed as a result of not following through; rather, they are simply confronted to examine what got in the way, which choices they made, and what they would like to do instead.

A Few Comments on Cultural Biases

Obviously, reality therapy, like so many of the models presented up to this point, is reflective of the North American dominant culture in which the theories evolved. They stress individuality, freedom, personal choice, and autonomy, which are so much a part of many Western cultures. Imagine, however, how inappropriate these models could be for other cultures (i.e., Native American, Asian) that have very different value systems that stress cooperation, co-dependence, and subjugation of individual needs over those of the larger community. In such cultures, issues like personal responsibility are less meaningful than collective responsibility. It is for this reason that all of the previous theories *must* be adapted to the specific population you are working with and the special culture of the group's members.

The Narrative Approach

Constructivist approaches to helping emphasize the ways that individuals construct their own perceptions of reality though their language, culture, background, and creations of meaning (Gergen, 1985; Harre, 1984). Among these socially and linguistically based theories is a form of narrative therapy originally designed for family settings because of its sensitivity to the stories that people learn about who they are and the ways their particular experiences are framed within a unique cultural context (White & Epston, 1990).

Constructivist (also called social constructionist with some subtle differences) approaches to individual or group work are incredibly complex and intellectually challenging. What they offer is a model for explaining how people co-construct a shared reality of their group experiences (Brower, 1996). Narrative approaches are among the most well developed, or at least more clearly described, theories that can be adapted for your purposes as beginning group leaders. Actually, it has only been in the last few years that a well-articulated model of narrative group work has been developed (Chen, Noosbond, & Bruce, 1998; Monk, Drewery, & Winslade, 1997; Silvester, 1997; Vassallo, 1998), although this is an approach that lends itself particularly well to group settings because of the ways it acknowledges individual and cultural differences among participants.

Like many of the other approaches, narrative therapy has been adapted from individual interview settings to a group format. It has evolved in a professional and cultural climate very different from what many North Americans find familiar, since its first proponents worked mostly in Australia and New Zealand. It is within this context that narrative group work is especially responsive to gender and cultural backgrounds of participants. It has been described as both a feminist theory, as well as one especially well suited to work with indigenous peoples (Silvester, 1997).

Narrative Assumptions

A narrative approach to group work subscribes to certain beliefs that may strike you as very different from others you will study.

1. *The group member's presenting problem is the problem to be addressed.* Whereas some approaches see the problem as symptomatic of underlying deeper issues, or perhaps as a manifestation of a disease, family dysfunction, early trauma, or a weak spirit, narrative group work treats the symptoms as the most legitimate focus of attention.
2. *Personal experience is treated as the ultimate authority.* Reality is constructed by the stories one has heard (by media, parents, books, and so on), as well as those one makes up about one's life.
3. *Human beings tend to "story" their lives.* Our brains appear to be wired in such a way that we feel a natural affinity for the narrative to provide a coherent record of what we experience. These stories *are* our reality.
4. *Behavior is not viewed as abnormal or pathological, but rather as functional adaptations to unique circumstances.* Rather than using a medical model to diagnose problems, the narrative approach favors one that uses the group member's own language and metaphors.
5. *The group leader takes on the role of a guide rather than an expert.* A position of "not knowing" or "curious questioning" is adopted in which the group leader attempts to model for participants a respectful, persistent, and probing style of exploring the dominant narrative.

Narrative Group Techniques

Narrative therapy introduces a whole new vocabulary of terms used to describe the novel techniques and interventions. Many of these have been adapted for group settings.

Narrative Metaphors. In the process of constructing meaning from one's life experiences, people tend to use particular words and metaphors to represent their narratives. For example, in telling a group about her life growing up at the hands of a neglectful father and abusive mother, Kristen described herself as worthless. "I'm like the recycled trash that people put in front of their houses when they've emptied the receptacles. That's why I've been in three marriages. I get used up and then thrown away."

Is this really what happened in Kristen's life? From a narrative perspective, this is her "constructed reality," pieced together from the "dominant story" that she has subscribed to. It is the job of the group leader to help Kristen, with the aid of other group members, to refashion a quite different story in which she feels empowered rather than victimized. Eventually, a new narrative would become internalized, not just by Kristen, but by others in the group who can relate to her problem. That, of course, is one of the beauties of group work: It may appear as if you are helping one person at a time, when actually many others are identifying with the narrative, personalizing the issues, and working on parallel processes.

Externalizing the Problem.   It is a very peculiar idea that instead of getting group members to accept responsibility for their difficulties, the way other approaches proceed, the narrative group leader gets people to disown their problems as a way to reduce scapegoating and self-blame. Contrast, for example, the way a cognitive-behavioral group leader would ask, "How are you *making yourself* depressed?"; a reality therapist might ask, "What are the consequences of *choosing* to be depressed?"; an existential group leader might say, "How are you using your depression as a way to avoid responsibility for your freedom?" On the other hand, the narrative group leader would ask, "How has depression ruined your life?" The tone and syntax, you will notice, implies that depression is not a choice, or even an internal condition, but rather an externalized problem that is creating misery. This clever strategy allows group members to work together to defeat the externalized problem.

Deconstruction.   How are your dominant narratives influenced by the ways your culture has taught you what it means to be a member of your gender, sexual orientation, ethnicity, religion, and geographical identity? Group members work together to "deconstruct" the ways that roles and stories have been learned. This is especially the case when group members have been taught to "pathologize" their experiences. Kristen, for instance, learned from a child psychologist when she was younger that she had a "conduct disorder" because she tried to stand up to her abusive mother. Group members help her to understand that an alternative version of those events is that she was appropriately assertive in the face of attempts to enslave her. One outcome of this exercise is that group members learn to question continuously the origins of their beliefs and how they have been shaped by forces representing the majority culture.

Relative Influence Questions.   Typical of many "brief" therapies, narrative group work helps participants to sort out the consequences of their behavior. What are the effects of continuing to act the way you do? What is the likely outcome if you continue in this way? When are some times that you have not felt controlled by your problem? How have you managed to keep the problem from disrupting your life at various times?

For a Class Activity

Narrative group leaders adopt a stance of "curious questioning" when they explore issues with participants. They demonstrate a respectful, naive, but intensely interested attitude that says: "Help me to understand your story. More than that, tell me about your experiences that are *outside* your dominant story." This strategy is intended to help people to bring out new ways of viewing their life narratives.

In group of three or four, take turns having one or more persons tell a story that represents an important lesson in life. Use a stance of curious questioning to help the person find exceptions to this dominant narrative. In other words, ask the person to tell alternative stories in which he or she was able to overcome the problem or ignore it.

Afterwards, talk about the effects of this exercise and what you learned.

Other brief therapies might call this "looking for exceptions," but in the narrative approach you are trying to do more than just balance the negative with some instances of success; you are also learning a process for tracking the effects of maintaining the current narrative.

Brief Group Structures

Some of the most powerful learning experiences you have ever encountered did not necessarily take a long time to work. I remember sitting in my very first group experience as a student in a beginning class. We were required to participate in a "real" group as part of the class, led by the instructor.

I sat in the group the first few weeks and thought to myself, "No way am I saying anything personal in here!" I did not trust my classmates and I surely was not going to put myself in a vulnerable position knowing that my instructor might some day be in a position to grade me.

Although issues related to "dual relationships" were addressed—we would only be graded on our papers in the class, not what we said or did not say in the group—I still did not feel inclined to stick my neck out. We were instructed about things like informed consent (accurate information about risks) as well, acknowledging that this experiential approach had its advantages and dangers. Personally, I could only see the downside of disclosing.

The group was humming along, already in its third session, when I was sitting in the background watching the proceedings as usual. To this day I do not know what pushed me to open my mouth but I almost could not stop myself. Without rehearsing what I would say, I blurted out that I felt trapped in my life, working in a job I hated, engaged to a woman I did not love. I received about an hour of attention (it probably felt like an hour but was really only a few minutes) before the group session ended.

During the subsequent week, I proceeded to change just about everything about my life that I could. I quit my job. I ended the relationship with my fiancée. I moved into an apartment in the inner city so I could go to school full time to be a therapist. I announced to my family and friends that I was no longer the same person; I did not hold the same values, nor covet the same dreams. I completely reinvented myself during that week. I kept thinking how cool it would be to return to the group and announce, oh so casually, that I had rearranged my life.

Perhaps you have had an experience similar to this—it might not have been sparked by a therapeutic group but by some other dramatic or traumatic event that got your attention in a way that nothing else could. The point of this story is that change need not take a very long time. If you are ready, if the environment is right, if the circumstances are in place, the briefest of interventions can initiate the most dramatic changes.

A Sign of Our Times

While not strictly a theory as much as an abbreviated approach to doing groups, brief methods have evolved in recent years in response to the demands of "managed care" in the mental health and medical systems, as well as pragmatic concerns in schools, agencies, and other settings.

Essentially, any of the preceding theories may be shortened in their scope as long as more modest goals are defined, time-limited sessions are negotiated (usually three to ten meetings), presenting problems are addressed (rather than deeper issues), careful screening is undertaken to include only good candidates, and follow-up evaluations are conducted (Bloom, 1997; Shapiro, Peltz, & Bernadett-Shapiro, 1998).

Planning a Brief Group

If you find yourself in a work situation in which you have far too many people to help and too little time available to do your job, you may very well design brief group experiences. In such structures you will want to take the following guidelines into consideration:

1. Set a definite time limit as to how long your groups will run.
2. During prescreening interviews, help group members to get a running start by identifying problems to work on. Remember that group work begins not with the first session but with the first decision to seek help.
3. Establish a thematic focus to your group, one that all of your group members can relate to. For this reason, it is often better in briefer groups to work with a central issue (i.e., divorce, anger, depression, weight loss, etc.).
4. Remain solution-focused rather than explanation-oriented. Include structured homework assignments that help members work on problems between sessions.
5. Don't get fancy. Stick with basic group process that keeps things in the present rather than the past and that addresses specific problems.
6. Work efficiently to establish trust and cohesion as quickly as possible so that you can move the group into the working stage.
7. Monitor closely those participants who may need longer, more intensive treatment, individual sessions, or more support than can be provided in briefer groups. Make referrals accordingly.
8. Remind participants that the clock is running, that time is limited and must not be wasted. Make group members responsible for using the group time in the most efficient manner possible.

For Reflection and a Field Study

Think of a time in your life in which you made a dramatic change in a relatively short period of time. Write about this experience, including what happened, why you were ready to change at that critical juncture, and what you believe was responsible for such a rapid shift.

Talk to other people about the times in their lives that they transformed themselves within a very short period of time as a result of some supportive or confrontive group experience. Compare your experiences with those of others you interview.

Based on what you learned, what would you do in brief groups to capitalize on those forces that you believe are most responsible for rapid, potent changes?

Other Theories We Did Not Get Around To

In the limited space available, we could only survey several of the most popular approaches to group work currently in practice. Depending on your interests, desired work setting, and type of group you wish to lead, you may wish to investigate other theories that might be of relevance to your work.

- *Transpersonal* group work has a spiritual, mystical flavor that is missing from the others we have reviewed (C.F. Clark, 1998).
- *Extensional* group work is representative of existential growth models that are used with relatively high-functioning individuals (Carroll, Bates, & Johnson, 1997).
- *Developmental guidance* groups are well-suited to school settings (Bowman, 1987; Gazda, 1989; Schmidt, 1999).
- *Feminist* group work is especially sensitive to issues of power and oppression that are so much a part of the dominant culture (Burstow, 1992; DeChant, 1996; Gilbert & Scher, 1999).
- *Social work practice* groups emerged as integrated and specialized applications of this discipline (Hepworth, Rooney, & Larsen, 1997).
- *Process consultation* groups are another specialized conceptual framework, but one designed specifically for business settings (Kormanski & Eschbach, 1997; Reddy, 1994).

An Integrative Model

Many group leaders choose one of the preceding theories of intervention and use its framework to guide behavior. Many others, however, prefer a more integrative model (Carroll, Bates, & Johnson, 1997; Corey, 2000; Hopps & Pinderhughes, 1999; Jacobs, Masson, & Harvill, 1998; Kottler, 1994a; Shapiro, Peltz, & Bernadett-Shapiro, 1998; Yalom, 1995) that combines the best features of several theories.

Perhaps later in your career you may choose to specialize in a particular theoretical orientation to group work, one that fits your unique style, client population, and work setting. As a beginner, it makes more sense for you to learn the basics of group leadership by following a fairly generic, universal model, one that can be adapted to a number of situations.

In the second half of this book, you will learn the means by which to make assessment and diagnostic decisions in groups, to read accurately the stage, dynamics, and processes that are operating, to apply basic leadership skills, to select appropriate interventions, and to function effectively with a co-leader. Most of this content will serve you well regardless of which kind of groups you wish to lead.

For a Group Activity and Field Study

We have just covered an extraordinary amount of material in a ridiculously short period of time. You could spend a whole lifetime studying any one of these group theories, so you can appreciate the depth of your challenge in trying to make sense of a dozen or more.

Form a study group with several classmates to review the various theories and talk about the features you like best and least. Based on your limited exposure, talk to each other about what draws you to a few of these models and what you find distasteful about others.

Make a commitment to investigate a few of these theories in greater detail. Read original sources written by the developers (Freud, Rogers, Perls, Ellis, Glasser, Adler, etc.). Read secondary sources as well by group leaders who have adapted the theories to various group formats. Peruse journals devoted to the particular theory of interest (i.e., *Psychoanalytic Psychotherapy, Journal of Humanistic Education and Development, Journal of Rational Emotive and Cognitive Behavior Therapy, Journal of Reality Therapy*). Finally, interview group practitioners in the field to find out about which theories they follow. Ask them to tell you about how they settled on those particular models.

Review of What You Learned

- Various group theories share a number of similarities in spite of their apparent differences. It is useful to search for common elements that can be integrated into your own leadership style.
- Group approaches differ in their focus on such variables as: past versus the present, symptoms versus underlying issues, cognitive versus affective versus behavioral dimensions, insight versus action oriented, individual versus family structures, group versus individual goals, process versus task completion.
- Most group leaders are flexible and pragmatic, borrowing concepts and interventions from a multitude of theories, depending on what the group or individual member needs.
- Some leadership approaches are best suited for certain settings and client populations.

CHAPTER

7

Assessment and Group Diagnostics

Each of the approaches reviewed in the previous chapter provides a framework for making sense of what is going on in a group. Depending on its philosophy, the theory may focus on assessing individual member issues or larger group dynamics. This is not really an either/or proposition: As a group leader you are responsible for closely monitoring what is happening with each participant, including presenting problems, interpersonal style, unique needs and goals, and progress toward identified objectives. Not only are you collecting and organizing information for each member, but you must also keep track of what is happening in the group at any moment in time. Who is bored? Who is anxious? Who is about to bolt? Which member should receive the attention next? Should you change directions or keep going with present flow? These are just a few of the questions that you will consider during every minute of your leadership responsibility.

What Is Assessment and Diagnosis in Groups?

There are three parallel assessment processes going on in a group. This creates some unusual challenges in that you must split your attention between each domain at all times.

Individual Assessment

First, you are watching closely the behavior of each member. It is likely that you have formulated some sort of working diagnosis for each person, including presenting problems and treatment goals. You will examine each person's behavior in terms of its relative contribution to the overall group objectives. Examples of what this might sound like inside the leader's head include:

- *For some reason, Patrick is being very quiet today. I wonder if something happened at home that he is not talking about.*
- *Nadia has chosen not to report on what she did last week. She may have forgotten, but I doubt it. I think she is hoping to avoid the issue altogether.*
- *I've just got to help Miguel become more concise. Here he has been talking for the last few minutes but nobody, including me, is even listening.*

- *Trina seems to lose track of what she has said previously, almost as if there are some memory deficits. I need to refer her for a neurological exam.*
- *Connie seems less than her usual lucid self. That could mean she has started drinking again.*
- *Luther either is showing signs of a conduct disorder or even more entrenched sociopathy. I need to watch his behavior carefully.*

For Reflection

Review each of the members of your class, identifying some of their most characteristic patterns that have been displayed consistently. What do you imagine are the issues that each of them would most need to work on in group (in your humble opinion)? What are some things about each person that puzzle you?

Now, since everyone else in the class is looking at you the same ways that you have been looking at them, what are some of the things they probably identified about you?

Group Assessment

Second, you are watching very carefully what is happening in the group, especially with regard to dynamics, stage development, and ongoing processes. Many questions will come to mind as you watch things unfold, as illustrated in the internal comments of a group leader:

- "I thought we were moving into a stage of cohesive engagement, but now it seems like more induction needs to take place first."
- "What would it take to develop more cohesiveness among the three different factions?"
- "Fred seems to be designated as a scapegoat by some of the others."
- "I see some collusion going on whenever attempts are made to get into risky areas."
- "What is the metaphor to describe what is happening right now?"

Self-Assessment

Finally, you are continually assessing what is going on inside of you throughout the experience. This internal monitoring will become a source for intuition and a "felt sense" about what is happening in the group. Far more that, however, you must be especially careful to watch for signs of countertransference toward particular members. How will you know if such a strong personal reaction is going on? Look for the following symptoms:

- The arousal of guilt from unresolved personal struggles that parallel those impulses and emotions of any member.
- Impaired empathy in which you find it difficult to feel loving and respectful toward a member.

- Inaccurate interpretations of a member's feelings due to your own distortions.
- Feeling generally blocked, helpless, and frustrated with a particular group member.
- Evidence of boredom or impatience when working with some members.
- Unusual memory lapses regarding the details of a group member's life.
- A tendency to speak about a client in derogatory terms.
- An awareness that you are working harder than the member.

For Personal Application

Again review each of the individuals in your class, including your instructor. This time, however, concentrate on your personal reactions, noting those people you have a strong attraction to, as well as those who rub you the wrong way.

Rather than concentrating on what others do that provokes, stimulates, or irritates you, look at what *you* are doing inside that prevents greater compassion, empathy, and understanding on your part. In particular, note the ways that you are critical of people who are most different from you, who engage in behavior you don't understand, or who are more like you than you would prefer to admit.

Obviously, you have considerable work cut out for you, simultaneously assessing yourself, individual members, and the group as a whole. That is one reason why it is so helpful to work with a co-leader to divide the diagnostic responsibilities. When that isn't feasible, you will need to consult with a supervisor frequently to check your impressions.

Models of Assessment and Diagnosis

There are several different diagnostic models currently in use by practitioners of various specialties and professional identities (Kottler, 2000). You are probably familiar with the "medical model," for example, the basis for the current "bible" in mental health diagnostics, the *DSM-IV* (*Diagnostic and Statistical Manual* of the American Psychiatric Association). Psychiatrists are not the only ones who use this manual, as psychologists, nurses, social workers, counselors, family therapists, and other mental health professionals must also refer to the diagnostic terms contained therein.

The *DSM* and Its Use in Groups

The medical model is, naturally, disease-based. This means that various emotional disorders are classified the same way as are other physical maladies. In the case of mental health problems, however, a complicated system has been developed that examines a given person's functioning in a number of areas. Although this method was not intended for group settings, per se, you will still observe various *DSM*-labeled diagnostic entities among group members you help.

Basically, the *DSM* looks at several features of a person's functioning, including personality characteristics, symptomatic behaviors, biological conditions, coping levels in the present and past, and other such variables. You will often overhear group leaders talking in this *DSM* language: "I've got this 'Axis II borderline' who is wreaking havoc in the group" or "I'm not sure if this guy's depression is reactive to his recent loss or if there is preexisting dysthymia." In the first case, the leader is describing a member with a manipulative personality disorder. In the second example, the leader is trying to differentiate between a form of acute depression that is a normal adjustment reaction versus a chronic, low-grade form of depression that may have been present before the crisis.

The most traditional type of diagnosis is one in which the group leader is required to develop a diagnosis for each member of the group, including present complaints, preexisting conditions, precipitating events, and a specific treatment plan. Insurance companies require this sort of information before they will process claims, and many agencies also see it as sound clinical practice. The problem, however, is that only part of the work in groups has to do with individual issues; the rest involves interactive and interpersonal contacts that do not lend themselves to individual diagnostic classification.

You may very well be required to keep records and update charts on each participant in your group, a challenging task that requires time-consuming paperwork. For each member, you would need to formulate a *DSM* diagnosis, develop an individual treatment plan, justify group work as the preferred modality to reach identified objectives, and then include progress notes documenting which interventions led to which outcomes that furthered the treatment plan identified earlier. If this sounds like it requires a high degree of creative writing, you are probably not far wrong. Nevertheless, it is a useful exercise to make notes after each group session, recording the progress of each group member and where you intend to go next.

Sample Progress Notes

As a beginner, you will most likely be required to keep detailed treatment plans and progress notes for each group member. This practice not only helps you to develop sound clinical habits but provides valuable notes for supervision. After group sessions, it is a good idea to jot down notes for yourself, including what each group member worked on, what goals or homework they have declared, and which directions seem viable next time. Such group session progress notes for a few members might look like this:

> *Sharon:* Quiet today, seemed withdrawn but denied there was anything going on. Was she looking for an invitation? If things don't change next time, I'll draw her out. I could also schedule an individual session. Reported making good progress on her relationship with husband but I suspect things are not going well. Is she overidentifying with Sam's issues?

> *Sam:* Seemed like a breakthrough for him today. For the first time he did not appear defensive, nor did he try to keep the focus off himself. Depression seems to be under better control with cognitive restructuring so medication may not be needed at this time. Agreed to talk to his wife about their lack of intimacy. We role played this scenario and gave him feedback. He left optimistic that he could change the way things have been going.

Mandy: No significant progress on her issues related to being more assertive either in the group or outside. Still engages in approval seeking with me and other males in group. Reports she is doing well but there is no evidence to support that. When confronted she tends to acquiesce. Would be interesting to try getting her to exaggerate her behavior next time. Need to get her honest feedback from group members about how they perceive her.

For Personal Application

After class one day, write up progress notes for the session. First, talk about general issues that you observed, applying everything you have learned already about group dynamics, group stages, and interpersonal patterns. Next, review the relative progress of each participant according to objectives that have been articulated. Finally, write reminders to yourself of things you would follow up next time.

It might take a half hour, at most, to write out these notes. They provide an ongoing record of the experience, suggesting possible treatment options for the future. In many groups, members are urged to keep their own progress notes in the form of a journal, sometimes even exchanging their writing with the leader or one another. The object is to make all participants more reflective about what is going on in the group.

Alternative Diagnostic Models

Almost all mental health professionals must use *DSM* language in their work even if they do not subscribe to the underlying assumptions of a medical model in which people are labeled with emotional disorders. Even those who do groups in inpatient settings, inheriting terminology like "the bipolar," "the borderline," and "the dual diagnosed" (sounds like a movie title), do not necessarily think in terms of this diagnostic schema that often reduces people to labels.

The *DSM* is clearly a valuable tool for group leaders in formulating systematic assessment impressions of a given client, including treatment considerations. It allows you to communicate with others in a common language and to be held accountable for your clinical decisions based on what is known about best practices for a given diagnostic entity. If, for example, you have someone in your group who has a form of major depression, with strong suicidal ideation, and you did not refer this person for a medication review and psychiatric consultation, you are probably being negligent. Likewise, if someone has a clearly identified personality disorder that is prone to interpersonal manipulation (borderline, sociopathic, narcissistic) and you did not screen this person out of your group of relatively high-functioning members, you are asking for serious trouble.

Although you will use *DSM* concepts and language in your assessment of individual group members, you may also wish to employ other diagnostic models that are more consistent with group methodology and a different philosophy. If you are leading a group that is working primarily on adjustment reactions to life stress, developmental adjustments, and growth issues, a medical model is highly inappropriate. Even if you are working with more severe kinds of problems in your group, you and your clients may still profit from employing alternative assessment models.

Developmental Assessment

In a developmental assessment process, you are not looking at pathology, disorders, or problems, but rather current developmental functioning when compared to what would be expected for a given person's age, culture, gender, life situation, and stated goals. You may recall from psychology courses that human growth and development is segmented into several broad areas including physical maturation. There are certain "developmental tasks" that are considered age appropriate—mastering scissors for a preschooler or driving a car without bumping into things for a 16-year-old. How are your group members functioning with respect to their developmental progress?

In a developmental assessment model, the question you are asking is not where are people dysfunctional, but rather where can they be encouraged and stimulated to move to the next levels of maturation. This is seen as a natural process that unfolds under the right circumstances. Your job as a group leader is to create the kind of climate that is most conducive to fostering developmental growth.

Behavioral Assessment

Ironically, humanistic and behavioral theories finally share something in common when it comes to diagnosis: Both frameworks believe that it is not useful to label people but rather to describe their behavior. Although the developmental model is concerned specifically with normative behavior, the behavioral model is focused instead on specific maladaptive behaviors in need of change.

Whether the group member is schizophrenic, depressed, or brain damaged, the important questions in behavioral assessment are which target behaviors can be changed and how might that best occur. Consistent with a theory that values specificity, objectivity, and measurability, the group leader operating from this framework would think in terms of which specific goals for each member can be worked on during the session and in between sessions.

A strict behavioral model would not be the only one that might adopt an assessment strategy like this; other approaches we have covered such as cognitive behavioral, reality therapy, and brief therapy also make use of procedures that identify specific behaviors in need of upgrading. Whether the focus is on observable behavior (assertiveness), verbalizations (shoulds, musts), cognitions (exaggerations), or other internal processes, the key is to describe specifically what is to be changed and how this will take place. The group leader would thus help members to formulate what they intend to change about themselves during a given period of time. These goals would be created according to the following criteria:

1. Specific, targeted behavior
2. Observable behavior
3. Measurable outcomes

4. Mutually negotiated contracts
5. Realistic, attainable objectives
6. Useful plans that are relevant to the main problem

What this means is that you would not ask group members to conduct self-assessments in a general way. Instead, you would help them to develop specific assignments that they could work on during each group session and between each meeting that would get them closer to their desired goals. This process in a group develops as follows:

MANDY: "I'm just so tired of getting in trouble in class. I do want to stop that but I just don't know how."

JOSE: "Why don't you just keep your mouth shut? That's what I try to do." [Laughs]

LEADER: "Well, that's one solution, Mandy. What else could you work on this week that would help you to make progress toward avoiding trouble and improving your grades?"

MANDY: "I don't know. That's why I'm here, right? Why don't you tell me."

LEADER: "Let's all figure this out together. What could Mandy do to work on her problem?"

STEPHAN: "Aren't we supposed to build on what we've done before? Last week, Mandy, you tried to do your homework every day but then you got frustrated because that wasn't realistic for you. You don't go from not doing any homework at all to then doing it every day. Maybe you could start off doing just ten minutes a few times."

So goes the discussion and negotiation among group members who assess for themselves what they need to do and then are helped to translate their goals into specific plans they can complete. This may not sound like diagnosis in the traditional sense of what you imagine that to mean, but the behavioral model does get you to assess behavior instead of diagnosing people.

For a Class Activity

In small groups, take the case of Mandy described in the preceding dialogue as a starting point. This is a 14-year-old girl who is repeatedly in trouble because she rarely turns in assignments and talks to friends in class when she is supposed to be paying attention.

One of you play the role of Mandy in the group, while everyone else will work together to help her identify what specific behaviors she wants to change and how she might do that. Help her to set goals for the next session that meet the six criteria mentioned earlier.

After you are done, talk to one another about how you found the exercise.

Systemic Assessment

Another alternative method of diagnosis is one that does not look at individual behavior at all, but rather at interactive patterns between group members. This is a diagnostic model favored by family therapists because it examines the systemic context for any problem. The problem in a dysfunctional family (or group) is rarely one person, or even his or her behavior, but rather the larger system that makes someone into a scapegoat.

You learned in Chapter 3 about the systemic, interactive view of cause-effect relationships contrasted with the more linear, traditional perspective of most individual therapists and counselors. Group leaders must actually apply both assessment methodologies, thinking in terms of individual disorders and dysfunctions à la the *DSM*, plus the systemic patterns evident in group behavior.

Crawl inside a group leader's head once again during a session and you are likely to hear something like the following:

Gee, Carole seems unusually timid and cautious today. I wonder if she is getting enough sleep. Her depression sometimes keeps her up at night worrying about things. I must check out her thinking these days.

Why does she keep looking at Merna? Now that I think about it, she's real quiet today as well. I wonder if they have had some sort of fight. They used to be so close but today, and last week, they barely speak to one another.

I notice that every time Gary talks, he makes a point to look at one or the other of them. The guy has such an incredible need for attention, big-time narcissistic stuff going on. He could be playing them against each other.

You will have noticed that there are two parallel assessment processes going on. The group leader is carefully scrutinizing each member's individual behavior, especially in light of what is already known. In addition, she is also looking at the ways that each member's behavior is both the cause and effect of others' actions. Just as an economist looks at the scope on a micro and macro level, so too does a group leader assess individual and group behavior.

Theoretical Models of Assessment

Not only does the behavioral approach have its own method of diagnosis, but all of the theories we have reviewed in the previous chapter come with their own assessment strategies. In summarizing these various approaches (see Table 7–1), the intent is not to overwhelm you again with choices, but instead to get you thinking flexibly and creatively about all the ways you can make sense of what is happening in groups and all the various facets that you can attend to.

Picture a group in which several different individuals are talking about their difficulties finding meaningful work. Each of them feels stuck in a dead-end job and they see few options for themselves that things will ever be different. The conversation has been going on for long enough that you know that you need to do something, to intervene in some way, but you are not sure in which direction to lead things next.

Should you interrupt the conversation and refocus back to a subject that is more optimistic? Should you get other group members involved who have been left out? Maybe you

TABLE 7–1   Assessment Models of Selected Group Theories

Theory	Assessment Strategy
Adlerian	Look for personal strengths that provide leverage for change; recognize patterns of early family dynamics in present interactions; conduct thorough lifestyle assessment of family constellation; identify faulty perceptions.
Narrative	Name the problem in person's own language; identify the themes in personal narratives; deconstruct the ways the dominant narrative evolved; externalize the problem; find out when the problem does not exert control.
Gestalt	Examine experiences in the present moment; recognize disowned or fragmented parts of members; label unfinished business; recognize when enactments might be useful; listen for distorted language; monitor awareness of own experience in group.
Existential	Observe avoidance of responsibility and freedom; recognize times of inauthenticity and avoidance of intimacy; look for themes related to meaninglessness, isolation, angst (generalized anxiety), death.
Cognitive	Recognize irrational beliefs evident in member thinking; listen for exaggerations, overgeneralizations, and overpersonalization in member speech patterns.
Reality	Recognize member needs; label irresponsible behavior; find excuses for inaction; assess consequences of behavior.
Psychoanalytic	Look for unconscious motives in behavior; label defense mechanisms; find sources of present difficulties in past traumas; diagnose projections and transferences; monitor own countertransference reactions.
Behavioral	Define specific behaviors to be changed; recognize skill and information deficiencies; identify reinforcers of dysfunctional behavior; delineate specific, measurable goals; follow up on previous assignments and evaluate progress.
Person-Centered	Decode underlying feelings; look for blocks to intimacy and trust; recognize when people are being judgmental, disrespectful, dishonest, unauthentic, or uncaring; identify areas for people to grow rather than problems to fix; monitor own feelings during process.
Brief	Define the problem; reframe the problem in a way that it may more easily be solved; look for exceptions when the person is problem free; specify solutions already tried that do not work.

could help them to see some possibility in hope in the future? Confront their excuses? Reflect their feelings? Interpret the underlying despair? Connect their experiences to other things you know about their past? Where to go and what to do?

In order to make any sort of informed decision about what action you should take, you must first form some diagnostic impression of what you believe is going on. There are so many dimensions of this brief interaction that you could attend to. If you look at Table 7–1 you can generate a thousand different questions you could ask and more than a dozen different hypotheses about what might be going on and which would be the best course of action.

For a Class Activity

It's time to apply what you learned in the previous theory chapter to an actual situation. In small groups, you will practice applying several different assessment strategies to a particular case.

One of you in the group should take about five minutes to present some issue going on in your life, or if you prefer, role play someone with a problem. During the presentation, you can take turns asking a few probing questions to draw the person out further and fill in some of the missing details.

After the case presentation, apply several of the assessment methods reviewed in Table 7-1 to form a diagnostic impression of what you think might be going on and to suggest a treatment plan. After you have tried out at least three different approaches, all of you come to a consensus as to which facets seem most useful.

Review of What You Learned

- Assessment activities are divided between diagnostic impressions of each group member, readings on group dynamics, and close self-monitoring of one's own personal reactions.
- It is sound practice to get in the habit of keeping progress notes each session for every member, as well as observations about group stages and issues. In your notes, include critical issues to follow up, such as future goals, declared homework assignments, and unfinished business.
- Several different assessment models (*DSM*, developmental, behavioral, systemic) allow you to focus on those aspects of group behavior that are most relevant.

8 Unique Leadership Skills

It is clear that leading groups is quite similar to other forms of helping, yet also somewhat different. The same skills that might be used during individual sessions would also be entirely appropriate during groups. If you have learned about "active listening" skills, for example, then you must realize that in group settings you can also easily reflect the content and underlying feelings that you hear. Likewise, all the other skills that would be commonly employed during interviews can be adapted for group settings as well (see Corey, 2000; Dye, 1980; Dyer & Vriend, 1975; Gladding, 1999; Nolan, 1978). Just as you might interpret or confront or summarize or clarify with a single person present, you would apply these skills when people talk in groups. In fact, one of the most amazing benefits of participation in a group is that members will learn to apply these same skills by watching and imitating the leader.

Group leaders must not only learn to adapt their usual helping skills to the requirements of a larger setting, but they must also master a set of unique behaviors. In this chapter we will review how you can take what you already know and make needed adjustments for groups, as well as cover additional skills that will be useful to you.

Helping Skills in Groups

If you would make a list of all the things that make a group leader so effective, you might come up with a number of broad areas. Certainly what group leaders know is important—their knowledge of theory and human behavior, their understanding of what gets people in trouble and what gets them out, their familiarity with research that guides professional behavior. You would also likely mention several personal characteristics—integrity, responsibility, dependability, charisma, and so on. No doubt, experts would also have logged a lot of experience in groups, feel comfortable in those settings, recognize important signs, negotiate through difficult passageways. After all, a guide should be familiar with the territory.

Knowledge, background, and experience are indeed important for group leaders. In addition, so are the skills needed to communicate effectively, clarify issues, mediate conflicts, and negotiate through the various stages in the journey.

When participants in groups are asked to contribute to this discussion by listing those skills and behaviors that they appreciate the most in their leaders, they mention such things as a leader who (Ray, 1999):

- Has a clear vision for the group
- Is someone who really cares about me
- Can teach me things I don't know
- Listens and responds to me
- Helps everyone work together as a team
- Makes everyone feel valued

Although this survey is related primarily to work groups in organizations, the same set of skills would also apply to any context or setting. Assuming that you agree with this assessment, the question now becomes: How do you propose to learn these skills?

For a Class Activity

Conduct your own piece of research with classmates. In small groups, each person shares an experience with the best group leader that has ever been encountered. This could have been in a therapeutic type of group, but may also have been in a class, business setting, or any other group.

Talk to one another about the *skills* that this leader demonstrated, rather than any personal qualities or other dimensions that were present. In other words, what was this person able to *do* that made him or her so effective?

You can read books and journal articles to learn the conceptual background. You can talk to more experienced group leaders and supervisors to find out about the stuff you need to make sense of groups. In order to master the skills of leadership, however, structured experience is the only legitimate path. You must find ways to practice these skills, receive constructive feedback on your progress, and then make needed adjustments. Of course, if you are *really* paying attention, group members will continually give you feedback on what is working and what is not; the problem is that often we are not listening to what they are telling us.

My favorite skill in groups is called *immediacy*. This is when you access what you are experiencing in the moment and then communicate aloud what you sense and feel. It is an especially potent intervention to use when people are talking about something in a detached way. For instance, I love saying something like, "I'm aware that right this moment, as you talk about your strong desire for closeness, you are doing everything you can to put distance between us."

After saying this, I feel so proud of my brilliant observation that I fail to notice that the person is very threatened and offended by what I said. I see him pull his chair back further and so I decide to use immediacy to reflect that as well. I just love the intensity of the encounter, the realness of the feedback that forces a person to confront behavior—that is, if the time is right. In this case, because I was not paying close attention to the feedback I was getting from the group member, I failed to make needed adjustments. He was saying to me clearly, "No, thanks. I don't want what you are selling right now. I'm not ready to deal with this yet. Could we go at this from a different angle?"

Now if you were watching closely, perhaps you could have pointed this out to me. The best thing about groups is that even when the leader is off base, other members will jump in to save the day. Indeed, another person did intervene and let me know that what I was doing did not appear to be helping very much. It takes this kind of feedback in order to get better at your leadership skills. In order for that to happen, however, you are going to have to figure out ways to get supervised experience and practice.

Soliciting Honest Feedback

It is not as easy as it sounds to hear the truth from others—that is, to find out what people really think about what you are doing. More often than not, when you ask for input you will get "yearbook feedback," the kind of platitudes that people write in their high school yearbooks: "You're so sweet. Don't ever change."

For Personal Application

Select three people who you trust to be completely open and honest with you. Although these could include family members, it would be better to pick classmates, acquaintances, or others whose thoughts and opinions you don't normally hear.

Tell these individuals that you need to collect feedback as part of a school project. Impress how important it is that they be as honest and forthright as possible. Explain, as well, that the best feedback is specific with supporting examples. If needed, provide a few examples.

Ask each person to tell you three things you might not already know about yourself that could be considered strengths, as well as weaknesses. Most people will struggle with doing this for a number of reasons. For one, it is really hard to be honest. Second, it is difficult to see things that are beneath the surface. Finally, they might not be sure what you are really looking for. That's okay, though. Whatever you hear from others gives you some notion about the challenges involved in giving and receiving feedback.

Ask someone to review your tapes or observe you in action, and more often than not they will tell you that you are doing a fabulous job. Trust me: They are lying. You could not possibly be doing even an adequate job after limited training and experience. Even after twenty-five years of leading groups, I leave every session with my head hurting over all the things I wish I had not done, all the things I could have done instead, all the gaffes and mistakes I made, and all the different courses of action I wish I had considered. After I talk to colleagues about the session, I find out a few hundred other things I missed.

Do not get me wrong. It is important to be forgiving of our mistakes. What I enjoy so much about leading groups is there is always so much to learn. No matter what you do and how you do it, there are always dozens of other things you could have done that might have worked better. I shrug at the possibilities. Oh well, I think, it is easy to second-guess ourselves after it is over, but quite another to make a choice in a fraction of a second.

The point I am making is that you must get lots of honest feedback from peers and supervisors if you are ever to improve your skill levels. One useful structure is to purge from your vocabulary the words "positive" and "negative" when applied to the activity of receiving feedback. After all, is it "positive" when someone tells you that you did a good job? What can you learn from *that* statement? And is it "negative" when someone tells you that you raise your voice at the end of statements, communicating doubt and undermining your persuasive influence? Rather than using those terms, it is better to think in terms of "supportive" and "constructive" feedback. That way, you get both encouragement and useful ideas that you can work on.

For a Class Activity

It's time to practice giving and receiving feedback regarding your basic skills. In groups of four, divide up your roles as follows: One of you will be a client and talk about some issue (real or imagined), another will be the helper, and the other two will be observers who will take detailed notes on the proceedings. You are to conduct a 5-minute interview in which you practice helping skills that you have already learned. You might want to stick with the basics: open-ended questions (those that can't be answered by yes or no), rephrasing (reflecting content), and reflecting feelings. At the end of the 5 minutes, close the brief session with a summary statement.

It is really the observers who have the tough job. Your role is to write down at least three things your partner did that you thought were especially good and three things that you think might be useful to work on. You are not responsible for being "right," or seeing the "truth." Your job is simply to express your opinion about what you observed. There will be two of you to compare notes and your partner can make the decision for him- or herself whether what you offer fits. If this is the first time this particular feedback was heard, maybe it is more about the observers' perceptions (or experience level) than about the helper's behavior. End the round by giving the observers feedback on their feedback. Remember, this is really an exercise on the importance of being honest and constructive.

Switch roles after each round so that each partner gets a chance to give and receive feedback.

Sample Observer Notes

Supportive Feedback
1. Good eye contact and attending behavior, communicating intense interest.
2. Good rapport established early when you told her what you understood.
3. Restatements were clear and concise, natural rhythm and flow to the conversation.

Constructive Feedback
1. Vocabulary of "feeling" words too limited. Kept saying "sad," "mad," and "frustrated."
2. Waited too long to insert comments. Let client ramble too much. Seemed reluctant to say the "wrong" thing.
3. Try not to ask so many questions. At times you seemed impatient. Rather than waiting for her to think, you'd ask another question before she had a chance to answer the previous one.

Skills Adapted for Groups

It is assumed that you are not taking this course in isolation, that you have had, or will take some time in the future, a class on basic helping skills. It might be useful for you to review or familiarize yourself with these skills (see Egan, 1997; Evans, Hearn, Uhlemann, & Ivey, 1998; Kottler, 2000).

One of the dangers of groups over individual sessions is that it is so much more difficult to customize your skills and interventions to the special needs of your clients. Remember that each of the group members comes from a unique cultural background in which the things you do and say will be interpreted differently. Thus, acquiring competence in these skills is one thing; it is quite another to become sufficiently sensitive in their application that you can make adjustments according to the group members you are working with (Conyne, 1998, Corey, 2000).

Recently, I have led groups in different settings in which there were Mexican Americans, Native Americans, Hawaiian Americans, Icelanders, Australians, or Hong Kong Chinese in attendance. Each group is distinctly different in predominant culture and tone. Even though the struggles and personal issues are much the same, the skills I must use in each group, and how I use them, are distinctly different. In a mixed group representing both genders, heterogeneous cultures, and varied ages, you must be even more flexible in choosing your skills wisely and employing them with appropriate sensitivity. Some of the following skills you might not use at all with some group members; others will need to be adapted according to their values and comfort level.

Rephrasing

Also known as paraphrasing, restating, or reflecting content, this is probably the most common and benign helping skill that is used to confirm what was heard. In groups, the leader uses this behavior to model how important it is to listen carefully and respond sensitively to what is said. Ideally, group members catch on to this interpersonal style and begin using it naturally.

> **DON:** "I'd like to try to do more with my life, but I'm so afraid that I'll just be disappointed again. Like always."
>
> **LEADER:** "It'll be another time in your life in which you put yourself out there and set yourself up for disappointment."
>
> **DON:** "Yeah. What's the point? If I'm just going to end up stuck where I am, maybe I shouldn't even try any more."
>
> **MARSHA:** "So you don't even want to try any more?"

The leader is trying to demonstrate solid listening and responding behavior, letting Don know that he has been heard. Marsha tries to follow his lead, but as you would expect from a beginner just learning this skill, she turns it into a close-ended question. Nevertheless, the intention is good. Members are learning how to listen and respond appropriately. The leader is showing that he cares and understands.

Reflecting Feelings

A companion to rephrasing, this skill also reflects back what was heard but at a deeper level. This is infinitely more difficult to do because you must listen to not only what was said, but what is felt beneath the surface. When group leaders employ this skill, they are not only taking the discussion to a deeper, more emotional level, but they are again showing group members how to listen and respond to emotion. As with all behaviors used in group, there is a parallel process going on in which members learn their own helping skills by observation and personal experience at the same time they are working on their personal issues.

DON: "Well, I don't want to give up completely. It's just that . . . I don't know . . ."

LEADER: "You really do have some hope, you're just so frustrated and tired of being let down."

MARSHA: "I sure know what that's like too. I remember when . . ."

LEADER: "So Marsha, you're really relating easily to what Don is going through. Maybe you can talk directly to him and tell him what you sense he's feeling."

Notice the way the leader uses the reflection to interrupt Marsha's digression: She was about to go into her own stuff, which would have taken the focus away from Don. The leader is prompting Marsha to use reflections herself to communicate that she understands. The leader keeps the discussion on a more emotional level, rather than just talking about the content.

Interpreting

This is still another way to listen carefully to the communication, decode underlying meaning, and offer that interpretation back to the client to promote greater self-understanding. In group settings, interpretations can take place on an individual level in which you venture a hypothesis about what might be going on for a person, or such explanations can be offered about group dynamics and process. Since this is potentially a threatening intervention, you would want to make sure that the timing is appropriate or people will become defensive or shut down.

DON: "Marsha, I appreciate sincerely what you are saying. And I know that you have had some tough times as well, but it's not just the same."

LEADER: "Don, Marsha was trying to make contact with you, to show you that she cares, and now it seems that you are negating her experience and pushing her away. You've reported you did this with others as well."

DON: "No, it's not that exactly. I mean, you're right, of course, that I have a hard time letting people get close to me."

KENA: "I have that same problem too, Don. Don't feel too bad about it."

NANCY: "Hey, you aren't the only ones. You remember I told you . . .'

LEADER: "I think that's great that you are all jumping in to give Don some support and that you can relate to his problem. I wonder, though, if what might be going on is that many of you are feeling uncomfortable with this issue and so trying to distract the focus away from Don."

In this scenario, the leader interprets both Don's statement and the group's behavior. Since such skills are based on assumptions and limited data, you would want to phrase them tentatively and sensitively.

For a Class Activity

Form small groups and practice basic listening and responding skills. As each person speaks, rephrase the content of what was said or reflect the underlying feeling that is being expressed.

Questioning

Often the previous skills are effective in eliciting all the information you might need in working with group members. Sometimes, however, you must resort to more direct inquiries. Here are three guidelines when asking questions: (1) Use them only when indirect means do not work or you may come across as interrogating, (2) structure them in an "open" versus "closed" manner so that the answers require elaboration, (3) avoid "why" questions (people usually don't know) and ask about "what," "where," and "how" instead.

For Reflection

In the group that is being enacted for these demonstration of skills, what are some questions that you could ask Don that might collect valuable information and further the process of exploration? Write a few down here:

1. _____

2. _____

3. _____

Remember, it is not just what you ask, but how you ask that is important as well. Compare the ways the following questions might be directed towards Don.

Close-Ended Questions	Open-Ended Questions
Have you always had this problem?	When did you first become aware that you had this problem?
Are you feeling upset with us for intruding so much?	How are you feeling right now?
Do you have brothers and sisters in your family?	Who is in your family?

Notice that open-ended questions facilitate a much greater level of elaboration and collect more information. In group settings, you will likely do some tutoring with members, teaching them how to ask good questions. For example, if a participant was to ask one of the closed questions just illustrated, you might insert, "I wonder how you could frame that question in a slightly different way to get more information."

Reframing

Many of these skills originated with particular theoretical orientations. You might have recognized, for example, that interpretations evolved from psychoanalytic theory or reflections of feeling from the person-centered approach. In the same vein, reframing is a skill that was once part of brief and family therapies, although it is now as "generic" as the others. The object of this more advanced intervention is to help group members to change the way they view their situations or their problems.

When it is used optimally, reframing creates a perceptual shift that makes it much easier to work with an issue. It is as if you are taking a painting, removing it from an ugly frame, and putting it into a new context that reveals it in the best possible light. This is something you might want to do in a group when you are aware that you cannot do much with the present issue as it is conceived.

In our previous group, Don says, "I've got a problem with intimacy. Everyone in my family does. It's just in our family genes."

For a Class Activity

Work with a partner to devise several ways to reframe each presentation of a problem by a group member.

1. "I guess I'm kind of promiscuous. At least that's what my parents say. I've only had sex with three different guys, but I didn't really date them very long before we slept together."
2. "I'm stupid. I've always been stupid. I mean, how else can I explain my inability to get a decent grade in this class?"
3. "It isn't my fault that things keep going wrong. It's this damn system that is so screwed up."

What would you do with a situation like that? As long as Don believes that he has "poor intimacy genes," there is very little you can do for him, short of genetic engineering.

If you attempt to disagree with him or argue with his interpretation directly, he may become defensive. In reframing, you take his conception of the problem, and put a slightly different cast on it.

"What you are saying, Don, is that many members of your family have shared your fears about getting close to others."

Notice that in this "rephrasing" of Don's statement, there are some subtle differences. The leader uses "many" instead to "all," implying there are exceptions to his family disorder. Second, the problem is changed from having a genetic predisposition toward lack of intimacy to a learned fear of intimacy. This is a problem that could actually be worked on in the group, whereas the previous one could not.

Confronting

The best confrontations are those in which the person does not know he or she is being confronted. It should be so sensitive and diplomatic that the person remains open to hearing what is said, taking it in, and metabolizing its essence. In the working stage of a group, there will be many confrontations. Group members are usually not very good at either confronting one another or responding to these honest statements. That is why the leader models this behavior as much as possible to point out discrepancies between words, body language, and behavior, either in the present or between what was said or done earlier and right now.

> KENA: "Don, I think you're just saying that shit about your family as an excuse so you don't have to change."
>
> DON: "That's not true!"
>
> LEADER: "Whoa! Kena, as you can tell, Don is feeling angry and defensive about what you've just said. Perhaps you could try that again, but this time say it in a way that Don can hear you."
>
> KENA: "Sorry, Don. What I meant to say is that maybe you have your own fears of getting close to others, and getting close to me, that have nothing to do with your family."

The leader has obviously been working in this group to help members learn to confront one another effectively. Since this is one of the hardest skills to learn, it takes considerable practice to find a balance. Otherwise, group members will "make nice" and avoid confrontations altogether (a conspiracy to avoid deep, threatening work) or they will become too aggressive and assaultive.

Disclosing

Among all the basic skills, this is the one that is most important for the leader to demonstrate. The object is to make it safe for group members to reveal themselves in an honest, open way. If the leader, who has power and status, can show members how attractive it is to be open and vulnerable, then others will follow. Careful, though, as leader self-disclosure can be easily abused since the focus is taken off the members.

In our illustrative group, the leader might address Don's reluctance to talk about his intimacy issues in the following way:

"Don, I can see that you are feeling uncomfortable with all this attention and even getting into this issue. I recognize this because I once had similar problems. Yes, I can see you're surprised, but I came from a very dysfunctional family in which the only way my parents showed intimacy was to scream at one another, or at me. I decided that I would never trust anyone to the point they could hurt me.

"What made the difference for me was realizing that although there are risks involved in trusting people, letting them get close, the alternative is far worse. I don't know about you, but I often felt very lonely relying only on myself all the time."

Hopefully, Don would feel encouraged by this disclosure. If this powerful leader, who obviously is now quite skilled at intimacy, can overcome this problem, maybe he can, too. It gives explicit permission that it is okay to be vulnerable and afraid. It also shows that the problem can be overcome with commitment and hard work.

Before using self-disclosure, you should ask yourself two questions to ensure that it is the most appropriate skill at that time:

1. Is there another way that I can do this without putting the focus on me?
2. How can I say this in the most efficient way so as to not keep members' attention for very long?

For Reflection

Think back on the times your instructors have used self-disclosure to illustrate a point, tell you a story about their lives, or reveal themselves in some personal way. When were the times that you found this most and least helpful?

Review the self-disclosures that I have used throughout this text. Which were those that seemed especially effective? Which ones struck you as distracting or self-indulgent?

Suggesting

As I mentioned in the very first chapter, giving people advice is not a good idea. For one thing, they hardly ever listen. For another, if what you tell them to do does not work out as they had hoped, you will be the one to get blamed. On the other hand, if what you suggest does turn out well, then you have inadvertently reinforced the idea that they should come back to you in the future.

Just as self-disclosure, confrontation, and other skills have unforeseen side effects, so too must you be careful whenever making suggestions. Ideally, they should be framed tentatively, in such a way to get group members thinking creatively, rather than providing specific advice. Such a skill might be used whenever someone is about to do something that you know is unsound or unsafe, or whenever you believe that others may profit from a gentle probe in a particular direction.

> DON: "So, I was thinking that maybe I would approach this girl that I like, and tell her I want to be close to her."
>
> LEADER: "If I might make a suggestion, Don."
>
> DON: "Sure, I'll take all the advice I can get."
>
> LEADER: "This isn't so much advice as an observation. In the past, you have managed to scare people away in various ways, usually by withdrawing."
>
> DON: "Yeah. So? This time I'm doing the opposite."
>
> LEADER: "Exactly! Anyone want to help Don understand what might happen?"
>
> KENA: "All I can tell you is that if you came on to me like that, I'd run so fast you wouldn't even find my trail."
>
> DON: "I'm confused. So, are you saying I shouldn't tell her how I feel? I thought that was the point."
>
> MARSHA: "No. I agree with Kena. It's just that you gotta be a bit more subtle."

In groups it is so much more challenging for the leader to get the members to do the work, rather than doing it all him- or herself. That means you have to thoroughly master these skills before you can ever hope to teach them to others. Your job is to get the ball rolling, to recognize that a suggestion is indicated, and then to cue members to do what needs to be done. You can always fill in with whatever they miss.

Summarizing

Just as in individual sessions, there are opportune times in which it is helpful to review what has just been covered. This can bring together disparate themes, connect related elements, link together several issues that have been discussed, or put some sort of closure on a topic as a transition to a new area.

Summaries should generally be initiated any time you are about to leave one topic or subject and move to another, when discussions are disjointed and chaotic, or when a transition is needed. Most of the time, sessions would end with some sort of summary statement.

Probably the best way to do a summary is to ask the group member who has received the most time to review what he or she is leaving with. Then you can fill in important things that were missed.

> LEADER: "Don, you've heard a lot of valuable feedback today. You have thought about a number of things related to your fears of getting close to people and letting them get close to you. I wonder if you wouldn't mind summarizing what you think this was all about?"

DON: "We were talking a lot about the things I learned growing up in my family about not trusting people. I had a lot of excuses for using that stuff as a reason for not having many good relationships now. That's about it, I guess."

NANCY: "Don't forget the part about the uncertainty you still feel about changing this pattern. At least I heard that."

KENA: "Yeah, and what about not coming on too strong with people you like."

LEADER: "Thanks. That's helpful to Don. In addition, you talked a lot about the closeness you felt to others in this group, how this felt like a good beginning for the kinds of relationships you want in your life. You got excited about possibilities and even identified one young lady that you wanted to get closer to. We talked about ways that you could make that happen and how you might sabotage things. Finally, you declared that you wanted to try some new things and report back to us. Maybe you could tell us some more about exactly what you intend to do."

Notice the way this summary naturally leads into a homework assignment that Don can complete between group sessions. Not all group leaders structure things in this way, but generally speaking, it is agreed that unless members work on issues between sessions, lasting change is not very likely.

For a Class Activity of Field Study

Participate in a group discussion for several minutes about some topic of mutual interest. If you are doing this with classmates, you could take turns talking about your strengths and weaknesses in various skill areas, including what you think you do best and where you feel less prepared. After each person speaks, spend another few minutes giving the person feedback based on what you have observed. Remember to include both supportive and constructive comments.

Before each person begins, select someone else in the group to act as a scribe. He or she will take detailed notes on what you say about yourself and what others tell you in the way of feedback.

Once a person has heard the feedback, he or she must summarize what was said, highlighting the most important areas and commenting on new things that were learned. Afterwards, the scribe will fill in things you missed by referring to the notes taken.

Group Skills

The previous section reviewed skills that are common to all helping encounters, although they were demonstrated in a way to show how they might be adapted to group settings. This next set of skills is somewhat unique to the practice of group leadership.

Linking

One challenge in leading a group is that people will be all over the place in their comments and input. One person will talk about some poignant moment, and before she can even finish, someone else will say, "That reminds me of a story . . ." Then another will make a comment about something else that seems completely unrelated.

Another challenge you will face is that group members will initially direct all their comments to you, ignoring everyone else. They want the leader's approval and validation. If left unchecked, you will end up with a "leader-centered" group in which all communications are filtered through you.

Linking involves building as many bridges and connections as you can between members, connecting their issues, and fostering direct interaction. You will do this in two main ways.

The first form of linking involves a type of summary in which you connect several comments together:

"Carole, when you were talking about how it's hard for you to sleep at night, I noticed that both you, Jamie, and you, Ronnie, were nodding your heads. Earlier, you both were talking about how you get stressed out as well, but in different ways. It seems to me that this is also related to what Megan was talking about earlier when she said she doesn't like to go to parties because she gets all jittery and then drinks too much. It seems that one theme that's emerging has to do with managing stress in new situations."

The second type of linking is more elegant, since you get the group members to do the work:

JAMIE: [Talking to leader] "I know just what Carole is going through 'cause I also get . . ."

LEADER: [Pointing to Carole] "Talk to Carole. Tell her what you were telling me."

JAMIE: "Yeah. Well, it's just that I get pretty upset about things too. It's not my sleep that gets disrupted so much as I start eating too much."

LEADER: "Ronnie, I noticed you were nodding your head when Jamie and Carole were talking, as if you can relate to what they're saying. Talk to them about your experience."

The leader is building cohesion and trust in the group by linking group members together in their common experiences. Every time a communication is directed to the leader, a gentle reminder is directed to speak directly to one another. In some cases, the group leader will refuse to make eye contact with the speaker, which often forces him or her to find a more attentive audience. In such instances, I prefer to explain what I am doing so I do not appear rude. I tell group members that I am training them to talk to one another rather than just to me.

Cuing

You already witnessed a bit of cuing in the preceding example. This skill involves scanning the group *very* carefully every minute or so, watching for the slightest nuance in nonverbal behavior. It is like taking the pulse of each group member, checking to see how each person is reacting to everything that is happening. You would be amazed how much you can read in people's expressions, body posture, and nonverbal behavior.

One of my favorite secret weapons is to become aware that I am having a strong reaction to something going on in the group. Maybe I am bored or frustrated. Perhaps someone said something that struck me as unusually insensitive or misinformed. Generally, there are negative side effects to the leader's being the one to say something, since he or she has a lot of power. Comments are often taken as a censure or as critical. Often it is far better to get others to communicate aloud what you think needs to be said. One way this can happen is by inviting members to say things that you think they are feeling based on nonverbal cues you observed.

I am aware, for example, that as a group member is speaking, I find it difficult to listen. I've heard this stuff several times before. Yet the guy is oblivious to how he sounds. I know that if I say something to him, he will feel hurt. If he interprets the slightest sign of disapproval from me, he pouts. So I scan the group to see who else might be feeling the same thing that I am. I notice that among the several members who appear bored, one in particular is very sensitive in the ways she gives feedback to people. "Samantha," I say, startling her out of a fantasy, "I noticed that as Mickey was talking, you seemed to be somewhere else, as if you were bored with what was going on. Perhaps you could tell Mickey what was going on for you."

Cuing is used whenever you believe someone needs an invitation to speak, or when you want to redirect the discussion to another area. It is a way to control the flow of the group, to cut off rambling, and to get maximum participation from the widest number of members.

Blocking

If cuing is an invitational skill, then its counterpart involves stopping those member actions that are deemed inappropriate, insensitive, or unnecessary. When are the times in which blocking might be indicated? Remember the following instances:

- When someone is being pressured to do or say something that he or she does not feel ready for
- When someone is being ridiculed or picked on
- When someone is rambling or distracting
- When someone uses intellectualizing as a defense
- When someone starts making excuses
- When someone is disrespectful or abusive toward others
- When someone uses a racial or cultural slur
- When someone is doing anything that is interfering with the productive flow of the group
- When someone is talking about events and persons outside the group that can't be controlled

Note in the example below the ways the group leader tries several different blocking strategies before she is successful:

MURRAY: . . . So I was thinking maybe that it wasn't that important after all. I mean . . ."

LEADER: "What you're saying, Murray, is that . . ."

The leader first interjects a summary statement as a way to help this member stop rambling and be more precise, but that doesn't work.

MURRAY: "What I was *trying* to say is that . . . I don't know. It's just hard to put in into words."

LEADER: "Maybe it would be best if you stopped for a little while, gathered your thoughts, and then we can come back to you later."

This intervention is a lot more direct, but Murray is very persistent and doesn't like to be side-tracked. Ordinarily, you might let him go on a bit longer, but you are trying to model for other group members ways that they can engage one another in direct ways.

MURRAY: "No, that's okay. I'd rather finish now."

LEADER: "Before you continue, Murray, I couldn't help but notice that some other things seem to be going on while you were talking. Kammy, you seem to be feeling impatient while Murray was talking. Your foot was moving up and down. You kept squirming in your chair. And at one point, you even start snorting. Perhaps you could tell Murray what has been going on for you?"

In this case, rather than confronting Murray directly, and risking that he might feel further censured by an authority figure, the leader instead scans the group to see who else is having a similar reaction to her own. She cues Kammy to do the confronting work because the leader knows that she will be direct and honest with Murray, yet sensitive.

The particulars of what you try in your efforts to block inappropriate or counterproductive behavior are less important than the realization that some intervention is called for. Often, the first thing you try won't work anyway, which is not a problem if there is basic trust operating in the group. Sometimes, it might take three or four attempts before you find the best strategy to set limits.

Supporting

When you work with one person at a time, it is relatively easy to monitor closely how the person is doing throughout the experience. In a group, however, you have a dozen different individuals who are all responding to what is happening in their own unique ways. It is not unusual that some people inadvertently get in over their heads, either because they have gone too far or find themselves surprised by the intensity of their reactions.

In the example from the previous section, for instance, Kammy confronts Murray, then feels filled with guilt and remorse afterwards. You are actually quite proud of her courage in demonstrating honesty, so it is important that she feel supported in her efforts.

KAMMY: "I'm sorry, Murray. I didn't mean to hurt your feelings like that. I guess I should learn to be more patient."

MURRAY: "Yeah. Well. That's okay. But what I was trying to say earlier . . ."

LEADER: "Excuse me, Murray. [Notice more blocking on the leader's part] Kammy seems to be struggling with her decision to be honest with you in saying that she finds it hard to listen to you when you take so much time to repeat yourself. In fact, I notice you are about to do it again."

MURRAY: "Yeah. I guess so."

LEADER: "I'm wondering, though, how the rest of you feel about Kammy's attempt to give Murray feedback. Do you think she was out of line? You can tell she is beating herself up pretty good right now."

FRED: "I'm in awe of her. I think . . ."

LEADER: [Pointing toward Kammy] "Fred, tell Kammy."

Notice the leader's attempt to recruit support for Kammy by encouraging members to talk directly to her. The leader wants to make darn sure that Kammy ends up feeling supported and reinforced for her courage. This was a critical moment in the group—the first time a member has confronted another. Even though the action was initiated by the leader, it is crucial that this behavior is rewarded as much as possible so others will follow the lead.

For Personal Application

Experiment with using support as a helpful skill during times in this class, or others you are in. Whenever someone says something that you especially appreciate or that you believe took courage to initiate, show the kind of encouragement to others that you would most appreciate if roles were reversed.

Group members need support when they become overemotional, when they do or say something they are unsure about, or when they are feeling mistrustful. At the most basic level, you would support a group member any time he or she does something that you want to reinforce enough to continue this behavior. This could occur in the following instances:

- When someone says something kind or caring to another
- When someone discloses him- or herself in a personal way
- When someone takes a risk
- When someone confronts another appropriately
- When someone uses the language of self-responsibility
- When someone catches him- or herself doing something inappropriate and then stops it
- When someone does what he or she says would be done (completes an assignment)
- When someone acts forgiving of a mistake or failure

- When someone shows unusual sensitivity toward others' cultural or personal differences
- When someone does or says anything in the group that is constructive or facilitates the process.

In other words, every time something occurs in the group that you like, you will want to support that behavior. Remember that you have an audience watching so that vicarious reinforcement is going on at all times. When you communicate that you like a particular member's contribution, most everyone thinks inside, consciously or unconsciously, "Hey, I want the leader to like what I'm doing as well!"

For Reflection

Think of a time in class when your instructor used overt support to reinforce desirable behavior. Recall the effects of that intervention not only on the target person's behavior, but your own inclinations to do something similar in the future.

Make a list of all the specific behaviors, actions, and contributions that are consistently supported by your instructor in class. Make a separate list of specific behaviors that your instructor has tried to extinguish or discourage. Try to trace how the norms were established that certain behaviors are supported and others are blocked.

Energizing

If group members are not fully engaged in the experience, they will not learn much. Even worse, if they are bored, they will not return.

During a session you are taking continual readings of the group energy level. Are people paying attention to what is going on? Who has checked out? What is the intensity level in the group? Essentially, you are trying to maintain an optimal level of engagement in which people are fully present, thoroughly enamored with what is happening, but not overstimulated to the point where they feel threatened and shut down.

You can assess the energy level of the group in two ways. The first is that you check your own internal reactions to what is happening. This can be a very useful tool since, presumably, you have full access to what is going on inside you. The only problem with this measure is that your reactions may not be representative of what others may be feeling, especially if you have a lot of experience in groups. I get bored very easily, for instance, not only because I have been doing this for so long but because, generally, I have a high threshold for stimulation. This is a struggle for me that I am constantly working on. It also explains why I enjoy group work so much since it has much higher energy levels than individual sessions.

The second, and probably more reliable way, to detect current levels of engagement is to scan members for nonverbal cues. Anyone yawning? Who appears to be lost in fantasy? Who seems antsy and impatient? What about voice tone and sense of drama?

For a Field Study

Find a group that you can observe that is being led by an experienced leader. Just as useful would be to watch a video of a group in session. Your department or library probably has several, demonstrating expert group leaders in action. A third option would be to complete this exercise any time there is a demonstration group in class.

It is important to increase your awareness of leadership skills. Using the following checklist as a guide, make a notation every time the leader employs a particular skill. If the leader does something that you do not recognize, then make a note to yourself that you can check on later to find out what it was. Do not focus on the "interventions" or "techniques" that are used (these are more complex), since we have not covered most of those yet. The emphasis here should only be on the leader *skills*, meaning those specific, simple behaviors that respond to individual and group actions.

A warning: The action is likely to happen so quickly at times that you may not have time to make sense of what the leader did, much less figure out which of these skills were selected. The object of this exercise is just to get you in the habit of watching what various leadership skills look like when they are used in groups.

Rephrasing _____

Reflecting feelings _____

Interpreting _____

Questioning _____

Reframing _____

Confronting _____

Disclosing _____

Suggesting _____

Summarizing _____

Linking _____

Cuing _____

Blocking _____

Supporting _____

Energizing _____

It does take real skill not only to read this mood accurately (you can easily misinterpret what you see) but to do something effective to change the energy level. One thing you can always do is simply bring what you observe to the attention to the group and let them deal with it. Another favorite method is to use self-disclosure to talk about your own low energy level, or better yet, to cue someone else to do the same.

Groups are about entertainment as much as learning and growth. If participants are not having fun, laughing as well as crying, then they will not be fully engaged in the experience. As much as within your control, you want to do everything you can to keep people excited and stimulated by what is going on.

Review of What You Learned

- Although there is similarity between helping skills used in groups versus those used during individual sessions, some adaptions must be made to let the other group members do most of the work.
- Group members especially appreciate leaders who have the skills to listen and respond sensitively, demonstrate respect and fairness, protect member safety, teach new ideas, provide appropriate structure, and help things to progress smoothly.
- Skill proficiency is developed only through practice. In order to master leadership skills, you must find opportunities to demonstrate what you can do and then receive feedback from others about what worked best and ways you can improve.

CHAPTER

9 When and How to Intervene

With basic theory and skills now in hand, the next challenge is what to do with them in specific group situations you will face. As a beginner, you will likely be concerned (make that obsessed) with doing or saying the "right" thing. You may even have the mistaken notion (still) that there is a single correct intervention for any given situation that will arise. Although it is true that there are best practices, some rudimentary things you would or would not wish to do, at this point I am more concerned with your knowing that *something* has to be done.

There will be times when you are sitting in group, things pleasantly humming along, and you are thinking to yourself, "Gee, this isn't so bad after all. I've really got the hang of this." Then wham, out of nowhere it seems (there were probably warning signs but you missed them), you are faced with the dilemma that you have to *do* something.

Maybe someone said something incredibly stupid or insensitive and everyone is looking at you to make things right. Perhaps you notice that nobody seems to be saying much, no matter what you do to prompt them. Or long periods of silence go on without any indication that they will stop. Worst of all, someone starts freaking out, right before your eyes, and the rest of the group starts to become very nervous.

Believe it or not, at this juncture it is not that important that you know what to do as long as you know you must do something. Your instructor or others might disagree with this point, with justifiably good reason that you are supposed to know what to do in most situations you face. My true confession is that even after so many years of doing this stuff, I still do not know what to do much of the time. That is not to say that with a minute's consideration, I will not be able to come up with something suitably appropriate; it is just that as I face unforeseen events, my first reaction is usually panic: "Oh no! What the heck am I supposed to do with this?"

I do not feel too badly about this, however. I pat myself on the back because at least I recognized that something needs to be done, even if I do not yet know what that should be. Based on my experience, anyway, the first thing I try probably will not work anyway. It often takes several different attempts before I stumble on, uh, I mean *select*, the right combination of skills and interventions to deal with a situation.

For Personal Application

Think of a time recently in which you were sitting in a group situation—in class, at a social gathering, in a meeting—when it was clear to you that some intervention was needed to keep people on task, or to keep them from rambling or hurting one another.

Although in this particular episode nobody did intervene, review in your mind all the things that you could have done that would have made things better. Think of at least three different options, although more would be better.

Consider each of the alternatives you could have employed, reasoning through what the advantages, disadvantages, and likely consequences would have been. Based on this assessment, select what you think might have been the best choice.

This process is *exactly* what you do in group leadership situations every time the idea occurs to you that something might need to be done. The only difference is that instead of having a few minutes to consider your intervention options, you have a few seconds!

It Is Not Always What You Do, but When and How You Do It

If it sounds like I am trying to let you off the hook, take some pressure off, you are right. You have enough to worry about without having to second-guess yourself constantly about choosing the most appropriate intervention. With experience, supervision, and lots of practice, you will become better and better at choosing the most effective response.

Certainly, you have no business leading groups if you do not have a good idea about what to do in various circumstances you will face. That is exactly what I am saying: You should have a good idea, but not necessarily a rigid agenda. It is very important to remain flexible, to read and respond to how members are acting and reacting. If the first thing you try does not work, it is usually no big deal—you have time and the opportunity to try something else. That is why in this chapter on when and how to intervene in groups, I am less concerned with exactly what you do than that you do something that is based on sound clinical judgment.

Differences of Opinion

I think you will find that if a half dozen different group leaders were faced with the identical situation, even if they all perceived the incident the same way (which is very doubtful), they would not necessarily do the same things. Let's take as an example a situation in which a group has been merrily going about its business when, all of a sudden, someone announces that he will not be returning again. Members register their surprise. They attempt to explore with this person why he is leaving but he is evasive. Some people become angry, feeling manipulated. Others feel hurt and abandoned. This whole episode has lasted all of four minutes.

All of our expert group leaders would agree that this clearly calls for an intervention. But what exactly needs to be done? Here is a sampling from our experts:

> Leader A: "I see this as an attempt to control the group and get attention. With the limited information I have, it seems like he needs to be confronted about more appropriate ways to get his needs met. Even if he does desire to leave the group, this is probably not the most responsible way to do so."

> Leader B: "Granted, the guy is awkward in announcing his decision. His timing is also a bit strange. Still, I'd take him at face value and applaud his courage in doing what he needs to do to take care of himself. I would respect his right to not disclose any further, but I would ask his permission to have members say goodbye by offering him some final reactions. This closure would be critical."

> Leader C: "I would ignore the guy for the moment and go with the intense feelings he has stirred up, the anger and the hurt. This is not really about his announcement but about their own issues. Everything that happens in a group represents an opportunity for growth and work. I would reframe the situation as that. Only after that would I return to the guy who said he is leaving and explore the meaning of this for him and for others."

I could go on with other possibilities, but I think you get the point. There are really a number of viable intervention options, all that are legitimate, professional responses to the situation. If we surveyed enough experts, surely we would get some sort of consensus about what the best course of action might be. With experience, you will have faced this situation enough times that you will be able to pick what you believe is the best option. Of course, if that does not turn out as you hoped, you can then try something else.

Perhaps I am belaboring the point. I just want you to concentrate on knowing the specific situations when you must intervene in a group. This will form the framework for the various therapeutic options that you collect.

For a Field Study

Think of a difficult scenario that you fear could arise in a group that you will lead. This could involve a group member challenging your authority and saying aloud that you do not know what you are doing. Another possibility could be a group member who consistently comes late to group, but always has a good reason. Or perhaps a silence lasts for long minutes, continuing no matter what you do. It does not matter which challenge you pick as long as it is a very specific situation.

Present this scenario to a half dozen different group leaders and ask them how they would handle this situation. Compare the different answers. Try to find a consensus among all their various opinions.

When to Intervene in Groups

I hear these little bells ringing in my head when I lead a group. No, I am not hallucinating. I have trained myself to "hardwire" warning signals in my brain when I face various situations that require some intervention. When something happens in a group that requires my immediate attention, the jangling starts, first as a little tinkle, then building to a gigantic gong if I ignore it too long.

For a Class Activity

Your instructor, or an experienced group leader, will conduct a group session in a "fishbowl" in front of your class. This group should be composed only of volunteers who are willing to talk about a particular theme that is introduced, or perhaps simply what it is like to be part of this group. The leader's role will be to employ as many group interventions as can be reasonably inserted into this limited format.

Observers on the outside of the group will serve as process consultants. Your job is to take notes on what you see unfolding in the session. Pay particular attention to the following:

1. What specific interventions, techniques, and strategies do you see the leader using?
2. Applying concepts you have read about or learned in class, which dynamics and processes do you observe in the group?
3. Who in the group most closely speaks for you, expressing your own personal reactions to what occurs?

After the session is completed, the observers will now take center stage by forming their own group in the middle of the class. Talk to one another, as if you were alone, about what you observed and experienced during the group session.

After sufficient time, the leader and group members will then join the discussion, talking not only about how they experienced the group, but also their reactions to the observers' comments.

Compile a list of all the group interventions that were witnessed. Discuss alternative strategies that could have been employed as well.

So far in your training you have been exposed to considerable disagreement among researchers, theoreticians, and practitioners about the best way to proceed in your work. Rest assured, however, that there are not only generic skills that almost everyone agrees are useful, but also certain predictable situations that will crop up that require an intervention. There may be some debate about the most effective course of action, but almost everyone agree that bells should be ringing in your ears if you face any of the following situations.

Lack of Group Cohesion, Trust, and Intimacy

You should by now be thoroughly convinced that not much constructive work will take place in the groups you lead unless you are able to build collaborative relationships among participants. Cohesion, trust, and intimacy are among the most important building blocks for any therapeutic activities that take place (Yalom, 1995).

How do you know when you have a problem in this area? Bells and whistles should go off in your head whenever you see evidence of the following:

1. Remarks made in group are consistently superficial and safe.
2. Self-disclosures are minimal and forced.
3. Members come late, leave early, or skip sessions.
4. More than one participant says that it does not feel safe.
5. Risks and honesty seem to be avoided.
6. Confidentiality has been breached.
7. Ground rules and established norms are not respected.
8. People seem to get offended easily.
9. Members are not caring and respectful in their communications.

The preceding symptoms could mean that something else may be going on in addition to mistrust issues. It is generally a good idea to return to basics when things are not proceeding as expected. Ask yourself what you need to do to build closer trust and intimacy.

For a Class Activity

1. In small groups, share a time when you did not feel safe in a group. Talk about what it was about the experience that made it difficult for you to trust others.
2. After each person speaks, summarize the main barriers to cohesion and collaborative relationships.
3. Apply the variables you identify to your own group experiences in class.
4. Brainstorm ways that you could develop more closeness and trust in your class so that you would be more inclined to work at a deeper level.

Disrespect and Abusive Behavior

This should be an easy one to detect. And the direction I offer will be unequivocal and definitive: Do not allow anyone to speak or act disrespectfully toward anyone else. No matter how heated things become, how emotional and passionate the interaction, it is never permissible for people to become abusive.

Remember that people come from varied family and cultural backgrounds in which there are different tolerances and definitions for what is considered inappropriate communication. For one person, calling someone an "asshole" is an affectionate term; for another, screaming at the top of his lungs is simply a way of saying that he loves you. In other cases, making "aggressive" eye contact, interrupting someone before they are finished, or even using a nickname may be interpreted as disrespectful. Since you will miss many of these slights, and perhaps commit a few yourself, you must make group members responsible for telling others when a line has been crossed.

In general, there are some fairly obvious signs when a group member is abusive enough to require intervention:

- A group member physically or verbally attacks another.
- Someone shows a marked insensitivity toward others.
- Someone makes a racist or gender-biased remark.
- A participant becomes so out of control that he or she does not notice the negative effects that are resulting.
- You notice that someone appears offended or withdrawn as a result of some comment or action.

What all this means is that you have to watch and listen very carefully to make sure that nobody is harmed. In some ways, you are like a playground monitor: Your job is to make sure that while everyone is interacting, learning, and having fun, nobody gets so careless that others are hurt.

For Reflection

Think of a time when someone in a group said or did something that you found extraordinarily hurtful—toward you or someone else. What happened inside you as a result of this disrespect or insensitivity? How did your behavior change in the future as a result?

Rambling

Nothing can kill the energy of a group quicker than one member who talks and talks and talks, not saying much in the process. Others become bored. They check out. Time becomes squandered by the filibuster so that you are unable to address other issues that need attention. Unless some intervention takes place, the whole session can become lost.

For all you know, the person who is rambling thinks that he or she is doing what you want. "Well, heck," she explains, "nobody else was talking so I thought I might as well use the time."

There are a lot of reasons why people ramble—they do not know better or they are not aware of what they are doing. They could even be encouraged unconsciously to do so by others in the group who want to avoid attention. Rambling can also mean that the person talking is trying to push others away, keeping people from getting too close.

The first signs that you need to do something is when you notice that (1) you are bored and impatient with someone who is speaking, and (2) you observe other members showing nonverbal signs of restlessness and boredom.

The most direct intervention is one in which you interrupt the person, saying something like: "I notice that you have a lot to say about this. I wonder if you could summarize this concisely."

Depending on whether this is a chronic problem or a single episode, you may wish to use the opportunity to elicit feedback for the person: "Candy, if I could interrupt you for a second. I noticed that while you were talking that several others seemed to be restless. Clyde's foot is moving a mile a minute. Nigel is yawning. And Loria is looking off into space. One reason might be because you are repeating yourself and taking a long time to get to your point. Before you continue with what you wanted to say, it might be helpful to hear how others are reacting to you."

An intervention such as this accomplishes several things at the same time. Number one, it stops the annoying and time-wasting behavior. Second, it gives the rambler valuable feedback that might change characteristic patterns, not only in the group but outside as well. Finally, it demonstrates ways that group members can confront one another effectively during appropriate times.

For a Class Activity

In small groups, take turns playing the role of a rambler who takes far too long to make points. Talk to one another about the power and other benefits that are enjoyed as a result of dominating the group time and avoiding deeper issues.

Practice different ways of getting the rambler to stop the self-defeating behavior, but without wounding the person to the point that he or she withdraws, pouts, or feels defensive.

Withdrawal and Passivity

It is often difficult to tell when someone has withdrawn in group for some reason that needs attention. Some members are naturally quiet, so you have to examine behavior in a normative context.

Immediately after someone has been addressed, you watch carefully to see how the comments were processed. If the person pulls his or her chair back, refuses to respond, or folds his or her arms and looks pouty, then you can obviously tell that something is wrong. But what about other members in the group who may be having their own strong reactions to what happened?

Since passivity or withdrawal represent an absence of participation, it is important to monitor carefully how each person is doing. I think of it a little like periodically taking the pulse of each member, checking in with my eyes if not a direct inquiry. "I notice you are unusually quiet today," I might observe, "What's going on with you?"

If someone does appear to have withdrawn, you have the choice of ignoring the behavior if you think it is intended as attention-seeking and manipulative, or to call on the person to talk about what the nonverbal messages are communicating.

Apprehension and Anxiety

As part of your responsibilities to monitor each member's current condition, you will at times notice that some people show overt signs of intense agitation. They may be upset about something that has been triggered inside them as a result of group interaction, or they might be feeling extremely uncomfortable about someone else's disclosures.

Imagine a group session in which one member starts speaking rather casually about the sexual abuse she suffered as a child. It is apparent from the way this person is talking about the experience that many of the issues have already been addressed and resolved. But as you scan the group you can see that another woman is fidgeting. Her foot is tapping nervously. Her hands are wringing. Her eyes are darting around the room but refusing to remain settled on any one spot. Obviously, she is upset about something.

Now you must decide what to do. You have a responsibility not only to this person who is anxious, but also the woman who is speaking, not to mention everyone else in the group. Anything you do or say to help the apprehensive group member is likely to affect everyone else as well.

The first thing you try to figure out is whether this group member is merely embarrassed about the explicit, casual talk about sex, or whether she might be identifying strongly with the disclosure. Has she been sexually abused as well, but has not yet dealt with this trauma?

There are actually a hundred possible reasons for her behavior, including the possibility that she just has to go to the bathroom. There is no way that you can know what is really going on and choose an appropriate intervention until you collect more information. The simplest way to do this is to just label what you observe: "Nancy, I noticed that while Frieda was talking about her sexual abuse, you seemed to be uncomfortable. I wondered if you might want to talk about what is going on for you."

Notice that the punctuation above does not include a question mark at the end of the sentence. This is because the intervention is offered as a statement in a neutral tone of voice rather than as a direct question. Nancy is given the opportunity to go as deeply as she wants at that moment. If she is ready to pursue things, she can do so; if she would rather pass, that option is available as well. Everyone who is watching this intervention will observe to themselves, "Gee, our leader is watching us very closely to see how we're doing. I didn't even notice that Nancy was upset but she did. I like the way she invited Nancy to talk but didn't pressure her to do so."

Some members are pouting and do not feel ready to talk yet. Others are too threatened or scared. Even if the invitation to speak is declined, the group members get the clear message that *all* behavior, even withdrawal, is subject to scrutiny and accountability.

Feedback

There are various times throughout the group when members could profit from feedback on how they are perceived by others. This could take place after someone discloses something personal, after an issue is worked on, or whenever someone is doing something that appears especially counterproductive.

People do not know how to give feedback effectively. They become evasive, too general, or even dishonest. It is your job to teach group members how to give feedback to one another. One way you do this is by modeling the behavior the way you would like others to follow.

Using feedback as an intervention accomplishes two goals. It lets someone know about the effects of some aspect of his or her behavior, and it shows everyone else how important it is to tell people what you observe.

There are lots of ways that feedback can be offered, whether in the form of self-disclosure, confrontation, or immediacy. Basically, what you are doing is telling someone how he or she comes across to you. One of the wonderful things about group settings is that members do not have to take your word for it; they can check things with others.

> **MYRON:** ". . . It's just so hard to get anything done when everyone else doesn't keep up their end of things. I don't mean to . . ."
>
> **LEADER:** "Let me interrupt you for a minute, Myron. You've been talking about what everyone else is doing and not doing for some time. I was thinking to myself as you were talking that you sounded like a little boy who was whining. I was finding it difficult to listen any more. If you're interested, you could ask others how they were reacting as well."

While this intervention may come across as very direct, and perhaps too honest, the group leader was watching Myron's reactions closely as she was giving him this feedback. It was offered in the spirit of pointing out what was observed, which may or may not be valid in light of how others react. Sometimes the best thing that can result from such a discussion is a promise on the part of the member receiving feedback to check out others in his life to see if they have similar perceptions. In the example above, Myron will report to the group the following week on what he learned from his family and friends about his perceived whining.

Threat to Harm

The ethical codes of all helping professions mandate very clearly that if someone is a danger to him- or herself or someone else, you *must* do something to protect the safety of all concerned. In groups, just as in individual sessions, people will occasionally reveal—directly or implicitly—that they are thinking about hurting themselves or someone else. This could involve any of the following:

- Suicidal ideation or recurrent thoughts, often with a specific plan
- Threats of homicide or physical assault
- Past or ongoing child or spousal abuse
- An HIV-infected individual continuing to have unprotected sex with strangers
- Engaging in criminal acts

What do you do in situations like this? A very good question. Presumably, you have included a statement of "informed consent" as part of your intake procedures so group members are well aware of your responsibility to protect others' welfare. When group members reveal threats to harm in group, often they are asking for help and intervention since they are well aware of what you must do.

As with most critical incidents that occur, the best course of action is often to bring the issue up for everyone to discuss and resolve. That does not absolve you of your responsibility to report suspected abusive or criminal act, or to protect others' welfare, but it does demonstrate the kind of collective decision making that is so important for promoting continued mutual responsibility and accountability.

Boredom

At some point, many groups become predictable and stale. You can tell you have reached this point when you find yourself unable to maintain focus and notice others showing restlessness as well. If left unaddressed, this marked lack of energy will encourage members to slip into complacency. You must do something to stoke up the energy level.

As for what you can do, the sky is the limit. This is a time to be creative, dramatic, and provocative. Boredom stems from predictable routines so you must do what you can to break these up.

Here are just a few things that group leaders have been known to do during times of boredom:

- *"I am really bored! I don't know about the rest of you but I've been sitting here for the last few minutes looking at the clock, just counting the minutes until we get out of here. Anyone else feeling the same way?"*

    In this first example, the leader says out loud what he senses the others are feeling. This gives permission for group members to talk about the low energy and then to brainstorm things they can do to change it.
- *"Okay, everybody stand up. Time to stretch."*

    In this case, the leader changes the level of engagement, from passive to active mode. Rather than allowing members to sit quietly, she stirs them up.
- *"Let's stop for a moment and reflect on what's going on right now."*

    Rather than doing the work herself, she simply takes a time out and invites participants to label and describe what is happening. This reinforces the idea that they are responsible for what happens, or what does not happen.
- *"If I were a member of this group, I sure would be feeling cheated about now. I mean, taking all the time to come here, to say that I want to change and become involved, and then sitting around waiting for someone else to take the lead."*

    Rather than a scolding, the group leader is actually creating a scene. He is trying to provoke some reaction from members and is likely to get one.
- *"Time to do something different. Count off by threes. I want you to talk to one another as consultants about what could be done to make this group more inspiring and responsive to your needs."*

    A change in structure and atmosphere is initiated. With this change in scene, dynamics, and a specific structured task to complete, group members are likely to venture into new territory.

This is just a sampling of possible interventions. The key here is recognizing there is a problem that must be addressed. When boredom gets a grip, when routines become entrenched, when energy runs low, it often takes a major effort to change the atmosphere. Just keep in mind, and remind members as well, that it is *their* group, not yours. They are the ones responsible for keeping the group responsive to their needs. If they are bored, then they are also responsible for taking care of their own problems. Of course, it does not hurt to remind them of this.

Lack of Direction

As a beginner, this may be the problem you face the most. If not, you are likely to encounter the opposite: too much structure. It is very difficult to create a balance between sufficient structure in which people know what is expected, what their roles are, what they can do to make good things happen, versus so much control that every minute is scripted.

When groups are overstructured, members feel stifled. The leader is firmly in control, but also totally responsible for what happens. Participants are along for the ride. Yet when groups lack structure, members do not know what to do, or how to do it.

How do you know that your groups lack direction? For one, ask the participants. Pay attention to the bottom line: Are they meeting their stated goals? You will also notice long silences, as if members are waiting for you to tell them what to do next.

Another key sign is that movement is all over the place. There appears to be little continuity, as is evident in the dialogue below:

MARGARET: "I've had this problem for, I don't know, maybe a year or more."

SIMON: "Yeah. That's a bitch when you can't get what you want. Like the song goes, though, you can always get what you need."

TAMAR: "Simon, what the heck are you talking about? I don't know what you're talking about half the time."

ANGIE: "Come on, Tamar, leave him alone. He doesn't know any better. He's just trying . . ."

MARGARET: "Do ya'll mind, but I think I was talking about something that was . . ."

SIMON: "Yeah. I mind. We heard that story before. Besides, I thought we were supposed to be talking to each other, not telling stories."

Obviously, without leader direction and intervention this group loses control very quickly. Members are not listening to one another. They are not responding well, either. They seem lost, moving from one topic or person to another. Unless the leader jumps in to mediate, to direct the flow of traffic, there are likely to be some casualties.

Lights. Camera. Action.

People can talk and talk in groups without doing much to make changes. There comes a point in which it often becomes necessary to move an individual member, or the group, from talk to action. "Now that we understand what is going on," you say, "what the problem probably stems from, and what you'd like to do about it, what do you intend to do?"

Moving into this action phase can take a number of forms:

- Declaring a goal to work on
- Committing oneself to some specific course of action
- Rehearsing, practicing, or role playing new behaviors
- Agreeing to complete a homework assignment before the next session

The transition from insight to action might look something like this with one group member, Jon, who has been talking at length about his struggle to control his temper:

JON: "It's not like I enjoy having everyone I love scared of me all the time or anything."

LEADER: "What about right now?"

JON: "Excuse me?"

LEADER: "Right now. You say you don't like having a bad temper but I've noticed lots of ways you have used that threat to get what you want in this group."

MIDGE: "That's for sure."

LEADER: "Tell him about it."

So far, the leader has started to prepare Jon for taking action with his temper problem instead of just talking about it, which he has done several times before with no discernible change. Next, the leader would help Jon to rehearse alternative ways that he could get his needs met other than resorting to tantrums. Group members could offer him feedback on the side effects of his current patterns. Next, he would be encouraged to declare something that he would be prepared to work on during the week that would demonstrate significant progress. Finally, other group members would be urged to talk about ways that they can also relate to this issue and what they would like to work on.

For a Class Activity

Write down some relatively minor concern in your life that you are facing right now. It could be something related to a primary relationship, your eating or exercise habits, or school work.

Think of a goal that you would be able to complete within the next week. Keep in mind the criteria of an effective goal: (1) it should be as specific as possible, (2) it must be realistic so that you are absolutely certain that you can do it (no excuses), and (3) it should represent a baby step in the direction of where you would eventually like to be.

Take turns declaring out loud to members of your group what you intend to do. Make an agreement to check in with one another next week so you are held accountable for what you said you would do.

Self-Defeating Language

There are some differences in what specific types of language various group leaders would intervene to correct. Depending on theoretical orientation and style, there might be more attention paid to thoughts over feelings, or vice versa, or shoulds, musts, can'ts, or other forms of syntax, vocabulary, or communication style that reinforce dysfunctional ideas. Remember that language is one of the best ways to know what is going on inside someone's head.

Following are some examples when you might wish to intervene:

- The use of "we," as in "*We* think it would be best . . ." This plural pronoun is a way that group members avoid responsibility for their own beliefs by spreading around the blame. Generally, when this happens, you can easily ask who else the person is speaking for, making him or her switch to "I."
- "He *makes me* upset." Verbalizations like this imply that someone outside of oneself is controlling internal emotional states. "He makes you upset? How does he do that?" you might ask. "Don't you mean that you *make yourself* upset over what he's doing?" Remember also that you are not only talking to the person who used the illogical language, but to everyone else who are learning this principle vicariously.
- "*It* is just so difficult." The "it" is called an ambiguous pronoun that allows the group member to speak in a general rather than specific way. "What is the 'it' you are referring to?" might be a way the group leader would help the person to be more detailed about what he or she believes is the source of her difficulty.

There are dozens and dozens of other instances in which you might also focus on the language employed, depending on the type of group and approach you prefer. When a group member says, "It's not fair!" a leader might reply with, "Who says the world is fair?" When someone says, "I really *need* that job," the intervention might be: "You mean you *want* that job." When people use the words "never" or "always" they might be challenged to substitute "sometimes," which is probably a more accurate description of frequency.

Just because you are aware of illogical, irrational, or self-defeating language patterns does not mean that you would necessarily intervene each time. Most people do not appreciate being interrupted, especially when they are in the middle of a heartfelt personal disclosure. Timing is therefore important when you choose to point out that someone is talking in a way that reinforces negative thinking or dysfunctional behavior. More than half the time, you might want to file the observation away and return to it at a more opportune moment.

For a Field Study

Keep a journal for a single day in which you jot down how often you hear people say things like "I can't" instead of "I won't," "I should," "I must," "never," "always," and other evidence of illogical thinking, overgeneralizations, and distortions.

Imagine the ways you might effectively point out what people are saying, and what this means, without offending them.

Manipulation and Attention Seeking

In spite of your best efforts to screen out poor candidates for your group, sometimes a few toxic individuals will slip through. In some cases, you will inherit particular members with little choice in the matter.

Manipulative and attention-seeking behaviors come in two basic kinds: situational and chronic. In the first case, the person might normally be reasonably cooperative, either in the group or in life. There is something about the group environment, or perhaps a given situation, that encourages the person to engage in self-protective behavior that involves a hidden agenda. In the second case, however, the person's manipulative tendencies are characterological, meaning that they are part of the individual's personality style. You have probably heard of such diagnostic labels like "borderline," "hysterical," and "sociopathic," which all have highly manipulative features.

Whether the group member acts manipulatively because of a particular situation or as a typical interpersonal style, you must intervene swiftly and decisively to stop this behavior. Otherwise, you may lose control of the group.

I am certain that you can recall any number of instances in which you have seen a whole class disrupted because of the persistent efforts of one student who keeps asking annoying questions, who tries to show the instructor how brilliant he or she is, or who operates behind the scenes to sabotage progress. In spite of your best efforts, lots of damage can be done if you do not confront those with hidden agendas or manipulative mindsets.

Here are just a few examples of what you can expect to encounter:

- Excessive approval seeking. "Thank you so much for your help. This is just the best group I've ever been. You are just so good at what you do."
- Attention seeking. "No. I don't have anything to say and nothing is going on with me." Folds arms and sulks.
- Power struggles. "You say that this is our group but you keep telling us what we can and can't do."

There are whole books written on how to handle situations like this (Anderson & Stewart, 1983; Edelwich & Brodsky, 1992; Kottler, 1992), as well as several excellent sources for group leaders (Gans & Alonso, 1998; Horne & Campbell, 1997; Leszcz, 1989). All the advanced training in the world will still not prepare you for the myriad of ways that group members can act manipulatively. At first, you will attempt to stifle this behavior by confronting it in group. If that does not work, a second option is to arrange for a consultation or individual session with the individual to deal with the issue. If that does not produce a change, sometimes you might have to ask the person to leave (which will create another set of problems).

This is among the most challenging of all situations for group leaders, which is why we will revisit this subject in a later chapter.

Coercion and Peer Pressure

TOMMY: "I'm not sure if I want to get into this or not right now."

ALICE: "Come on! We've all said stuff. It's your turn now."

JEAN: "Yeah, it's only fair."

TOMMY: "Well, I'm not sure . . ."

MICKEY: "Damn, you piss me off! I spilled my guts and you just sat there and soaked it up. Now when it's your turn, you wimp out. Man, you've got no balls."

This is not only a common scenario in group but a predictable one. If you recall the dynamics of groups moving toward cohesion and intimacy, then you know that there is strong—intensely powerful—forces that act to pressure people into revealing themselves. Sometimes this occurs before they are ready.

You have heard me say before, and research bears this out, that casualties occur in groups when people are pressured to do or say things that they are not ready to do. They are forced to take risks and then regret it later. They are shamed into revealing secrets and then feel such embarrassment that they do not return. They are emotionally "blackmailed" into saying things that, afterwards, they can disown because there was no freedom of choice. Worst of all, they can be pressured into letting down defenses to the point in which real harm can be inflicted.

In the group that began this section, it is the leader's responsibility to intervene on behalf of Tommy and to stop the others from applying so much pressure. This might take the form of the following:

LEADER: "I think it's really great that many of you feel such strong attachment and loyalty to our group that you want everyone to belong. Tommy, I guess what Alice, Jean, and Mickey are saying to you is that they have taken risks in here and they perceive that you have not. I don't think that's true, by the way. I think you *have* put yourself out there, but just in a different way. Right now, you seem reluctant to go further with this."

TOMMY: "No, that's okay. I don't mind. Maybe I should . . ."

LEADER: "That's up to you, Tommy. But I'd suggest you wait until you are certain you are ready. You seem almost there, but not quite. Meanwhile, I'd like to spend some time talking about what just happened."

The leader clearly intervened to stop Tommy from being coerced. She even did not allow him to go further at that time even though he seemed inclined to do so. It is very important that group members accept responsibility for their own behavior, rather than have an excuse if things do not proceed as expected. "I didn't want to do it anyway," Tommy could say to himself afterwards.

Whenever anyone is offered feedback, it is important to ask permission to see if it is welcomed. When someone is invited to join in, you should first ask if the person is willing to do so. You are not only protecting the rights of each member but you are demonstrating to the more timid participants that you are present and available to provide a safety net for them if and when they are ready to jump in.

Closure

One final instance when intervention is required is when time is running out. Somewhere before the end of session, usually anywhere from five to twenty minutes depending on the size of group, the length of session, and what happened that day, you will announce that it is time to bring things to an end. Often you must interrupt someone in the middle of saying something. The alternative is to let things go on to the point where closure is not possible, which is not desirable.

It does take considerable practice to do things in group that in the outside would be labeled as rude. "I'm so sorry," you interrupt someone who is talking about a poignant issue, "but we are almost out of time. What can we do for you right now to bring this to closure until we can resume next time?"

Typically, groups end with a final go-round in which members mention how they are reacting to what just happened, what they will take home with them, and possibly what they intend to work on before the next session. If time allows, you might then do a final check-in with the person who was interrupted at the end, just to see how things are going.

For a Class Activity

Take turns bringing the class to closure by using the last 5 to 10 minutes to process what happened and helping classmates to leave with something constructive to work on.

Review of What You Learned

- There are specific instances in group when you must intervene to protect member safety and facilitate progress.
- There is rarely only one single intervention that works best in any given situation. Prepare yourself with three or four options since the first try may not be successful.
- The best interventions are those in which you cue others to do the work.

CHAPTER

10 Group Techniques and Structures

Group leadership is not about techniques, although it is always handy to have options available, a bag of tricks you can reach into, to pull out just what the situation calls for. There are many sources that you can consult that suggest practical strategies that you might use in various group settings (see Barlow, Blythe, & Edmonds,1999; Corey, Corey, Callanan, & Russell, 1992; Dyer & Vriend, 1975; Jacobs, Masson, & Harvill, 1998; Rosenthal, 1998 as examples). I will warn you, however, that the challenge of running groups involves not a scarcity of options about what to do, but having too many choices and not knowing which seems most appropriate.

Over time, you will collect favorite strategies and exercises that you like best to start a group, break through prolonged silence, or close the group on an upbeat note. Many of these you will glean from operating manuals, attending workshops or conference presentations, and working with co-leaders who introduce their favorite methods. Some of the best ones you will make up yourself, in response to some challenge that emerges. Regardless of how you build your repertoire of strategies, you will want to customize them to any situa-

For a Class Activity and Field Study

In small groups, each of you shares your absolutely favorite method to enliven a party or social gathering that has run out of steam. Build on each other's ideas, discussing ways this method could be further refined or developed.

One of you acts as scribe and takes notes on each person's contribution. Agree to make copies for each person in the group.

Identify what you consider to be your one or two most creative or brilliant ideas and share them with the rest of the class. Have the scribe of your group add to the list by including others that were offered by other groups.

This is *exactly* how you might collect the "greatest hits" of each veteran group leader you ever meet. Make it a habit to find out what his or her favorite, most foolproof technique is.

As a corollary to the group activity, initiate a field study to interview experienced group leaders about their most effective, powerful techniques. Report back to the group (or class) what you learned.

tion, adapt them to the particular needs of the moment. There is nothing that dooms an intervention more than inserting it without consideration for its context and specific intent.

The goal of this chapter is not to equip you with all the techniques you might need, just at the theory chapter presented the merest sampling of useful structures. Instead, we will review a few representative techniques that might be used at various intervals throughout the life of a group. This will give you the background you need to understand the ways that techniques are constructed, as well as the means by which they are employed.

Ways to Prepare a Group

The group begins before anyone walks through the door for the first time. This is true for all learning/therapeutic experiences. Once the person first contemplates getting help, the process starts. It could take months, or even years, before the person is ready to seek help; nevertheless, the change process has already begun with the first awareness that help might be needed.

Before beginning any group, several practical factors should be considered (Corey, 2000; Gladding, 1999; Tomasulo, 1998):

- Clarify what kind of group you wish to run. Homogeneous groups are easier to market and get going; heterogeneous groups offer more resources and balance. Decide, as well, whether you will have a "closed" or "open" group in which new members can be added and whether it will be time limited. You will also need to decide on the theoretical orientation and leadership style you will adopt.
- Undertake far more promotion than you think you need to fill up the group. In my experience, only about half the people who say they will come actually show up. Some of those who attend the first meetings will not continue. That means that if you want eight active, committed members, you may need twenty viable prospects.
- Clear what you are doing with the administration or managing body so it will support your efforts.
- Provide written guidelines explaining confidentiality, informed consent, established ground rules, and appropriate member conduct.
- Keep the number of participants manageable—six to eight if you are leading alone, eight to twelve if working with a partner.
- If possible, work with a co-leader who is more experienced. If this is not feasible, make sure you have weekly supervision available to help you debrief each session.
- Remain clear about what you want to accomplish during the first induction stage. Think through the most appropriate structure for building trust and cohesion.
- Screen the participants to make sure that they are good candidates for the group. Avoid potential trouble makers. Help selected members to begin planning issues they want to work on in the group. Plant favorable expectations.

Whether you schedule pregroup screening interviews, talk to prospective participants on the phone or as part of large group, or distribute informational literature, you will want to prepare members about what to expect, get them thinking about ways they could use the group, and hopefully, even get them started in the change process.

As one example of this, I was set to do a workshop for therapists and counselors on their "personal transformations." I enjoy doing these experiential one-day retreats, but often feel frustrated because I know the effects don't often last very long. After all, how many workshops and seminars have you attended in your life, gotten fired up during the process, then a few weeks (or days) later you can't even remember what you were so excited about? The challenge for any group leader, whether structuring a one-day workshop or an ongoing group, is how to best prepare participants to get the most from the experience.

I decided to send out a letter to all 250 people registered for the program, stating the following:

As you are well aware, therapeutic learning experiences are often time-consuming and lengthy processes. In order to get the most from a "single-session" growth experience, it is critical for participants to do some preliminary work so they come prepared and open to deal with critical issues in an efficient manner. Most of us struggle with similar challenges in our work with clients—how to promote significant growth in a brief period of time, and most importantly, how to make the changes last.

I urge you to review the following reflective questions prior to attending the workshop, preferably writing out your responses. Although pleading a lack of time is surely not a legitimate excuse, at least think about each of the inquiries as they apply to your life and goals for this workshop.

- *What are your greatest strengths and weaknesses as a practitioner?*
- *Throughout your career, which clients have you struggled with the most?*
- *What has been your most consistent mistake or failure with clients?*
- *What have been the most common interpersonal struggles you have faced at work?*
- *What is the most recurrent conflict you have experienced with family and friends?*
- *Where are the blocks and blind spots for you in supervision?*
- *Where do you most fear to tread?*
- *What do you yearn for the most in your life and work?*
- *What are some ways that you would most like to grow?*
- *Where have you been and where are you going in your journey as a helper?*

The reasoning behind this letter to workshop participants is similar to what any group leader would consider in setting up a group. If you don't already know the people who will be participating in your group, it would be useful to collect some preliminary information from them, either by interview or questionnaire. Almost all clinical settings employ some type of intake form that can be easily adapted to group formats. Essentially, you would want to know such things as the following about each prospective group member:

- Why did you choose to join this group?
- If you were pressured or forced to join the group by someone else, explain the situation.
- What are you hoping to gain from the group experience?
- What previous experiences have you had as part of groups such as this?
- What are other group/counseling/therapeutic experiences you have participated in? Describe what you liked best and least about them.

- What are some of the characteristic roles you usually play in groups? How might you like to change these patterns?
- Describe any emotional problems or mental disorders that you have experienced or are currently struggling with.
- Describe any medical history or physical problems that concern you at this time. List medications you are taking.
- Describe your history related to alcohol and drug use. How much alcohol do you typically consume in a week? Describe other drugs that you use for recreational or "self-medication" purposes.
- Who are the most important people in your world? Describe the people you live with, extended family members you interact with, and others with whom you share closest intimacy.
- List at least three goals that you hope to accomplish as part of this group experience.
- What else would be helpful for me to know about you that would be relevant to this group experience?

No matter how you choose to collect basic information about the group participants, your interview or questionnaire should help you to screen out those who might not be suitable. Ideally, such an exercise should not only help you find out things you need to know, but also help the group members to begin thinking about how they want to make the best use of their time.

Ways to Begin a Group

For Reflection

Before I even begin talking to you about what you want to do to launch a group, think through on your own what objectives would need to be addressed. What are all the things you would wish to accomplish in any introductory structure to get a group going? Make a mental list of the most crucial factors.

Hopefully, if you took the time to think through the possible objectives for launching a group, you came up with several goals that struck you as most important. Obviously, for instance, you want to devise a way that helps members to learn each other's names very quickly, as well as to build initial trust. In addition, any technique you use to begin a group should accomplish the following:

- Plant favorable expectations. Get the members excited about their journey.
- Create efficient intimacy and cohesion. Help them to get to know one another immediately, with a minimum of fuss.
- Establish a productive atmosphere that covers ground rules.

- Capture and maintain the members' attention so they are focused on the tasks at hand.
- Identify goals and problem material to be worked on.
- Get the members to come back.

This may sound like a lot to do in a single session, must less one introductory structure, but most of these objectives are actually linked together. The last one, getting the people to come back another time, is the most important of all: If you can't do that, you can't help anyone.

Obviously, the choice of what you do to launch your group is *very* important. You want to "hook" the participants in such a way that they feel they have made a good decision to come. You want to make sure that *everyone* gets involved, that nobody is left out. And you want to make sure you provide the kind of meaningful experience that meets their needs but doesn't scare the timid ones away.

This is indeed a tall order. Fortunately, there are loads of introductory techniques that work well to accomplish these goals.

For a Class Activity

Get together in groups of six to eight. Pretend you are all meeting in a first group session for the first time. Take on the role of someone else you know, someone you can play realistically and fluently, preferably someone with a problem or two.

Introduce yourself to the others in your group by talking about how you feel about being in the group, what you want from the experience, and what concerns you have.

After you are done with the exercise, abandon your adopted roles and talk to one another about what the experience was like and what you learned from it.

Icebreakers are designed to build a working level of familiarity to get a group going; there are hundreds of such exercises. Generally, I like to start a group by having members talk about who they are and what they are looking for. Since you want to minimize small talk, rambling, digressions, and self-indulgence, the key is to get people to say something new about themselves, something unrehearsed. I will actually say this out loud, and then model the kind of introduction that I would like them to try. I present myself as authentically, genuinely, and spontaneously as I can, showing them how it is possible to be vulnerable and appropriately disclosing.

Since group members are unskilled at this task, used to giving their standard "speeches," and "canned" introductions, I make everyone responsible in the group for calling each other to task if they sense that something is said that is part of one's usual way of presenting oneself. That is why modeling the introductions is so important to show them how it is done, something along the following lines:

My name is Jeffrey. I have been in groups a lot, which is not altogether a good thing, because I can hide easily by figuring out what others want and then pretending to be that person. I have struggled throughout most of my life with winning approval. I want everyone to like me. All the time. And when that doesn't happen, I get hurt. I recover quickly, however, and that is a testimony to all the good things I've learned from being in groups like this.

What do I want you to know about me at this time? I am pretty playful and will act silly at times. I like to stir things up, to be provocative, to get my heart beating quickly. I like to take risks, too.

As far as what I could work on in a group such as this—if I were a member rather than the leader—I could use some help clarifying what I want to do with the rest of my life. I have been very ambitious thus far, driven toward success and achievement, and now those things don't feel so important any longer.

Who would like to go next?

This introduction took less than two minutes to deliver. I tried to be precise and efficient, since there is so much to do in this first session and so little time to do it. Notice what I did *not* include in my introduction. I didn't talk about my job, my family, or the usual roles I play. It's not that these things are not important; they will certainly emerge later as people get to know me. For now, however, I stuck with revealing as much about my "essential" self as I could in the briefest period of time. I also demonstrated a degree of vulnerability in which I shared a number of issues that I might use the group to work on.

For Reflection

In your journal, write out one way that you could introduce yourself to a group for the first time that reveals as much as possible in less than two minutes of time. Include not only the most essential parts of who you are, but the particular personal issues that you could work on in group at this time in your life.

This is the basic structure for beginning a group, in all its various forms. There are limitless twists and variations that are possible to include as well.

- You can have members work in dyads, triads, or subgroups, interviewing one another for the purposes of introducing one another.
- You could have people share their first impressions of one another after each introduction.
- You could have them reveal something about themselves that nobody else knows or has heard before.
- You could have them talk about how they are feeling in the present moment, what it's like to be there now.
- You could structure the introductions in such a way that attention is directed towards one facet that is relevant to the group. In a grief support group, members could talk

not only about the present losses they are currently suffering, but also the most dev-astating loss they have *recovered from* in the past (notice the emphasis on recovery).

In any structure you use, remember that you must watch the time so you have the opportunity to start working on issues in the very first session. In groups with voluntary participants, each person is making a decision as to whether it is worthwhile to come back another time. Therefore, one good way to end that first session is ask members to talk about how they are feeling about things so far. You might also ask them to mention what they are taking with them as the session ends, or what they already learned from the experience.

Ways to Build Cohesion and Intimacy

Whenever you deduce that trust in the group is not sufficient for deeper work, it is time to initiate some intervention to correct this matter. How will you know when you have reached this point?

Several signs and symptoms will be displayed (Corey, Corey, Callanan, & Russell, 1992):

- Members make overt statements that the group does not feel safe.
- There seems to be a marked reluctance for people to volunteer or reveal themselves.
- Members engage in rambling, distractions, intellectualizations, and other means by which to hide.
- Verbalizations are vague and lack personal meaning.
- Repeated silences last long periods of time.
- Participants confide to you privately that they do not feel comfortable.
- Members deny that they have any problems to work on.
- Conflicts and disagreements are side-stepped.

These, of course, are quite natural reactions to a strange, threatening situation. In order to move things along to the next level, and as a prerequisite for risk taking, you must do what you can to build a greater sense of community.

Rather than employing a "technique" in order to create deeper intimacy and cohesion, the most direct route is simply to label what you observe (this is often the preferred choice): "I notice that some people seem unwilling to move beyond the superficial. I wonder if we could talk about what is going on."

Depending on the type of group you are leading and the setting, there are dozens of manuals that supply thousands of trust and community-building exercises. As just one example, adventure-based group activities involve people in a series of games and physi-cal activities that are designed to break down barriers, improve communication, and build a sense of community (Nadler & Luckner, 1992; Rohnke, 1989). You probably played a lot of these games as a kid, like the "trust walk" in which you walk around blindfolded, led by partners, or the "trust fall" in which you fall back into others' arms who catch you. Some programs, like Outward Bound and Project Adventure, have incorporated such structures into their warm-ups as a way to facilitate team work before venturing off into the wilderness together.

Ways to Promote Risk Taking

Once you are well into the working stage of a group, you will want to introduce structures that take things to a deeper level. This is a tricky part of your job because the readiness levels of members to take risks are so variable. Some participants feel free to say whatever they want, to say out loud anything that comes to their hearts or minds, while others find it utterly terrifying just to make direct eye contact with someone else in the room.

Any risk-taking exercise should be undertaken to deepen the levels of intimacy, sharing, and cohesion in the group. Safeguards should be in place to give people choices about how much (or little) they want to reveal. Efforts must be taken to make sure that people are not coerced to say or do more than they feel ready for. On the other hand (that means a paradoxical message is coming), your job is also to *encourage* people to go beyond what is comfortable and risk new ways of being.

Probably, the first step in this process is to talk openly about the fears of risking. I like to ask participants to imagine that they will say out loud their deepest, darkest secrets, or that they will blurt out all the things they have been thinking and feeling but can't imagine ever having the courage to reveal publicly. As they think about what it would be like to reveal these things, I ask them to look around the room, making eye contact, and imagine how each person might respond to their revelations. This usually provokes a rather spirited sharing about fears of risking and of being judged by others.

There is always someone in the group who is relatively fearless, or who is highly motivated to take risks. You can often use this person's courage as an entry point for others to join in as well. Remember, however, that such structures must always include volunteers rather than those who may be pressured.

The "hot seat" is always a good icebreaker for risk taking, in which members take turns agreeing to answer any personal question directed their way. In another variation, members can be randomly divided into subgroups, or allowed to choose those they trust the most, and then share with one another aspects of themselves that have yet to be revealed. Afterwards, participants can talk about what it felt like to take risks such as this, and then be encouraged to do so in the larger group.

Here are some other risk-taking structures:

- All members write down something so personal about themselves that they would be unwilling to reveal it except anonymously. Make sure that all members use the same kind of paper and pens so their disclosures will not be revealed unless it is their choice to do so at a later time. Collect the papers, shuffle them up, and pass them out so everyone gets one to read out loud. Afterwards, see if anyone is willing to own their disclosure.
- Ask members to choose someone in the group with whom they feel some unfinished business. Have a volunteer sit right in front of someone else (who also agrees to participate) and then take turns telling one another things that have not yet been said.

- All members share a time in their lives in which they took a major psychological and emotional risk that ultimately had a positive outcome, even though it was initially very difficult.
- Ask for and receive honest feedback from others in the group.
- The most risky thing of all to do is to speak in the present about something you are feeling toward someone else in the group. Imagine, for instance, what it would be like to tell a classmate how attracted you are to her or him, or how difficult you find it to be around this person.

For a Class Activity

Sit around in a small group so that you can easily make eye contact with everyone else. Sit as close as possible to one another to create an intimate atmosphere.

Each of you takes a risk by sharing something about yourself that nobody else knows about you. You have wide latitude about what sort of thing you can reveal, depending on the trust level you feel in your group, as well as your own inclination at this time. Select from the choices above, or others that might occur to you.

Before you decide to say your risk out loud, rate on a 1 to 10 scale how risky it feels to reveal this. A "1" means that it isn't risky at all while a "10" means that your heart is thumping so hard inside your chest you can barely breathe. A "5" is medium risky, whatever that means to you.

First tell your group members what your risk is, then tell them how relatively difficult it was for you to share that.

If time allows, do a second or third round in which you go a little deeper.

Afterwards, talk about what happened for you in this experience, what you learned about yourself, about others, and about the role of risk taking in groups.

Ways to Solve Problems

Problem-solving and other skill development models have been invented for use in group settings. The intent is to teach participants the systematic steps involved in making good decisions in their lives, a process that can be applied to a variety of situations.

Quite spontaneously, a member may signal that he or she needs help making a decision about whether to end a relationship, quit a job, relocate to another state, or take a dramatic step in another direction. The leader may then announce to the group as a whole that it would be profitable for them all to learn a process for making sound decisions.

Several problem solving models, such as those developed by Johnson and Johnson (2000) and Ray (1999), follow a process that invites members to:

1. *Identify the problem and define the issue.* It is preferable to select one part of an issue that can be specifically addressed and that lends itself to resolution within the time and resources available.

2. *Gather information that is relevant to the situation.* Explore the nature of the difficulty and its context. It is helpful to know, for instance, such things as what has been tried before, under which circumstances is the problem *not* present, and who else is involved in this situation.

3. *Consider alternative courses of action.* Initially, as many different options as possible should be considered. Afterwards, these can be narrowed to those that seem most feasible.

4. *Examine barriers to making a decision.* This is where you anticipate where things might go wrong and prepare ways to overcome the obstacles.

5. *Decide on a solution.* Based on the exploration, analysis, and discussion that has taken place thus far, what is the person willing to do at this time? Preferably, this goal, or at least a small part of it, can be completed before the next session.

6. *Take action.* In groups, action takes two different forms: rehearsal or practice in the group (role playing, confrontation) and homework outside the group. In either case, the group members act on what they understand.

7. *Evaluate the outcome.* Any problem-solving attempt should be assessed in terms of its relative effectiveness in reaching desired goals. Most of the time, adjustments need to be made for continued efforts in the future.

For Personal Application

As with any technique or structure you use in groups, you must develop sufficient familiarity that you can make needed adaptations. One way to do this is try out every one of them with yourself first.

Working with a partner or on your own, proceed through the problem-solving stages to address some unresolved issue in your life. As you go through the process, notice the places where you feel stuck or resistant. Consider how group support, input, and feedback might make this procedure go more smoothly.

As a technique in action, whenever a group member seems stymied between courses to follow, unable to decide on the best solution, you can invite the whole group to become involved in the process of learning about problem solving. This kind of skill development approach can be used with a whole variety of content areas, depending on what emerges in a group and what the are identified as needs.

Ways to Facilitate Task Completion

One of the challenges you will face is finding ways to help group members apply what they are learning to their lives in the outside world. You will recall that the insights that are generated or the changes that people make do not endure unless they have the opportunity to generalize concepts and practice new behaviors.

There are a number of standard operating procedures that are used to facilitate this task completion (Rosenthal, 2000). The "go-around" is often used to end each group session in which members take a minute to declare one thing they learned that day and one thing they intend to do before the next meeting. Depending on the type of group and your leadership style, these "homework assignments" can be rather specific, such as confront a specific person or take particular action. The next session would then begin with each person reporting on what he or she thought about and what he or she did. This lends consistency and continuity to the structure of the group so that members understand they are held accountable.

For a Class Activity

In small groups, or in the class as a whole, do a "go-around" in which each person says something that he or she intends to think about before the next class. Then declare one specific action you intend to take in your life that will get you closer to your ultimate goal. This can be related to what occurred in class, or it may be connected to some lifestyle or personal change you are working on.

Journaling is another adjunct structure that is commonly introduced as a way to promote work between sessions and process insights along the way (Kottler, 1994a; Rainer, 1978; Riordan & White, 1996). This can be a relatively unstructured assignment in which members are encouraged (or required) to write in journals several times each week and then share them periodically with the leaders, or more structured logs can be introduced in which members must complete self-assessment forms. In some cases, journals can be shared systematically not only with the leader, but also with one another.

The intent of such journaling is to help members to accomplish several tasks, many of which you could review during the first session:

- Reflect systematically on what transpired in group and personalize the content
- List important points or ideas to be remembered and retrieved at some later date
- Talk to the leader(s) in a private forum
- Explore more deeply personal issues that were triggered by work in session
- Describe vividly what is seen, heard, observed, perceived, and felt during the session
- Create memorable portraits of each participant
- Release pent-up feelings and unexpressed emotions
- Declare personal goals that can be worked on
- Construct letters (never intended to be sent) that express heartfelt reactions that have yet to be expressed
- Express creativity through poetry, art work, or free form writing
- Practice new ways of thinking or acting, rehearsing planned strategies
- Monitor progress and growth over time
- Carry on self-dialogue about some conflict or issue
- Capture the moment by writing vividly about something that has been observed, felt, or experienced

Believe it or not, this is only a *partial* list of possibilities. Generally, when I first begin a group, I spend considerable time talking about the ways that a journal can be used throughout the experience. At various intervals, I will ask members to talk about what they are reflecting on and doing in their journals. Sometimes they even bring them in to use as resources or share especially poignant entries.

One of the most meaningful comments you will ever hear from an ex-group member is if he or she comes up to you on the street and says, "Guess what? You know that journal you had us keep in group? Well, after all these years I'm still writing in it almost every day!"

Ways to Rehearse New Behaviors

You have heard before that groups have the distinct advantage of providing opportunities for members to practice new behaviors in a safe environment. Role playing and psychodramatic enactments make it possible for people to confront antagonists or experiment with alternative styles, all the while receiving continual feedback on what works best.

As originally conceived by Jacob Moreno, psychodramatic techniques were synonymous with therapeutic groups. In fact, he is the one who first coined the term *group therapy* to describe what happens when people get together to help one another work through unresolved issues (Tomasulo, 1998). The object of these methods was to help someone to work through a struggle by acting out feelings toward a "double" or "empty chair." Since that time, a number of refinements have developed role-playing techniques into standard procedures for groups.

The essential notion behind these methods is that rehearsal is provided for the real world, with appropriate support and critical feedback. Basically, the following structure is followed:

1. *Explore and understand the situation.* The member talks about what is most troubling. Others ask questions and draw the person out, exploring fully what is going on. The issues are clarified, defined, and narrowed to one situation that can be worked on profitably.

    LEADER: "So let me review what you've said so far. You resent the way your husband tries to control you. When you tell him how you feel, he either ignores you or says that you are imagining things. Then you withdraw and pout."

    FELICIA: "Well, I hate the way that sounds, but that about covers it."

2. *Have the client select the cast.* The member chooses people in the group who she believes are most capable of playing the various parts. In addition to the main antagonist, the husband in the previous example, there are other characters involved in the conflict such as her two children and her mother-in-law.

    In addition to the active characters, the leader may designate others in the group to act as "auxiliary egos." These members serve a supporting role as needed, reflecting unexpressed feelings, offering encouragement or advice, serving as a consultant when action is stopped, or saying out loud things that are sensed but not articulated.

> LEADER: "Felicia, let's reenact the typical way that you might attempt to confront your husband, and then we can try some alternative strategies that might work better."
>
> FELICIA: [Hesitantly] "Ah, okay."
>
> LEADER: "You seem a little reluctant."
>
> FELICIA: "Well, maybe a little. I'm just a little scared doing this."
>
> LEADER: "That makes sense. Maybe a first place to start would be to pick someone in the group who you trust completely, someone who can sit at your side and be there for you during the whole episode. This consultant's job will be to whisper in your ear when you get stuck. So, who could that be?"
>
> FELICIA: "Um, how about Michele? I mean, if that's okay with you?"
>
> MICHELE: "Sure, I'd love to! It pisses me off to hear you cowering like you describe. You just seem so much stronger than that to me."
>
> LEADER: "Okay, Felicia, next let's pick the others in the cast. Choose those who you think would be especially good at playing your husband, your mother-in-law, and your kids."

3. *Role switching.* Since the group members do not know what the family members look, sound, and act like, they need some coaching from the client. Even better than describing the people is to ask the group member to *become* the person in order to *show* the way he or she behaves. This has the added advantage of forcing him or her to experience what it is like to be the antagonists and to get inside their heads. Many clients report that this experience alone helped them develop greater understanding and empathy for others.

> LEADER: "Felicia, we don't know what Antonio is like, except as you've described him. Why don't you show us what he's like? Sit in the chair just like he would . . . That's right . . . Now, talk like him. Use his tone of voice and vocabulary. Gesture just like he would . . . Come on . . . Really get into it."
>
> FELICIA: "Well, he'd probably . . ."
>
> LEADER: "Don't tell us. Show us what he's like."

Clients are often a little resistant to doing this part. Not only might they feel a little inhibited acting in front of peers, but on another level, it is very threatening to become the person you fear the most. Nevertheless, clients should be gently encouraged and guided to proceed with the role switching, because it is critical to see and hear, as realistically as possible, how the antagonist behaves.

4. *Set the scene.* The next step is to arrange the situation exactly as it would take place in the real world. Set up the room just as you would a stage. Ask the person to explain the exact circumstances in which the confrontation will take place. By the way, notice the use of the future verb, "will" in the previous sentence, reinforcing the idea that what is being rehearsed will actually take place.

LEADER: "Felicia, please describe for us exactly when this conversation would take place between you and Antonio. Place everyone in the room just as they would be at home. Arrange the furniture anyway you like. Then tell us how this interaction will begin."

5. *Act out the confrontation.* In this first round the performance will be dismal. After all, the client is not really doing anything differently. And the group members playing their parts will probably really enjoy their antagonistic roles, giving the person a harder time than usual.

FELICIA: "Um, honey, I was wondering . . ."

GROUP MEMBER

PLAYING ANTONIO: "Hey, will you get me another beer?

FELICIA: "Yeah, sure, but first I wanted to . . ."

ANTONIO: "Not now! Can't you see I'm watching the game?"

Even with the support available, Felicia lapses into the same old patterns of being deferential. That is actually quite a good thing since it means this simulation will be as realistic as possible.

6. *Analysis and feedback.* At various intervals, the leader will stop the action and elicit feedback from the group and the assigned consultant in order to create alternative strategies. At this first juncture, Felicia hears that choosing to confront her husband in this situation is probably not wise, especially with all the distractions of the television and her kids.

During the course of the scenario, the action can be stopped frequently in order to give suggestions, suggest alternative strategies, and offer support. In some cases, other group members, or even the leader, can take Felicia's chair in order to demonstrate different styles that could be introduced. I'm also inclined to jump in if the client is getting discouraged or beaten down by the experience, so as to show how different outcomes are possible with alternative strategies.

This, of course, is just one role-playing format. You can use this method in many other ways:

- Invite group members to write a letter out loud to someone in their life (dead or alive) who needs to be confronted. A designated scribe can take notes and give the draft to the person afterwards.
- Talk to an empty chair, imagining that the antagonist is seated there, tied up and gagged, so the person can say anything he or she likes without being interrupted.
- Imagine that the empty chair contains another part of yourself. Talk to that alternative part of you, then switch chairs, and respond back.
- Reenact an incident from childhood, but add a different ending.
- Act out a fantasy.

For a Class Activity

Get together in groups of five or six. One member volunteers to work on the need to confront someone in his or her life. Preferably, this would be a relatively minor situation, since you are working without a professional leader present at all times.

Go through the various steps described earlier, but do so in an abbreviated manner: (1) Say something about the situation, giving basic background information; (2) choose and coach the cast in how to play their roles effectively; (3) act out the confrontation; and (4) solicit feedback to incorporate into the continued enactment.

Talk about what you found most frustrating and most instructive about this exercise.

Ways to Work Briefly

If you intend to run groups in schools or community settings in which brevity and efficiency are necessary, you must adapt structures to the requirements of the time available. Several sources have been designed for this purpose (see Scott & Stradling, 1998; Shapiro, Peltz, & Bernadett-Shapiro, 1998; Tomasulo, 1998), responding to the demands of managed care, as well as to the need for more brief interventions. Such methods are considered more cost effective and make it possible to reach more people in a shorter period of time. Of course, there are limits and disadvantages to such methods as well, since they are certainly not designed for everyone.

If you find yourself in a work situation in which you must lead a group in an abbreviated format (say, less that a dozen sessions, or even fewer than a half dozen), then you must make certain changes to the structures you introduce.

1. Work with homogeneous groups so that it is easier to build cohesion, trust, and intimacy quicker.
2. Start the group way before the first session. Use advance preparation to get members working on goals and issues before they meet for the first time.
3. Remind participants that the "meter is running," that time is limited, so there isn't the luxury of waiting until the perfect opportunity to do something.
4. Help participants to set limited, realistic goals that can be reasonably completed in the time available.
5. Employ the use of adjuncts (like homework, journaling, field studies, readings) to supplement what is done in sessions.
6. Spread out the frequency of sessions over a longer period of time to allow for follow up.
7. Use action rather than insight methods more often, since observable progress must be attained rather quickly.
8. Teach problem solving and other skills that can be applied immediately.
9. Use group time for rehearsal, practice, and application of new behaviors and skills.

Ways to End a Group

I can't emphasize how important it is to end a group with momentum at its peak. One of the disadvantages of group work that we have discussed previously is that sometimes people do not follow through with their intentions. You must devise ways to end your groups so that several objectives are reached:

1. Main themes are reviewed and processed, with an emphasis on summarizing what was learned.
2. People are able to reach closure with the experience, expressing their grief and loss, but also their excitement for the future.
3. Unfinished business is named even if there is no time (there never is) to resolve everything.
4. Potential setbacks and relapses are discussed, including ways that they may be overcome.
5. Members are helped to say goodbye to one another in a way that honors their mutual caring but does not reinforce dependence.
6. Opportunities are provided for giving one another final feedback.
7. Plans are set in motion for continuing the work that each member has begun.
8. Follow-up plans are proposed and implemented.

You don't have to use any particular gimmicks, exercises, or techniques to end a group effectively. You can readily see from the objectives just listed that the structure runs itself. Essentially, you ask participants to talk about how they are feeling now that the group is drawing to a close. You provide a structure and sufficient time for people to talk about what they had hoped for initially, what they actually experienced, and what they want for the future.

One technique that often works well at this time is a final go-around in which each member has the chance to share what he or she learned that was most meaningful. Afterwards, other members give some feedback to the person as some "last words" to remember. Because it is so difficult to remember things that were said, it might be useful to have each person choose someone to write down everything that was offered. Alternatively, you can even tape record the closing "speech" that each person made, including the feedback they received, and then give them the tape as a final gift.

For a Class Activity

This exercise is called "the reunion" and is designed to help participants to set goals for the future in a dynamic, fun, and subtle way. In order for this activity to work well, you must really take it seriously and pretend that the assignment is real. There are aspects of this experience that participants may feel to be a little threatening, so you may feel the temptation to treat it as "only" a game. In order for this to work well, you *must* act as if it is real.

Everyone leaves the room and stands in the hallway but resists the urge to look or talk to anyone else. Go inside yourself until you can imagine you have journeyed one year into the future. Pretend that one complete year has elapsed since the last time you attended this class. During that interval, you have not seen anyone else in the room. You are now meeting for a class reunion.

From the moment you reenter the room act as if it has been a year since you have greeted one another. After you say hello, sit down in your "old" seat that you last occupied a year ago. Each of you takes turns telling one another about what has transpired in your life during the previous year. *You must speak in the present tense.* Talk about what you have done, how you are different since your classmates last saw you, and what significant events have transpired in your life. How has your living situation changed? How have your relationships evolved? Anyone new in your life? What about those issues you were struggling with a year ago? How are you doing now?

After each of you has had a chance to make a brief report, talk about the ways this exercise has helped you to clarify goals for the future.

It matters less exactly how you handle this closing phase then what you do to help members feel good about the group and what they have accomplished. You must reflect the underlying fears and apprehensions, just as there are in any transition. You must also plant the most favorable, but realistic, expectations possible for what will happen in the future.

I like to tell members something like this:

"Of course, you are going to have setbacks. At times, you will forget everything you learned and make the same mistakes you have made before."

Here, I like to wait a long beat to watch them squirm. I am saying their worst fears out loud.

"But this is no big deal. These setbacks are *only* temporary, if that is the way you want it to be. Just as you were able to apply in this group the new skills you learned, you can do this in your life, whenever you want. While it is true that you won't have this group to report to, we will all remain alive inside you, as long as keep us there. The support that you offered to one another here endures far beyond the tenure of this group."

There is one final point to make, related to the dependency that sometimes can develop in experiences like this. As you are well aware, "groupies" become addicted to one support group after another, unable to function on their own.

"The key question is what you are going to do to recreate a group like this in your own life. What you are willing to do with your family and friends and co-workers and neighbors to include the same spirit of trust and caring that you found here?"

This is a tall order, of course. The truth is that you can't really recreate such a spirit that has all of the same elements as a helping group. Nevertheless, you job in this final stage is to encourage members to take what they have learned and to apply all they can to the other facets of their lives. Changes truly last when people find as many ways possible to internalize the lesson learned, practicing every day what has now become second nature.

Review of What You Learned

- The one main problem you will face is having too many rather than too few techniques at your disposal.
- Any group technique must be adapted to the particular context, situation, leader style, and member needs.
- The best techniques and structures are not even recognized as such because they are introduced so smoothly.
- Techniques are best collected by asking experienced leaders about their favorite methods. The hardest part is cataloging the options so that they may be retrieved on demand.
- When introducing group structures, you may often wish to model the sort of spontaneity, openness, honesty, and authenticity that you want from others.

11 Supervision and Co-Leadership

The best way to learn group leadership is not from a text, from a class, watching groups in action, or even participating in a group. All of these are important components of the training process, but in an experientially based educational model the best way to learn is by doing it. Of course, practice by itself might not be all that useful if you end up making lots of mistakes and do not know enough to learn from those lapses. You need a way that you can test what you know, practice your skills and interventions, try out your theories, and then receive immediate feedback on their relative effectiveness.

If you know what to look for, and watch carefully, you will receive lots of valuable information from group members. It is stunning sometimes to watch videos of your groups in action, noticing all the cues you missed and all the signs that you ignored. But that is not enough. You need a more experienced colleague to monitor what you are doing carefully and then provide you with supportive and constructive feedback about what you can do to improve.

For Personal Application

Recall a time when you were learning a new skill that was a bit of a challenge. This could have been in school or a social situation or involved a physical activity. Think back on what your teacher/coach/tutor/parent did that was helpful to you in mastering this difficult behavior. How was that feedback presented to you in such a way that you were able to improve your performance?

Power of the Co-Leadership Model

In addition to the advantages of an apprenticeship model for beginning group leaders who are teamed with more experienced colleagues, this structure offers a number of unique advantages for the participants as well (Alfred, 1992; Dies, 1980; Kottler, 1992; Roller & Nelson, 1991; Shapiro, Peltz, & Bernadett-Shapiro, 1998). In fact, close to nine out of ten leaders prefer to work with a partner if given the opportunity (Yalom, 1995). This really isn't very surprising when you remember how much there is to do in a group and how little there is of you to go around.

Greater Coverage

I have mentioned before that when co-leaders sit on opposite sides of the group, not only can they communicate with one another easily but they can also monitor more effectively how everyone is doing. Generally, it is hard to see the people sitting right next to you, but a co-leader can be responsible for scanning your side of the circle while you take the other half.

If dual scanning provides for better coverage of member reactions, then the division of labor operates in other ways. Co-leaders can specialize in attending to some facets of group behavior over others, or even take turns doing so. For instance, if you are listening for content, then I can focus on process variables. Or while you are facilitating an interaction between a few members, I can take care of the rest of the group.

In order for teamwork to work effectively, you must communicate with your partner throughout the experience so that you are both functioning together in a synchronized way. There is nothing more frustrating than pushing in one direction when your co-leader is pulling in another.

For a Class Activity

Take turns working with a partner to lead a particular part of class, whether that involves discussing an issue, demonstrating an exercise, or even talking about a part of this chapter. Before you begin, talk to one another about the following:

1. One of you begins the group, while the other one will end it (the one with a watch).
2. Sit on opposite sides of the group from one another so you can see one another at all times and also observe different members.
3. Make an effort to continuously scan the room, watching carefully to see how each person is responding to what is going on.
4. Occasionally make eye contact with one another to ensure you are operating together.
5. Take at least one "time out" in which the two of you speak to one another in front of the group.

After your leadership is over, elicit feedback from the group regarding how you did. Structure the feedback so you hear constructive things you can work on in the future.

Make plans after class to spend time with your partner to debrief one another and process the experience.

Exert More Control

This can be a mixed blessing, as we will see in the section on limitations later in the chapter. Nevertheless, safety is a big concern in group work because members receive less attention; it is more difficult to protect people's rights. With two leaders present, the odds increase that someone will not slip through the cracks, remain ignored, or end up as a casualty. Especially when working with rowdier populations—hormonally charged adolescents, rambunctious first graders, prison inmates, outraged or angry folks—it is important to maintain sufficient control so that nobody ends up hurt.

Functionally, what occurs is that you both can divide up responsibility for watching certain group members and observing different parts of the room. As shown in the example below, you can also remind one another, as needed, when some follow-up is required:

> **LEADER A:**   "Okay, then, I think it's time to move on. I'd like to check in with you, Scott, to see how you're doing this week."
>
> **LEADER B:**   "Excuse me, but before we change the focus I'm not sure that Rita is done yet. I know she said she doesn't want anything more, but I sense that she . . . [Looks at Rita to address her directly] . . . that you, Rita, have some things you would still like to say."
>
> **LEADER A:**   "That's fine. I didn't notice that. But while you were pointing that out, I saw that others were nodding their head in agreement. So let's stay with Rita for a little while longer before we go to Scott."

Perhaps you can breathe a sigh of relief, vicariously, as you think about the security of knowing that someone else is watching your back. You don't have to remember everything, or check everything yourself, because you have a partner who is helping out.

Model a Good "Marriage"

In more ways than one a co-leader is like a marital partner. You must read each other's moods, be sensitive to nuances in behavior, take care of the other's welfare. You share "children" who occasionally need discipline but always need nurturance. Your effectiveness is based on the quality of your communication with one another.

Many clients have never experienced being part of a "family" with healthy parents. They come from broken and abusive homes. Even the ones who lived in reasonably "normal" families may still not have observed parents negotiating with one another in constructive, sensitive ways. For the first time in their lives, they will see two adults disagreeing with one another in a respectful, sensitive way. They will observe the ways that two parent figures make decisions, give and take, and negotiate the challenges of a family in turmoil (as most groups tend to be).

In the first group I ever attended, I was amazed at the ways our two co-leaders handled themselves. It was obvious they respected one another, even though they often disagreed. Growing up in a home with an alcoholic mother and an often-absent father—two people who clearly did not like one another and argued constantly—I felt so privileged to be part of a family with new "parents" who got along well.

In the dialogue below, for example, notice how the two leaders disagree with one another respectfully, demonstrating how it's possible to take an alternative position without jeopardizing the relationship:

> **LEADER A:**   "I'd like to ask you to pick someone out of the group who you think could do a good job of role playing your father."

LEADER B: "One second. Before we proceed with a role play, I'm sensing that she might not yet be ready for this. Perhaps we should give her some time to think about this before we push her into action."

LEADER A: "I disagree. I think she *is* ready, even though I appreciate your sensitivity for her pace. Let's ask her what she wants to do."

LEADER B: "Sounds good."

The members, of course, are watching this interaction very carefully, as it reminds most of us of those times when parents or other authority figures argued about their preferences. In this case, however, the participants are watching two partners talk things out and negotiate where they want to go next. In order for this to work well, the two leaders must invest considerable time and energy into their relationship, as would be the case with any partnership.

For a Field Study

Arrange to interview two leaders who have worked together for a period of time. Like most of the assignments in this book, it will take some persistence and persuasion on your part to make this happen. People will tell you they are too busy, that their schedules don't permit such an interview. In one sense they are right: After all, you aren't paying them for their time.

I have heard many students complain that they were not successful in finding anyone, much less *two* group leaders, to agree to talk to them about their professional activities. When I hear such reports, my first temptation is to offer sympathy, that is, until I hear a chorus of others who report quite a different experience: They had no trouble at all getting group leaders to meet with them. All I conclude from this discrepant feedback on assignments such as this is that you shouldn't give up if your initial attempts prove futile.

Assuming that you can find two co-leaders who will meet with you, or even visit your class, talk to them about the ways they work together. How do they resolve disputes between one another? How do they communicate with one another before, during, and after the group? What do they like best and least about working with one another?

Double the Expertise and Resources

Two co-leaders come from different backgrounds, hopefully different cultures and genders, and have different perspectives on life. They likely follow slightly different theoretical orientations and certainly behave with unique interpersonal styles. Each personality is different as well. This means that a group has double the potential resources.

One leader may be better at confrontation, the other at dealing with feelings. One leader is an expert at role playing, the other is a specialist in thought disorders or career indecision. One is low key in his approach, the other is passionate and dramatic in her style.

One leader likes to use metaphors in her speech while the other is a concrete talker. One is warm and the other is firm. One becomes the "mommy" of the group (not by any means determined by gender)—the nurturing figure—the other is the firm and forceful "daddy." All of these variations in style create more opportunities for members to respond to different aspects of leadership.

For example, when one leader gets out of line, loses objectivity, gets embroiled in a conflict (yes, this does happen), the other leader can intervene to get things back on track. There is always someone else available whom you can count on to help you out of a jam, or at least share the chaos together.

Opportunities for Identification

The transference possibilities increase with two different authority figures to project their feelings. The beauty of this, of course, is that when you are the object of such intense feelings, it is very difficult to remain neutral, detached, and uninvolved to the point where you can help the person work through the unresolved issues. With a partner, however, it is relatively easy to observe: "I notice that you are having some rather strong reactions to my co-leader. Let's explore what's going on."

Ideally, co-leaders should be from different genders and/or cultural backgrounds to maximize the opportunities for member identification. Although sometimes this is not possible, given the staff available, every opportunity should be made to team up with someone who can offer group members a different perspective than your own.

Although one criterion for choosing a co-leader to work with should include variables like a different culture, gender, and personality, those are certainly not the only factors to consider.

- Choose someone who complements your style, someone who can supplement what you know and can do but in a way that is compatible.
- Pick someone you can trust. This is such an intimate relationship that you would want to work with someone with whom you can be vulnerable, admit your mistakes and failures, and ask for help when you need it. Your co-leader is going to see you at your absolute worst and best.
- Make sure that your approaches to leadership are compatible. You are in for trouble if you like to work primarily in the past and your partner values only the present (or vice versa). There are certain theoretical orientations that blend well together and others that do not. Keep in mind, though, that flexibility is probably a more important consideration than espoused beliefs.
- If you have a choice in the matter, find someone who has more experience than you do but who respects you as an equal. You are likely to learn more from a partner who is an expert in areas that you are not; however, it is better if this person is also comfortable sharing responsibility in an equitable manner rather than treating you as a lackey.
- Start dating before you get married (much less have children). In other words, spend some time with your potential co-leader before you commit yourself to a working relationship.

Mentoring of Beginners

It should be of special interest to you, as a beginner, that the co-leader format is ideal for increasing your confidence and skills. In one review of the issues involved in mentoring group leaders, Hazler, Stanard, Conkey, and Granello (1997) talk about the various lessons that can be learned in such a collaborative relationship. Beyond the new skills and techniques that can be modeled, it is the mutual support that they found to be most significant—not just for the beginner but also the expert.

Co-leading with a more experienced colleague is the best source of on-the-job training. It is one thing to tell a supervisor or co-worker about your group and ask for feedback; it is quite another when that person is actually present as a participant. As you have probably realized, this sort of work can be very lonely. Confidentiality requires that we keep most things to ourselves. Yet with a partner involved in the process, the journey becomes a shared enterprise.

Even when you log sufficient experience to fly solo, you will often find it frustrating that there is nobody to talk to about what happened in your groups. Certainly you will review things with supervisors, or talk to trusted colleagues about what happened, but this is no substitute for the kind of camaraderie that occurs when you have worked together with a co-leader.

For Reflection

Remember a time when you worked closely with a partner on a project. What were some of the things you enjoyed most and least about this collaboration? What are some aspects of such teamwork that you struggle with the most? Jot down a few notes to yourself that you can eventually share with a co-leader you might work with.

For instance, when I begin with a new partner, I like to spend time telling each other about trouble areas we most consistently encounter. I warn my partner about my tendency to be impatient, to try to do too much on my own. If my co-leader is especially talented or skilled in one area that I am not (which is usually the case), I sometimes start to feel inadequate, then competitive.

Based on your own previous experiences in collaboration or partnership with others, create your own list of trouble spots that you can share.

Some Dangers and Limitations

Co-leadership presents some special challenges that must be closely addressed. Almost all of the problems result from some aspect of the relationship between the co-leaders that gets in the way. When jealousies or resentments arise, when one member feels misunderstood or unappreciated by the other, even undermined, then serious problems will leak into the group. That is why it is so critical for co-leaders to continue to monitor and work on their relationship, just as partners would in any business enterprise or marriage.

Realities

Even if it was true that co-leadership does result in better groups (and there is no *empirical* evidence to support that), the reality is that most practitioners have to work alone. It is often too expensive and impractical to assign two leaders to a group, especially in schools and organizations that already have a shortage of personnel (Carroll, Bates, & Johnson, 1997).

Second, in many work situations you do not have the luxury of choosing your partner; that decision might be made by a supervisor or mandated because only one other person is available. Just imagine how frustrating work can be when you are forced to work with someone you do not trust or respect. And if you think that group members will not sense this animosity or tension, you are very wrong. Many people in groups make a living by feeling and exploiting conflict in others; it is their favorite survival mechanism.

Third, if you are so fortunate as to work with a co-leader who does have skills and expertise you admire, that does not mean that person is favorably disposed to mentoring you. If you feel continually evaluated and judged by your partner, you are not likely to be very comfortable in this situation. Therefore, probably most of the problems and dangers associated with the co-leader model are the result of partner incompatibility or mismatch.

Tug of War

If co-leaders do feel competitive toward one another (and it is difficult not to), there will come times when each of you is fighting to go in your preferred direction. Let's say that you think you are onto something important with one person who is exploring issues related to mortality. Right in the middle of your exploration, your co-leader interrupts:

> CO-LEADER: "Excuse me for a moment. I think there is something else going on that needs our attention right now. Besides, I don't think this person is ready to go much deeper right now."
>
> YOU: "I'm not sure I know what you mean. I don't know who else you think needs time right now, but I'd like to finish up here first and then we can move on."
>
> CO-LEADER: "Well, if you want to. But I still think . . ."
>
> YOU: "Yes, I heard what you think. You always interrupt me. Why don't you back off, you sanctimonious jerk!"

Okay, I got a little carried away there at the end. But I couldn't help it. Whether you say the things you are thinking out loud or not (hopefully you would not), you can't help but feel a degree of annoyance and resentment when your partner does not agree with what you are doing. And if you think that it's best to just let your co-leader finish before you change directions, remember that lots of times the roles will be reversed: *You* will be the one who believes your partner is wasting time or heading down a blind alley.

Shortly, we will discuss some methods for coordinating your different agendas and resolving differences of opinion. That does not mean, however, that co-leaders always take the time to say what they are really thinking about one another's work. The differences, per se, are not disastrous. The problem arises when these issues play themselves out in your public interactions.

What My Partner Means . . .

When one co-leader is more experienced than the other, or has more seniority (and this is often the case), there may be inequitable status and power in the group. When members know this, they may react either by marginalizing the leader without real power, or by siding with him or her against the perceived oppressor.

Another variation of this theme occurs when one leader is significantly more dominant than the other as a result of differences in styles. Some people are naturally loquacious—they talk a lot (too much). Others have a more low-key, quiet style. If one leader is allowed to take over, to fill in the space, then the other is going to be left behind. In marital counseling this happens a lot when one partner speaks for the other, who then takes a deferential position. With a mediator present, adjustments can made to force the dominant one to back off so the quieter one can become more involved. In your co-leader relationship, however, it is up to both of you to monitor and adjust your relative contributions and involvement.

Splitting

It is not uncommon for group members to choose up sides and identify strongly with one leader in an alliance against the other (Yalom, 1995). This is particularly the case when members can sense any tension or conflict between the leaders, or when there is a clearly inequitable distribution of power. Imagine, for example, that individuals who already feel powerless notice that the less experienced co-leader is frequently trumped, censured, or controlled by the veteran. They may overidentify with the beginner's plight and attempt to side with him or her in an effort to defeat the powerful authority figure. The beginning group leader can end up participating in this rebellion, especially if there are unconscious feelings of resentment.

Cross Firing

In some instances, group members can be ambushed by co-leaders who gang up in an effort to get some therapeutic message across. Calling this "cross firing," Edelwich and Brodsky (1992) describe what happens when one leader initiates an intervention, the group member balks or resists, and then the co-leader presses harder. Instead of offering needed support and reflecting the reluctance, the co-leaders function as interrogators.

For a Field Study

Watch on television, or listen on the radio, to two media personalities who work together as a team. Notice the ways they have developed to coordinate their efforts. Although some of their routines are certainly rehearsed, others are improvised. Pay attention to the ways they play off of one another's energy. Notice the tension that sometimes develops when they are each moving in different directions, as well as how they resolve these disputes. Identify what you like best and worst about their co-leadership methods, resolving to incorporate the aspects you admire into your own style.

Value Conflicts

I have mentioned already the dangers when two leaders subscribe to radically different theoretical orientations. It can be equally problematic when you share the same approach to group work but not to life. There can be religious or lifestyle differences between you. One of you is very conservative, the other liberal. I happen to think that differences among co-leaders can actually be a great strength, but only if there is essential tolerance and respect for one another. If I think you are wrong because of your beliefs, or think your ideas are not sound, then we are probably in for some trouble.

During your "courtship" period, you should spend some time with your co-leader finding out potential sources of conflict between you. How will you deal with abortion, extramarital or premarital sex, recreational drug use, and other controversial issues? If you cannot work out these differences during your initial contacts, you may see them play themselves out in your group.

For a Class Activity

In groups of six or eight (or some even number) interview one another together to find which among you would be the most compatible co-leaders. Spend a few minutes with your partner identifying potential sources of conflict and disagreement between you—areas in which your values diverge or your beliefs collide.

Come back together as a group and talk to one another about what you learned. Find a consensus among you as to the best ways to resolve such differences with a co-leader.

Leader Dominance

Gladding (1999) mentions that with the presence of two leaders there is increased likelihood that the group can become overstructured. The members can get lost in the process of two leaders working hard (harder than they need to) to control every facet of the experience.

One of the consistent errors I tend to make as a group leader when working alone, much less with a partner, is trying to do too much of the work. As soon as I notice something going on that I believe is important, I have to bite my tongue to avoid jumping in to point this out. I am sometimes impulsive. I talk too much. Imagine, then, the problem with *two* of us present, each of us working our own agenda, maybe even showing off a little at times.

One principle to remember is that the more you do in a group the less there is for the members to do. That is not to say that you should do as little as possible, but rather that with two leaders you must take more than usual care to not overstructure or dominate the sessions.

Basics to Keep in Mind

Even with the limitations and dangers previously reviewed, the co-leader model is still the preferred way for you to develop your skills and expertise. Taking a beginning course is just not enough to prepare you for all the difficult challenges you will face. While supervision and further training will definitely help, there is no substitute for receiving the kind of immediate feedback that is possible with a partner in the process.

Choose a Partner Wisely, if You Have a Choice

If you are scheduled to lead a group and you do not yet have a co-leader, recruit one. Throughout my career I have been systematic in picking out prospective mentors I could learn from and then arranging to co-lead a group with them. In some cases, I worked just for the experience. When my prospective mentor was less than enthusiastic, I still did not give up until I found a way to work together.

If a more experienced colleague is not available to mentor you, then pick a peer who has experiences and qualities that you admire. If you can arrange for both of you to participate in supervision together, all the better as a means to structure your continued learning.

For Reflection

Look around the room among your classmates and consider the relative merits of working with each of them as a co-leader. Who would you want to work with most and why? Who would you least be inclined to work with?

Now imagine that you are paired with the person you would least like to work with. How could you address your apprehensions in such a way that it would be possible for you both to function effectively?

This Is a Shotgun Marriage

In all likelihood, your pairing with a partner is a rather quick arrangement. Spend as much time as you can together before the group begins so you work out details, plan your strategies, develop signal systems, and help one another set personal and professional goals. Talk to one another about how you will resolve conflicts between you. Mention some of the concerns you might have.

Sit Opposite from One Another

For reasons that have already been mentioned it is preferable to sit on opposite sides of the group so that you can observe different perspectives. This seating arrangement also facilitates easier communication between the two of you. In some cases, you can plan more intentionally to seat yourselves next to members who you think might need extra support or supervision.

For a Field Activity

During a class session or meeting, practice scanning the room rather than just attending to the instructor or person who is speaking. Try to be as unobtrusive in your efforts as possible, so you don't draw attention to yourself. Just naturally look around the room at intervals, taking in everything you can about how others are responding internally. Form some hypotheses in your head about the ways you think people might be feeling or reacting. Who looks bored? Who seems distracted or anxious? Who is completely engaged? Who seems only pretending to listen but is really lost in a fantasy? Who is making eye contact with whom?

Write down notes to yourself about all the things you learned as a result of scanning systematically that would ordinarily have escaped your notice.

Develop a Signal System

The longer you work together, the more hand signals you can develop to communicate with one another unobtrusively. At the very least, you would want to signal things like:

- Time to end the group (by pointing at watch)
- Let's move on to someone else (moving hand in circular motion)
- I'm confused and don't know where you are going (hands with palms up)
- Help! I'm stuck (pleading look)

As you work together over a longer period of time, you can customize your signals to the situation and to particular members. For example, if you have a difficult group member who has been rambling too much, you can signal one another when it is time to move in and redirect. The same might be true for a passive member who rarely says much.

Talk Across the Group

One of the more interesting options available to you with a co-leader is the technique of calling a "time out" in which you talk across the group as if the two of you are alone. This method can be used for a number of purposes:

- *When you and your co-leader are not together.* "Stop for a second. I'm not sure where you are going with this."
- *When you want to confront someone indirectly.* "Time out. I don't think we should proceed any further with him. I sense he's very resistant."
- *When you want to discuss strategy and allow the members to listen in.* "We keep pushing for greater intimacy but only get to the brink before people back off. What if we try something different . . ."

- *When you want to make a decision and demonstrate your cooperation.* "I'm not sure whether we should continue with this or move on to something else. What do you think?"
- *When you want to explain some dynamic that is happening.* "Let's stop for a second and look at what's been going on."

Of course, the co-leader dialogue is as much for the audience as it is for the co-leaders to synchronize their efforts. It is a subtle, indirect way of informing members about things beyond their awareness. It demonstrates the way that cooperative partners can work nego-tiate options. And it can become an impetus for getting members more involved.

Whenever I am stuck in a group, or don't know where to go next, I will talk to my co-leader about the dilemma. If I don't have a co-leader, then I will deputize one on the spot:

"Manny, I wonder if you'd mind helping me for a minute. I'm not sure what this silence means that's been going on for so long. I'm tempted to just let people stew for a while, but maybe it's better to rescue them. What do you think?"

Regardless of what Manny says, you have brought the issue into the open. Generally, the conclusion reached is that we should ask the group members what they think is going on and then move on from there.

For a Class Activity or Field Study

Team up with a partner to co-lead a group for five minutes. During that interval, find one excuse to take a time out and talk to one another in front of the group. This could involve something like not understanding where your partner is going or it could take the form of talking together about what you observe. A third possibility is to stop the action in order to make a decision in front of the group about where to go next.

After you are done, talk about what it felt like to use the time-out strategy. What are some concerns you have for applying this in the future?

Balance Your Contributions

Feel responsible to make certain that both of you are included in the process and "on the same page." Remember that you are modeling this behavior for group members as well, showing them how a high-functioning team operates. It is also a good idea to check in with one another to make sure that you are both synchronized (as you've just seen, you can even do this *during* the group). It is also a good idea after the session to talk about the extent you felt included and that the workload was shared equitably.

Cue One Another

Feel free to cue one another if an appropriate situation arises. If you happen to know, for instance, that your co-leader has resolved a particular issue in her life, you can elicit this contribution at the opportune time. If you need some help during an interaction, ask for what you need. You might say to your co-leader something like this: "I'm not sure where to go with this next, so feel free to jump in any time."

Surprisingly, group members often like it a lot when you reveal your uncertainties and doubts, showing them that you are human, too. They are also able to see more clearly how you manage to do what you do. One of the benefits of group work that I've mentioned before is that participants learn the skills of helping at the same time they work on their personal issues.

Remember That the "Kids" Are Watching

Everything that you do takes place on multiple levels. In groups, you are not only speaking to one person but to an audience that is also personalizing what is going on. That is certainly the case whenever you and your co-leader communicate with one another. Members are watching carefully how you react, how you negotiate, and how you resolve differences. They are learning as much from you through these interactions as anything else therapeutic you might initiate.

For a Field Study

Pair up with a partner. Plan and implement together a very brief presentation in another setting. This could involve a demonstration, activity, exercise, or just a talk about something. The particular topic is less important than the opportunity it presents to gain co-leader experience.

Apply the concepts presented in this chapter to help you plan what you will do and debrief one another afterwards. Solicit feedback from the audience on only one dimension: your relative effectiveness as partners in the process.

Respectful Disagreement

Some practitioners question the usefulness of public disagreement among co-leaders in front of the group, preferring to show a consistently united front. In one study of group participants, Yalom (1995) found unanimous agreement that such disagreements, if handled appropriately, were of great benefit.

How to Debrief a Co-Leader and Get the Most from These Sessions

At various stages in the group's development, there are inevitably certain issues that must be examined by co-leaders, not only to keep the group on track but also to support their working relationship. Most of these issues, summarized by Corey and Corey (1997), have been reviewed in previous chapters.

Stage	Major Issues
Induction	division of responsibilities, shared roles, clarified objectives, screening interviews, diagnosis and treatment plans, marketing and recruitment, getting to know one another
Experimental Engagement	equitable contributions, evolving structure, individual treatment goals for members, potential challenges, initial feedback on leader behaviors, finding a compatible style
Transition	personal and countertransference issues, relationship problems between co-leaders, difficult group members and resistant behavior, plans for transition into working stage and greater risk taking
Cohesive Engagement	ongoing evaluation of individual and group progress, obstacles to deepening intimacy and cohesion, characteristic process and dynamics of group, introduction of advanced or creative techniques, compatibility of theoretical orientations, parallel working at a deeper level on mutual feedback
Disengagement	closure issues, unfinished business, follow up plans for individuals, separation and loss issues, evaluation of strengths and weaknesses, review of turning points and critical incidents, sharing of experience and feedback, scheduling of post-group sessions

For a Class Activity

Get together with a partner who will act as your co-leader during a debriefing session. Identify in which stage you believe your class is currently functioning. Discuss with one another the various issues that have arisen thus far, as well as those that have yet to come up, but may need to be addressed.

Meet with two or three other co-leader teams in order to compare notes and reach some sort of consensus.

Reflect on the ways that you and your co-leader worked together as partners.

Debriefing a co-leader is one kind of peer supervision that has the advantage of avoiding dual-relationship issues of evaluation. It is *not* intended to replace traditional, hierarchical supervision in which you are held accountable to a supervisor, but provides a different kind of support, feedback, and stimulation (Gladding, 1999; Kottler & Hazler, 1997).

Whether you work with a co-leader who is a peer or supervisor, here are a few suggestions to follow during your debriefing process that should take place before and after each session.

Tell Your Partner What You Are Working on

Let your co-leader know with which areas of your professional functioning you have historically had the most difficulties. Review the work you have done previously in supervision (and personal therapy or counseling). Inform your partner in which areas you are especially interested in having your behavior monitored. Basically, tell him or her what you need most and what you are looking to learn the most from the experience.

If I was working with you as my co-leader, I would remind you of my struggles I alluded to earlier. I would probably tell you something similar to this:

"I tend to be impatient. I work too fast and push people to quickly. Please stop me if you sense I'm rushing things.

"I've been told before that I sometimes have a blank look on my face. Group members have told me that this bothers them, that they don't know where they stand with me and how I'm reacting to what they're saying. What's really going on is that I'm concentrating so intently that my face becomes frozen. I want to appear more warm and inviting so signal me when this happens so I can loosen up.

"There are a few other things to help me with as well. I tend to overpersonalize things too much. If you catch me becoming defensive, please stop me. One other thing: Sometimes I get a little too goofy and irreverent. I get bored easily so I make jokes a lot, sometimes at inopportune times. I'm going to ask for your feedback on that and would sincerely appreciate it if you would let me know when I'm going too far. You can just tell me right in the group; don't wait.

"Since you and I have different skill and experience levels, you might want to defer to me. I am going to be much quieter and less active than I normally would so this will force you to do more of the work. Sometimes, though, I get carried away with things. I just sink my teeth in and won't let go. Please let me know when this happens."

Ask for What You Need

As should be apparent from the previous example, it is your job to let your partner know what you need. If you are not happy with the way things are going, say something. If you are struggling in some particular area, ask for help. While your co-leader is not your therapist, and may not be a supervisor, there is a mutual responsibility you share to support one another as best you can.

- If you are about to try something new, tell your co-leader to provide a safety net.
- If you are feeling stuck about some aspect of your development, ask for help to break through the impasse.
- If you are confused about what has been happening in the group, stay with the process analysis until you are reasonably satisfied.
- If some countertransference or other personal issues arise, discuss these with your partner.
- If you are feeling resentful, frustrated, or dissatisfied with some aspect of the leadership experience, work this through with your partner.
- If you are having trouble with something your partner is doing, or not doing, then let that person know.

Observe Carefully What You Like Best and Least

It was mentioned elsewhere that the best sort of feedback is the kind that has both supportive and constructive elements. After a group session is over, ask yourself what you did that you liked best and least. Then reflect on your partner's behavior. Offer him or her a few constructive suggestions, as well as some observations on actions that you believe were particularly helpful.

After reviewing specific leadership behavior, then cover the group as a whole. Discuss the strengths and weaknesses of the group so far. What are the resources that you can draw on? What are some soft spots that need to be filled in?

Remember Points of Confusion

There will be at least a dozen times in every group session when you don't have a clue about what is going on. The process is really so complex and multifaceted that a team of scientists could spend their lifetimes analyzing a single group session and still not hit everything. So confusion is not only normal but desirable: If you don't feel confused, then you should be if you think you know what's going on.

Make notes to yourself about things that happen in the group that you do not understand. This could involve some interaction between members or between yourself and someone else. Your intuition could tell you that something funny is going on but you can't quite get a handle on what it is. Certainly, there will be numerous times when you tried one intervention but could have chosen many others. Make mental notes that you can return to after the session during the debriefing process.

After one group session, I had the following areas to explore with my co-leader:

1. What's with David? Why was he being so evasive? Normally, he's the first to jump in.
2. When I jumped in after Flynn spoke, I wondered if I was rescuing him. What else could I have done?
3. I had no idea where you were going with that them about "life decisions."
4. I noticed that several times in the session there were those long silences. At first I thought that people were just thinking about stuff, but now I'm wondering if something else might have been going on.
5. Did you catch that look that Megan gave Stella every time you spoke? Is there some resentment there?
6. I thought we were more than ready to move into the working stage, but now I'm not sure. There was a lot of reluctance today to get much deeper.

This happens to be a *very* abbreviated list. I can come up with a hundred questions about things I don't understand after any session. The true joy of co-leadership, though, is that you have a partner to talk these things through. You get the benefit of another perspective on matters. Even if you must remain confused, you will not feel so alone in your bewilderment.

For Reflection

In your journal or on a separate sheet of paper, jot down notes to yourself about all the things that happened in your class that confused you. I am not referring to the content, but to the dynamics and process of what happened.

Make a list of at least a dozen distinctly different things that puzzle you. These could include:

- *The instructor's behavior.* What are some things the instructor did or said about which you were not sure about the intended outcome?
- *Hidden motives.* What are some interactions that took place in class that seemed to involve hidden agendas?
- *Peer interactions.* What are some communications between individuals that appeared far more complex than you would first guess?
- *Dynamics and process.* What is it about the group dynamics of the class that puzzles you?

Compare Notes on Critical Incidents

One of the ways you will get better as a practitioner is to discover other ways that various situations could have been handled differently. During a critical incident, my brain can only process so much information in the allotted time available. I see what I think is going on; then I react. It is fascinating, however, to hear my partner offer an alternative view on what was going on (often completely different from my own perspective) and then suggest other ways the situation could have been handled.

Even when the choice of intervention might be exactly the same, it is still informative and stimulating to hear the different ways an incident or interaction may be interpreted. This is what will increase your flexibility and resilience to deal with new challenges that arise in the future.

For a Class Activity

Working in pairs, compare your perceptions of an identical event or situation that came up in class. Reconcile your differences of opinion to the point where you can reach a consensus about what probably occurred.

After you are done with this task, talk to one another about the *process* of how you worked together. Talk about strengths and weaknesses of your communication together, as well as what it would take for you to work better together in the future.

Work on Your Relationship

If working with a co-leader is a kind of partnership, if not a marriage, then there will be times when you will encounter difficulties. Occasionally, you will get on each other's nerves. You will feel slighted. You may feel competitive toward your co-leader, who can probably do some things better than you can.

Even if you get along almost perfectly, you will still need to communicate a lot about your respective positions. This may sound rather obvious, that the quality of your work together depends on the amount of time and energy invested in the relationship, but the reality is that co-leaders often take one another for granted.

You may think it's a great idea to debrief one another before and after group, but there are a lot of obstacles that get in the way. The legitimate excuses are endless: You were catching up on paper work, you got stuck in a meeting, or you have another appointment scheduled right before or after. Another real possibility is that you are tired and just plain don't feel like it.

Just as in a marriage or friendship, it takes a degree of commitment in order to make the relationship work; the same is true with your co-leader. You must build time into your schedules, just like running the group or any other professional appointment, so that you can meet on a regular basis.

I am presenting these debriefing sessions as a sort of obligation when I really mean to infer that they are the absolute best part of the job. You will remain so hungry for camaraderie in this type of work, so needy for feedback on how you are doing. You will get some of this from informal contacts with colleagues and supervision, but it still isn't nearly as fun as being able to compare notes with a "co-parent" who shares the same experiences. It is like the camaraderie shared by soldiers who have fought many campaigns together. You pulled one another out of trouble. You took your share of wounds but also enjoyed the glory of many victories.

Supervision Opportunities

When your work is being supervised by someone else, there are a number of advantages having two participants in the process. There is another set of eyes, another witness present, who can corroborate what happened or offer a different perspective.

A good supervisor will help you to examine the dynamics of your relationship. You have a mediator who can help you to resolve differences in philosophy and style. You can brainstorm together new strategies to introduce in session. You can review the relative effectiveness of what you have tried so far.

An outside supervisor can easily enhance the work you are doing together. The sessions become more collaborative with three participants instead of the usual two. In many ways, the experience can become less threatening and more stimulating. There are also a number of creative supervision strategies that can be employed with co-leaders such as the "reflecting mirror" in which time-outs can be called during the session and the supervisor can join the two leaders in a discussion about what is happening and what can be tried next (McGee & Burton, 1998).

Back to Reality

There is no doubt that two heads are better than one, especially in such a complex situation as a therapeutic group when so much is happening all the time. Alas, the luxury of working with a co-leader is not often available. In most organizations, resources are already stretched to the limit. Groups are launched in the first place to maximize staff. Schedules do not often permit two leaders who can show up at the same place at the same time on a regular basis. Just as likely, there may not be anyone around who knows any more about group leadership than you do.

Before you throw up your hands and write off this chapter completely, saying to yourself that this was a great idea but not all that realistic, consider that there are other ways that you could recruit a co-leader. Remember though, in making these suggestions, I do not want to hear your excuses and counterpoints about why this would not work. You must start from the premise that you *can* initiate a co-leader experience, given enough resourcefulness and creativity.

For Field Studies

1. *Volunteer to co-lead a group in another setting.* Approach someone you respect greatly who you know is leading groups on a regular basis. Ask if you can serve as an apprentice, just for the learning opportunity. Surely there is someone in your community who would serve in the role of mentor.
2. *Ask a faculty member.* Instructors tend to be *way* overscheduled and overbooked in their lives but sometimes they might be willing to co-lead a group with you where you work. If time does not permit an extensive commitment, sometimes brief observations visits can be scheduled.
3. *Partner up with a classmate.* This should be a last resort because it may be like the blind leading the blind. If, however, a more experienced candidate is not available, then the next best choice is to work with a compatible peer so you can mentor one another. Remember, as a beginner, you will be receiving some supervision anyway.

Review of What You Learned

- Working with a co-leader is both much easier and much harder than working alone. On the one hand, you have support and added resources available. On the other hand, you have another potential source of conflict.
- Spend time planning with a partner how you will divide up tasks, communicate during the sessions, and resolve disputes.
- If you have a choice, select a partner who is more experienced, yet who will treat you as an equal and devote the necessary time for debriefings.
- At times, you can talk across the group to your co-leader when you are stuck, confused, wish to confront someone nondirectly, or cue your partner to do something.
- During debriefings, talk openly to your partner about your needs, frustrations, and weaknesses. If you don't feel comfortable doing so, talk about that as well.

CHAPTER

12 Groups for Special Populations

So far, we have been exploring group leadership as a general procedure. Everything you have learned will be helpful when working with any population in any setting. Nevertheless, it is necessary to make some adjustments in the ways you structure your groups, as well as your leadership style, depending on who you are helping and the context in which this help takes place. Surely, you can imagine that you would not design and run a group the same for incarcerated, involuntary violent sex offenders as you would conduct an informational meeting for business leaders.

In this chapter we will look at the specific adjustments you will need to make for a number of special populations. Yalom (1995) exhausted himself trying to list just a few of the possible specialized groups that are led on a regular basis. There are groups for every imaginable physical disease and medical problem: HIV patients, cancer patients, victims of Alzheimer's, multiple sclerosis, asthma, or diabetes. There are support groups for compulsive gamblers, drinkers, and addicts. There are grief groups; psychodrama groups; groups for amputees, sexual dysfunctions, weight loss, depressed transsexuals, agitated schizophrenics, physically disabled, minority veterans, children of Holocaust survivors, among others. There are groups in churches and synagogues led by clergy, groups in hospitals led by nurses or social workers, groups in business led by human service experts, groups in schools, in clinics, in community organizations, and private practice. The list is endless and would take more space than this book could hold.

The particular groups and populations selected are not intended to be exhaustive but rather to illustrate the variations that are possible. From these examples, you should be able to extrapolate policies and procedures that would work with any situation.

Some General Principles

Before we get into specific special populations, keep in mind that while planning any group you will want to answer several questions:

1. What are the special needs of this population you wish to serve?
2. What adjustments will need to be made in the way you work considering the unique needs of this population?

3. Which goals are reasonable and appropriate given the population, time constraints, setting, and mandate?
4. What modifications in technique are necessary for this group?

For a Class Activity

In small teams, you have been assigned the task to lead one of the following groups:

- 20 senior citizens, ages 71 to 97, living in a sheltered community who want to talk about loneliness
- 16 convicted drunk drivers who have been given the choice to attend a group for ten weeks instead of going to jail
- 5 third graders whose parents have recently divorced
- 60 members of the police, fire department, and rescue squad who had been involved rescuing survivors from a tornado
- 12 male and 2 female department heads in a manufacturing industry who are attending a meeting to generate suggestions for better quality control
- 8 patients (and 6 of their spouses/partners) who have recently been diagnosed with terminal cancer

Feel free to add others to the list that might interest you.

Plan how you would structure and lead these groups, paying special attention to the ways you would have to customize your services. Talk about the adjustments in structure, methods, dynamics, process, and interventions that you would make. Discuss the unique challenges working with this special population.

Summarize what you developed for the rest of the class.

A Survey of Some Special Groups

For each of several different kinds of groups, I mention some unique issues that would have to be addressed. In each case, you would want to do some more specialized research in the literature and among practitioners in order to prepare better to lead any one particular kind of group. If, for example, you were assigned the task to lead a support group for minority women in the midst of mid-career transitions, you would want to check out general group journals (i.e., *International Journal of Group Psychotherapy*, *Social Work With Groups*, *Journal For Specialists in Group Work*), as well as those specific to that population (i.e., *Psychology of Women Quarterly*, *Women in Therapy*, *Journal of Multicultural Counseling and Development*). There are also a number of handbooks and source materials you could consult on this specific population. Once you have the necessary background, then you would talk to group leaders who have already done some work in this area, or at least in the general vicinity.

For Personal Application

Identify at least three specific populations that you hope to work with in group settings. Take into consideration not only the cultural/gender/ethnic background of your likely client groups, but also their presenting complaints.

Go to the library and find at least three articles and three books that relate to each of your client constituencies. Familiarize yourself with the types of groups that are preferred with each audience and the unique challenges that are faced by leaders.

Find an expert in the field who has already led the type of groups that you one day hope to start. Interview this professional via the phone, internet, or in person, in order to find out what unique challenges are faced and the ways your training would need to be adapted for this population.

By the way, this same process is exactly what you would do each time you are faced with the challenge of leading a new kind of group that is outside your current repertoire. Better yet, try to apprentice yourself as a co-leader with someone who is already doing the work you wish to do.

Working with Young Kids

It is not too difficult to highlight some unique requirements of a group with younger children. They would obviously have a lower attention span and higher energy level than would groups for adults. I remember when teaching preschool that I began each morning running the kids around in circles, timing them in races (with no finish lines), just so I could calm them down enough to learn to use scissors. This experience is supported by others who specialize with this population, advising that groups be small in size (5 to 6), short in duration (30 minutes), involve physical activity, and include sufficient structure regarding rules for interaction (Berg, Landreth, & Fall, 1998; Rose, 1998).

Unique Needs. The first thing you would need to keep in mind when organizing and structuring groups for children are their levels of functioning in a host of areas including physical, social, moral, cognitive, and emotional development. You will recall from your study of developmental tasks and stages that children have particular capabilities and needs at various ages. First graders think on a concrete level. They need a high degree of structure. They interact well with agemates of both genders. Compare this age with a group of seventh graders who do have some capacity for abstraction, require less structure, but are often polarized by gender.

Second, children present concerns and issues that are often different from (and sometimes the same as) those of adults. Whether you intend to lead groups in schools, agencies, or other settings, you are likely to see kids who present some of the following problems: bullying (or victims of such behavior) shyness, truancy, class disruptions, defiance, fighting, sexual or physical abuse, family problems, depression, loneliness, anxiety and school phobia, drug abuse, poor self-esteem, excessive approval seeking, poor school performance, and delinquency.

Third, you are likely to use different group methods with children than you would with adults, or at least adapt the ones you know to the needs of specific age groups. If you are working with adolescents, for example, you know there is going to be a greater interest in issues related to friends, sex, drugs, careers, and family. Furthermore, with hormones raging, you will need to maintain sufficient control to keep discussions on task.

These same control issues would be present when working with very young children as well. In this case, you would also want to adopt group methods that do not require everyone to be involved in the same task all the time. Imagine trying to get ten preschoolers to all do the same thing at the same time! For this younger population, therefore, you would want to employ play therapy methods that have been adapted for group settings (Ginott, 1982; Landreth & Sweeney, 1997).

Special Challenges.   As far as special challenges you will face with this population, you will have one problem that is rarely the case with adults (except in prison) and that is discipline. Kids have so much energy and are relatively unrestrained in their enthusiasm to the point that they vibrate most of the time and you will have your hands full keeping things under control. Children are always hitting and jabbing one another, squirming in their seats, screaming out whatever comes into their heads, staring out the window, making weird sounds, throwing things at one another, interrupting constantly with jokes—I could go on and on and on. Either you love this sort of thing (I do!) or it drives you batty. If you work with kids, these discipline problems come with the territory.

In addition to maintaining control, you will also have the challenges of greater peer pressure, especially during adolescence. In one group I led recently, a seventh grader disclosed only that he didn't know what a particular word meant and he was teased mercilessly by everyone else. This was the last thing he said out loud for a long time.

It is a challenge to keep the momentum going with children's groups. When adults are bored, they resort to fantasy and other socially appropriate behavior. When kids are bored, they act out. You know exactly where you stand, not that you appreciate the dramatic ways they often let you know (a fake or real belch or fart).

As if these challenges are not enough, you must also contend with parental sabotage . . . I mean, parental *involvement*. Kids are often not allowed to think for themselves or to make their own decisions. All your best work can be easily undone by parents or other family members who are threatened by your efforts. It is not at all unusual that some of your most valuable group members will be unceremoniously yanked out of your group by their parents without explanation; even the kids don't understand what happened or why. That is why it is critical that you have the support of parents before you attempt to work with their children. If they do not like what you are doing or how you are doing it, you will not be allowed to continue.

Finally, if you are working in a school environment, then you must contend with the realities of briefer groups that must be compacted into 40-minute time segments. This is not a disqualifying factor, but it does require a degree of efficiency to get things moving quickly.

In spite of these unique challenges, I actually prefer leading groups of kids. I love their honesty. I love the fact that I can help them before it's too late. I like the idea that I can help children negotiate better some of the problems that I struggled through without help.

For a Field Study

Go hang out in a playground, mall, or other setting in which children interact in a naturalistic environment. Better yet, get permission to observe groups of children in action.

Pay attention to what children do with one another that they find most fun and satisfying. Notice the ways they get one another's attention, the ways they try to win approval, and the ways they are marginalized. Observe as well their communication patterns.

In your role as a group leader think about what you could do to organize their experiences so they would learn good stuff about themselves and others. Beyond techniques, what would you hope to facilitate?

Groups with Older Adults

Applying the same developmental schemata to this population, ask yourself the question, What the particular needs and interests are of this group?

Imagine that you are now 80 years old. Your life's work has been largely completed. Except for a few memory problems, your mind is relatively clear. You spend a lot more time thinking about the past than you do the present, which, frankly, is not as satisfying as you would prefer. Your body is shuffling along, but not at the speed or efficiency you once enjoyed. You have decided to join a group to talk about the things that matter most to you, as well as some concerns you have.

It is highly likely that older adults are going to be among the most frequent and popular consumers of future groups. With a rapidly aging population and a longer lifespan, older adults will have more discretionary time, longer periods of retirement, and a greater need for recreational and growth experiences that do not require physical skills. What better place is there then a group for senior members of our culture to have a forum in which to make sense of their lives, talk about their concerns, connect with one another, and work on their problems?

Challenges with the Elderly. Although groups are absolutely ideal settings for the elderly because of the emphasis on community and connectedness, there are some realities that make this type of work challenging. You are dealing with a population that is living within bodies that are deteriorating. They have sensory and memory deficits. Some members don't hear too well and will interrupt constantly with, "What's that you say?" Among the members who have their sensory faculties intact, they may have short-term memory problems, often forgetting what they were saying, or what they said before. There could be problems with participants rambling a lot or talking too much, failing to listen and respond to others. There may also be some people present who are unduly skeptical of group work or live totally in the past and appear to have little interest in the present. Finally, elderly group members may have medical problems or medication side effects that prevent them from being fully attentive and present.

Let me stress that the challenges you would face with this special population may be different than those with others, but no more difficult to overcome than the previous issues with children. With sufficient preparation and a sound plan you can work wonders, helping elderly individuals address many important struggles in their lives.

Typical Issues in Group Sessions.   Just what are the unique problems that this population faces and is likely to bring up in group? Later adulthood is a time of reminiscence, a period of reflection, and an opportunity to put one's life in perspective. To various degrees, the elderly may feel satisfied and/or disappointed with what has been accomplished. In either case, they want to talk about what they have lived and seen and experienced. They want to feel acknowledged and valued for what they have done and the contributions they have made. More than that, though, they want others to learn and profit from their experiences.

The elderly bring a number of other needs and issues to groups. Isolation and loneliness are big themes that are explored. Members also talk a lot about their families, including the joys of grandparenthood, as well as the resentment they may feel in being neglected or unappreciated. They may not feel they are getting the respect and attention they deserve (and they are probably right).

Another major theme is related to physical deterioration, body image, and medical problems. Almost everyone will have something that has gone wrong with their bodies. This is frightening—make that terrifying—not to mention annoying and disruptive. If given half an invitation, you could fill up ten group sessions just listening to all the complaints.

There are major grief and loss issues to deal with. There has been a significant loss of power and control over their bodies, their families, their work, and their lives. It is likely they are all grieving the loss of loved ones—friends, spouses, partners, acquaintances, even the loss of their own vitality. Their essential jobs in life at this stage are to give meaning to what they have lived and to pass on lessons to the next generations. It is your job to help them do that, and make no mistake, they need a lot of help.

Customized Methods.   Screening participants is especially important to make sure that older members can meet the minimum skills to be attentive and responsive to others. You would also wish to screen out the incessant whiners, the belligerent, the ramblers, and those not based in reality.

Several authors suggest a number of structures that are useful with this population (Burnside, 1993; Corey & Corey, 1997; Gladding, 1999; Knight, 1996; Molinari, 1994; Myers, Poideveant, & Dean, 1991):

1. Use lots of structured exercises.
2. Allow members to reminisce and tell their stories, but in limited doses.
3. Help them to tell their family histories, their significant moments in life, as well as their disappointments.
4. Deal with death rather than avoid it.
5. Touch people physically as a way to communicate caring.
6. Emphasize listening in the group so everyone has a chance to be heard.
7. Attack the myths associated with aging.
8. Help people to make the best of their situations rather than lamenting what is missing.
9. Teach coping skills that help members to remain functional and cogent.
10. Motivate people to live in the present as well as the past.

11. Get families involved in the treatment so that members feel less abandoned.

12. Focus on specific themes or topics (grief and loss, isolation, sexuality, creativity, etc.).

13. Get the members up and moving at times to generate some energy.

14. Deal with the transportation and logistical needs of the members so that they can attend on a regular, consistent basis.

In addition, be careful to monitor your own impatience and need for action. Some people need to vent, to talk, to tell their stories, to feel heard, even though they don't intend to do anything differently. Watch your own countertransference issues related to aging and death.

For Reflection

Picture yourself in retirement. Close your eyes and really try to see yourself, what you look like, how you sit and talk and walk. Imagine where you are living and who you are living with. Run through a typical day in your life.

Now, remaining in this fantasy, imagining yourself as elderly, look back on your life. What did you accomplish that feels most satisfying? What are your greatest regrets? What do you wish you had done differently?

Returning to the present, consider what it would take to live your life in such a way that you would have no regrets as you get older.

Groups with Homogeneous Populations

This is a huge specialty area as there are literally thousands of such groups for populations like struggling college students (Brinson & Kottler, 1995; Jennings & Anderson, 1997; Lipincot & Robinson, 1994; Meissan, Warren, & Kendall, 1996), overwhelmed adults (Hopps & Pinderhughes, 1999), HIV patients (Alfonso & Cohen, 1997), breast cancer patients (Gore-Felton & Spiegel, 1999), or abused adolescents (Glodich & Allen, 1998). If you think logically about the advantages of working with people who all share the same problem you can imagine how much easier it is to develop cohesion and trust since everyone can relate to the same issues. Also, participants are likely to feel a common bond that outsiders would not understand.

You can also customize the groups to meet the special interests and needs of the participants. In a group specifically designed for group leaders who work with HIV patients, the whole experience was structured around special grieving and guilt issues, survivor guilt, and post traumatic stress of the helpers (Cho & Cassidy, 1994). You can do something similar with any group that has a homogeneous population, insuring that attention is directed toward the areas you know are most relevant and useful.

On the other hand, when everyone has the same problem, they may also have the same weaknesses and blind spots. One of the distinct advantages of group work is the way that people of diverse experiences can help one another. One member may be lousy at intimacy and feels very inadequate in love relationships but is a superstar when it comes to problem solving. Another member may be guilt-ridden and filled with shame, but is very helpful to others when it comes to combating procrastination. Everyone is allowed to shine at times.

Yet when you have a group of shy individuals, all looking to become more assertive, they struggle with the same problems; the same with drug addicts or grieving spouses. Not only is there a marked diversity in experience and strengths, but homogeneous groups can also lack zest because of the continued focus on one problem over and over and over again. Members become identified with their problems, rather than as individuals who may have difficulties in one or more areas.

Another challenge you will confront with homogeneous groups is the tendency for polarization to occur when members can gang up against the leader. Pretend you have a group filled with resistent teenagers, alcoholics, or sex offenders. Now picture what happens when you get through to one participant, someone who admits he has a problem and commits himself to change. The others now have a choice to follow his lead or sabotage his efforts so they don't have to invest the energy to also change. Which do you think is easier to do?

Generally speaking, homogeneous groups are easier to market and harder to run. It makes more sense to "sell" a group for a specific population. Prospective consumers immediately identify with the target issue, whether that is developing study skills or working through loss. Once you get the group together, however, you will have other challenges on your hands that must be counteracted.

For a Field Study

Interview group leaders as to whether they prefer leading homogeneous or heterogeneous groups. Find out why they like one kind over another. What do they do to address the problems that inevitably arise?

In homogeneous groups it is good policy to emphasize what everyone has in common in the beginning to develop cohesion and trust, and then to stress individual differences. The fact of the matter is that everyone does not really have the same problem; they are all just calling it the same name. What I mean by this is that if a dozen people say they have a problem with divorce adjustment, they really do not have the same exact issues even though they might share a similar predicament. One member struggles with feeling lonely, another has unresolved rage toward the rejecting spouse, another is concerned primarily about economic problems, another experiences severe bouts of depression, while another is prone to panic attacks. In other words, the precipitating event may be the same, but their reactions are very different.

When leading homogeneous groups, prepare yourself for the predictable struggles as best you can. Stress more than usual the importance of using "I" rather than "we." Be careful not to exacerbate "us against you" power issues by doing anything that appears as a direct attack—get the group members to confront one another rather than your being the target of retribution.

For a Class Activity

Role play a group in which you all have the same problem. Revel in how good it feels to be part of a shared community in which everyone understands what you're going through.

Groups in Church and Religious Settings

Many of the groups that are offered in any community take place in local churches, synagogues, and religious organizations. Some of these groups like Alcoholics Anonymous and Parents Without Partners are without professional leaders. Other are led by members of the clergy and other professionals to address themes such as divorce adjustment, sexuality and fidelity, anger management, as well as discussions groups and Bible study.

Several resources are available for those who intend to work in these settings (see McBride, 1998; Turner, 1996), although the procedures are not essentially different than any other group. The main difference to consider is that you are probably operating within a particular moral philosophy that is consistent with the host religious institution. This may include integrating prayer, Bible study, Twelve Steps (AA, NA), or other religiously oriented doctrine as part of the group content.

Inpatient Groups

If you are working with this population, then your group members are probably not among the highest-functioning individuals. They are likely incarcerated in prison, involuntarily committed to hospitals, recovering addicts, or those manifesting psychotic or extreme mental symptoms. The good news is that you have far greater control over what they do, both inside the group and out.

Typically, these groups are time-limited, often as adjuncts to individual therapy. The themes are often devoted to coping skills and specific objectives such as reducing isolation, cognitive strategies, and general support.

As you are probably not surprised, there are lots and lots of inpatient group approaches including and educational, interpersonal, systems, developmental, cognitive, behavioral, or problem-solving models (see Brabender & Fallon, 1993). All of them must be adapted for the relatively captive audiences that form the consumers of these groups.

Some differences to note include the living situation in which group members are likely to see and interact with one another on a daily basis. Whatever you do in your groups represents a very tiny proportion of the time they actually spend in one another's company. This presents some special challenges, as well as therapeutic advantages, since you can plan interventions that make it possible for others to monitor behavior on an ongoing basis.

Critical Incident Stress Debriefing

Increasingly, group leaders are being called upon to apply their craft in alternative contexts than their home turf. One such model, called *critical incident stress debriefing groups*, are intended to help victims of disaster, as well as the rescue workers who were involved in their attempted intervention, deal with the consequences of the trauma (Mitchell & Everly, 1993).

The Symptoms.   People who suffer trauma associated with natural disasters, violent assault, abuse, or accidents manifest a number of symptoms that must be addressed, the sooner the better. CISD groups are actually designed primarily for those helpers who are involved in the rescue attempts, and in so doing, were exposed to dead bodies, severe grief, intense emotional upheaval, and other upsetting circumstances.

Just imagine what it would be like to show up at the scene of an earthquake, bus accident, or other disaster in which dozens of torn, broken bodies lay around. Survivors are hysterical and lost. Chaos abounds. And it is your job to pick up the pieces, literally as well as metaphorically. Few humans can walk away from such a scene without being profoundly affected, no matter how many times this has happened before.

Relief and rescue workers experience a whole range of emotional reactions from grief and loss to anger and "survivor guilt." Sleeplessness, loss of appetite, and other signs of depression and anxiety are not uncommon. Personnel can be plagued by nightmares and recurrent flashbacks of the disturbing scenes. Relationships can be disrupted, as would daily functioning. Attempts at self-medication may include alcohol or drug abuse. Under severe conditions, even seasoned professionals break down.

The Structure.   CISD groups are usually scheduled as a form of one-session intervention lasting several hours, although follow-ups can also be part of the treatment. Since the participants in such programs are in the midst of acute distress, the first priority is to administer psychological first aid, that is, to facilitate a supportive environment in which people can regain their composure after being subjected to traumatic events. This would not only apply to the actual victims of the disaster, but also to those law enforcement and rescue personnel who may have also been exposed to death, destruction, and chaos. In general, such group sessions are scheduled within a few days of the incident, since effectiveness seems to be related to a quick intervention (Rank, 1997).

For a Class Activity

Bring into class someone who specializes in doing CISD groups. Ask him or her to design a mini-workshop for you, equipping you with the basic structure and skills used in this modality.

In conjunction or apart from this guest speaker, have a number of volunteers come to the middle of the class in a "fishbowl." These should be individuals who have suffered some sort of trauma in their lives as a result of a natural disaster and interpersonal violence. Talk to one another, as if you are alone, about what helped you to recover from your trauma.

Afterwards, serve as panelists in a question and answer session in which classmates can learn more about what you went through and what helped you most.

Once participants are calm and stabilized, a forum is created to help people to share their feelings with one another, metabolize the incident in constructive ways, and work through residual negative reactions. An informational component is also included so that group members can learn about what to expect, as well as coping strategies that might prove useful.

What is interesting and quite unique about this group approach is that it is specifically designed as a form of single-session rather than ongoing treatment. Your job is to very quickly find out what symptoms are being manifested, to apply immediate relief of those symptoms, to build a more stable support system, and then to plan for continued self-administered interventions. Needless to say, that is a lot to do in a single meeting. Fortunately, there is specialized training you can receive in this type of group leadership that prepares you for what is needed.

One of the more important considerations in preparing to lead such groups is preparation about the professions and cultures that you will be working with. Not only do police, rescue personnel, and other groups have distinct codes of conduct and values, but debriefings are handled quite differently in various countries and subgroups (Dyregrov, 1997). As with all other group interventions, you must be intimately familiar with the language, customs, and beliefs of the people you are attempting to help. Nowhere is this more crucial then when working with individuals who are members of professional cultures that normally do not value psychological intervention or expression of feelings.

For Reflection

Imagine that you have been part of a team that just helped a community recover from a devastating hurricane. People lost everything during the storm—their homes, their possessions, in some cases, members of their family. For three straight days you have been providing assistance that included rescuing victims trapped underground, transporting people to the hospital, administering first aid, digging up dead bodies, reuniting family members, and providing comfort where you can.

Consider the ways that such an experience would affect you and how you would attempt to heal yourself before you could continue your work. What is it that you would want from a debriefing group that would help you to recover?

Conducting Business Meetings

So far, in this book and chapter, we have been primarily discussing group leadership with respect to growth, educational, or therapeutic experiences. The same principles and methods, however, may be applied with equal effectiveness to *any* group situation in which people need facilitative skills in order to complete tasks and work. Obviously, this makes sense. Yet it never ceases to amaze me how supposedly expert group leaders fail to apply in other areas of their lives what they do with their clients.

If you don't know what I'm talking about, you should witness the way many faculty members in a university or staff members in a mental health setting conduct their own business. Meetings are not only inefficiently run, but the exact things you would *not* want to do in a working group are nevertheless the dominant norms. People are rude and disrespectful to one another. Competition and one-upmanship prevail. Individuals are allowed to do all the disruptive, counterproductive things that you would stop in a second in one of your groups. In other words, sound principles of group leadership are not always applied in the circumstances in which they are needed most.

If you consider the things you have learned in this text and course and review the concepts of group dynamics, process, and intervention, you will find that you have a clear blueprint for how to lead any meeting, whether that is in a corporate, community, or any organizational setting. You can apply sound principles of leadership to help groups solve problems, function more effectively, and complete assigned tasks.

For a Class Activity

In small groups, brainstorm all the ways that you can think of to apply what you have learned about leadership to conducting a business meeting or task group in which the focus is on solving problems. Make the list as exhaustive as possible, including ways you would structure such meetings, observe dynamics, and facilitate the process in such a way that work would be completed efficiently, yet members would feel heard and valued.

Review your list and reduce the items to a few general concepts that you believe are most crucial. Since there is likely to be some disagreement about what is most important, work toward a consensus that you can all live with.

After you are done with the task, talk about the process that unfolded. To what extent did you apply what you were talking about to your own functioning during this group?

A number of authors (Bradley & Jarchow, 1997; Conyne, Rapin, & Rand, 1997; DePree, 1992; Hulse-Killacky, Kraus, & Schumacher, 1999; Kormanski, 1999; McBride, 1997; Ray, 1999) have suggested guidelines for applying leadership strategies to task groups and other meetings. The goal of such efforts is to balance a focus on productivity with attention to the quality of participant experiences. In other words, the best group experiences are those in which you get the work done, efficiently and effectively, *and* members also feel good about their contributions and the outcome. There is appropriate focus on content and tasks to be completed, as well as attention to process, both before and after business is undertaken.

When leading meetings, follow these basic suggestions:

■ *Plan and prepare for maximum success, capitalizing on member expectations.*
    "Before we get together in the meeting, I'd like you to give some thought to what you want to accomplish, what you'd like to get from the experience, and what roles you can play to be most helpful."

■ *Spend some time with warm-up so that members are favorably inclined to participate.*

"Before we get going, how about if each of us tells something funny that happened to you in the last 24 hours."

■ *Define the goals for the meeting clearly and realistically so there is a high probability for success.*

"Our job is to solve this problem. In this meeting, we will concentrate on getting a handle on what the problem is exactly and what impact it has on other areas. When we are done today, we should all have an assignment to research and then report back next time."

■ *Establish and negotiate ground rules that are conducive to productivity and satisfaction.*

"We need to agree on what the rules will be in these meetings. Who would like to begin with a nomination?"

■ *Make the group safe so that people are free to express themselves honestly.*

"In this group we will not tolerate ridicule or criticism of individuals. It is fine to disagree, perfectly acceptable to question ideas, but never to attack the person."

■ *Demonstrate in every way possible that you not only value the work being done but that you care about each person.*

"I really appreciate the effort you have taken to bring this to our attention. It really means a lot to me."

■ *Balance contributions so that everyone has the chance to participate.*

"Thanks for your input on the subject, Martin, but I'd like to hear from others as well."

■ *Don't try to do all the work yourself but make the members responsible for the outcome.*

"So, this is *your* group. How do you want to handle this?"

■ *Reflect back what you hear people saying, including content and affect.*

"You are saying that you really think we should move in this direction, but you also have some concerns about how quickly changes are being made. You've been here a long time and it doesn't feel like your opinions matter very much."

■ *Draw connections between what is said and what has been said by others.*

"Although you say that you disagree with Clarisa, really you have several points of consensus. You both think that we should hold off making a decision right now, even if for different reasons. In fact, Antonio and Leeza also made the same point a while ago."

■ *Interpret dynamics and processes that you observe occurring that may be facilitating or inhibiting progress.*

"I notice that we are stuck right now. People seem frustrated because there seems to be a lack of direction."

■ *Remember the developmental stages of groups so that you do not ask people to do things for which they are not yet ready.*

"It might be premature for us to move into that area right now. I'd suggest that we stay with the basics."

■ *Model the kind of group member you would like others to be.*

"I don't know about the rest of you but I feel resentful that we got stuck with this job. I'm willing to put those reactions aside, though, and do the best I can with this assignment."

■ *Conflict* can *be constructive, but don't let it get out of hand.*

"I appreciate that the two of you feel differently about this issue, but I'd like to ask you both to calm down before we revisit this matter."

■ *Do not allow disrespectful or abusive behavior.*

"Becky, it's not okay to speak to anyone here in that condescending tone. I'd like you to take a deep breath and try again."

■ *Stop rambling and digressions.*

"Let me interrupt you because I'm very interested in what you have to say but I'm getting lost."

■ *Don't humiliate anyone publicly.*

"I appreciate that you feel very strongly about this. Let's get together and talk about it after the meeting is over."

■ *If you feel lost or stuck, recruit a co-leader.*

"Wanda, maybe you could shed some light on what might be happening right now. I don't have a clue."

■ *Suggest structure or ideas to break through impasses.*

"I'd like to recommend that we leave this item on the agenda since we can't reach consensus. Who would like to be part of a committee to work on this issue some more and get back to us next time?"

■ *Don't rush people but move things along so that time is used efficiently.*

"I hate to interrupt here because this discussion is so useful but I see our time is running out. How do we translate this into some specific action?"

■ *Reward, reinforce, and validate people's valuable contributions.*

"I really appreciate what you just said. It took real courage to disagree with others."

■ *Provide a forum for giving and receiving feedback.*

"Let's talk about how this went today and what we can do in the future to operate even better."

■ *Use humor and play to make the experience fun.*

"Let's take a break for a few minutes and relax."

■ *Make summary statements at times to review progress, link ideas, and move toward transitions.*

"Let me see if I've heard what you are all saying. It seems that there have been . . ."

As long as this list might seem, these are just a *few* of the concepts that you might apply to business and meeting groups. You have actually learned so much more that you should feel free to apply to any group setting in which you want things to proceed productively.

For a Class Activity

Get together in small groups and talk to one another about the best meeting that you were ever privileged to participate in. Highlight what it was about the session that struck you as so productive and satisfying. Detail what the leader did to facilitate the process in such an effective manner.

Review of What You Learned

- Group procedures are adapted not only for the cultural/ethnic/gender backgrounds of people, but also their type of presenting complaints and the setting in which they are seen.
- When working with the very young or very old, maintaining attention span and focus are critical in order to accomplish desired goals.
- Homogeneous groups are easier to get going but often more difficult to move into deeper level work. Cohesion and trust develop rapidly, but so do protective alliances.
- Everything you've learned in this book and course can be applied to the leadership of any group including family gatherings, staff meetings, case conferences, or even social situations.

13 Challenges and Obstacles

It is not altogether rare that many people will end up in your groups who do not really want to be there. The honest ones will say directly, "I don't want to be here." The *really* honest ones will add how they feel about that: "Not only do I not want to be here, but I think it sucks that I have to come." Almost nobody will state what they intend to do about the situation: "Since I don't want to be here, and I am being forced to come, I intend to make everyone else's life as miserable as I can."

There is little sense complaining about involuntary participants because they make up so much a part of the people with whom you will work. Kids are referred by teachers or parents against their will. Adults are blackmailed by their partners. Substance abusers are mandated by the court. Hospital or prison inmates are required to attend as part of their treatment. And a whole lot of folks, who look like pretty cooperative people, are secretly very resentful about the idea of having to be in the group.

The question is not whether you have resistant, noncompliant, difficult, uncooperative group members, but how many there are in any group and how determined they are to take others down with them. They will protect themselves and test the limits of what they can get away with through two main strategies: fight or flight (Edelwich & Brodsky, 1992). In the latter case, they will simply withdraw, appearing passive or superficially cooperative. More directly (and probably indicative of a more healthy ego), they will fight back.

Critical Incidents

There are a number of critical incidents and predictable problems that come up in groups, mostly signs of resistance or confusion (Conyne, Rapin, & Rand, 1997; Donigian & Malnati, 1999). Alternately, the transitions between each of the stages are often precipitated by particular incidents that occur with a sense of drama.

Imagine, as examples, that the following situations arise in a group you are leading:

- When everyone in the group is asked to report on what happened during the preceding week, one member responds with, "Nothing," and indicates that he should be skipped.
- It is revealed in the group that one member broke confidentiality by telling others what happened, identifying specific people by name.
- A group member attacks you as being incompetent because you confronted someone before she was ready.

- A member walks into group fifteen minutes late. This is the third time in five weeks that this has occurred.
- A group member says to someone in the group who asks him how he's feeling: "Get the fuck outta my face!"
- A group member is about to disclose something rather powerful, when another attempts to make a joke.

This is just a sampling of critical incidents you will face on a regular basis. In each case, you must figure out what the behavior is all about and what you can do to prevent collateral damage to others, before you can intervene effectively.

For a Class Activity

In groups of two or three, discuss ways you might handle the critical situations described above. For each of them, list what the motives, goals, and hidden agendas that might be operating for the individual who initiates the incident. Next, figure out what you might do to limit the destructive aspects of the behavior, as well as use it as a learning experience in the group.

Share your strategies with other groups, coming to a consensus as to preferred methods.

Responding to Challenges

As you no doubt realize, there is no single best way to respond to a critical incident that occurs in a group. There are, however, some sound strategies that can be employed. If we take, as an example, the rather structured sort of group of a school classroom, you can see the way a number of common challenges can be responded to (Kottler & Kottler, 2000). This will give you a flavor for how you might deal with similar situations in any group you might lead.

The situation: A member asks you a question to which you don't know the answer.

The response: "Good question. What do *you* think?"

Group leadership (and all helping) is often like tennis; the object is to keep the ball in the other person's court.

The situation: When a member shows resistance, makes excuses, or argues about why something wouldn't work.

The response: "Don't argue with me but with yourself."

Don't try to talk someone into something that he or she is not yet ready to hear. Extricate yourself from arguments by reminding yourself that sometimes people don't want what you are selling.

The situation: When you ask people a question and they say they don't know.

The response: "Take a wild guess."

Many times, people are just unwilling to risk being wrong. Once you give them permission, they will often surprise you (and themselves) with how much they really do know and understand.

The situation: When a member is wandering, digressing, or being distracting.

The response: "I wonder if you wouldn't mind summarizing your main point."

This is much more polite and less threatening then saying, "I'm lost," or "You aren't making much sense," or "I wasn't paying attention."

The situation: When a member is passive, withdrawn, or quiet.

The response: "You seem awfully reflective."

This is, of course, an invitation to join in. On the one hand, you can't ignore members who are withdrawn; on the other, you don't want to pressure them to do more than they feel ready to do.

The situation: When what you're doing is not working.

The response: "I'm aware that what I'm doing isn't working."

Members often like it when you own your confusion, making it easier for them to do so. This also allows members to take more responsibility for what is going on.

For a Field Study

Talk to several experienced group leaders about the critical incidents and challenges that they struggle with the most. Find out what they have discovered works least and most effectively when faced with such situations. What would they recommend you do to best prepare yourself for similar struggles?

Difficult Group Members

Although this may surprise you, what makes someone difficult to work with is often in the eye of the beholder. The persons you may experience as tough to deal with would not necessarily be those with whom I have the most trouble. I know some group leaders who prefer their participants to be well-behaved and relatively compliant, whereas I consider this a form of resistance, much preferring people to "act out" if that is the way they are really feeling.

For Reflection

Think about the people you have had the most trouble with in your life. This has likely been a consistent pattern in which the same sorts of individuals consistently get underneath your skin. What are the typical characteristics of these people?

For instance, I have trouble with people who are smug, who act like they already know it all. In other words, I struggle with those who are *like me.*

How do you typically deal with those individuals who push your buttons or otherwise provoke strong reactions inside you?

In spite of the differences in the ways some group leaders react to particular kinds of group members and provocative behavior, there is a consensus about which ones are the most challenging to work with (Gans & Alonso, 1998; Kottler, 1992; 1994a; Leszcz, 1989; Roth, Stone, & Kibel, 1990; Silverstein, 1997; Smith & Steindler, 1983).

Silence and Withdrawn Behavior

Beginning group leaders often list prolonged silence as the situation in group they fear the most. Just imagine: There you are—you just gave what you believe are very clear directions and asked people to respond. The members sit there staring at the floor. Or the ceiling. Or at you. But nobody says a word.

The silence seems to go on forever, although you glance at your watch and see it has only been forty seconds. Should you say something? Maybe you should wait just a little longer?

What you do in a situation like this depends on what the silence means. I suppose you could say this about any critical incident that arises in a group: *The first thing you have to do is decode what the behavior means.*

If we take silence as one example—it can mean a whole bunch of different things:

- Your instructions weren't clear and members are so confused they don't know what you want or expect from them.
- They are taking needed time to reflect on things, to formulate what they want to say, and how they want to say it. In this sense, the silence is very helpful.
- One or more members are being manipulative and playing power games in order to test you.
- Members may be quiet because that is their usual style.
- Trust may be an issue for participants and they are not saying anything because they don't feel safe.
- They may be experiencing some trauma that renders them mute.

In cases when only one member stands out as particularly passive or quiet, you still must decode what the behavior means before you choose an intervention. Is this person characteristically shy or just situationally mute?

Depending on what you interpret the passive behavior means, you might address this problem in a number of ways. You must, however, deal with this individual, publicly or privately, or the withdrawal may have negative effects on others.

Manipulation and Hidden Agendas

Whether as a situational or characterological pattern, you will face individuals who have in mind little else except to undermine the group. They may feel some injustice has been committed against them and want to have their revenge. They may enjoy the sense of power and control that accompanies destructive acts. More than likely, they are just trying to keep you and the group off balance so you don't get too close to them.

This is one of the most difficult challenges you will face because people who are really good at being manipulative are also highly skilled at disguising their efforts—until it is too late. Assume that they are smarter than you are, at least in the domain of clandestine sabotage. Needless to say, you will have your hands full.

When encountering members who are being manipulative, the first order of business is to bring the issues out in the open. Since they are unlikely to respond to direct confrontation, except as another manipulative act to pretend compliance, you may have to resort to enforcing the strictest possible boundaries. In extreme cases, you will have to get the manipulative person out of your group, but that will come with its own price to pay since he or she is unlikely to leave without a fight.

I don't wish to frighten you with the possibility that there is a monster lurking in every group, just waiting to tear things apart. But you will wish to be vigilant to monitor carefully the extent to which group members are acting in ways that are not constructive.

Self-Centered and Entitled Behavior

A group is one place where you cannot tolerate excessive self-centeredness. Members will certainly compete for attention and time. They will do their best to win your approval. They will try to earn the award for most valuable participant. They will also try to keep center stage for as long as possible, or at least as long as you permit this to occur.

Many such individuals are not aware of their behavior; they just feel they are entitled to more than their fair share of time and resources and probably do this in all facets of their life. Others may very well understand what they are doing but just don't care very much about others' needs.

Your job is make certain that no one person dominates the group, captures an inequitable share of time, or keeps center stage. This will be far more difficult than it sounds (just look at your own class in which some individuals talk far more than others). Ideally, you can train everyone in the group to be responsible for intervening when necessary. In the early stages, however, the job will fall on you to do something to limit overindulgence by some members. The challenge is to give people feedback that they need to stop talking, but to do so in a way that they don't feel censured or threatened.

I am not nearly as good at this needed intervention as I would like to be; in fact, it is the one situation that I dread the most. First, I try waiting things out, hoping the person will either run out of steam or someone else will jump in and tell him or her to shut up. This almost never happens in the beginning of a group.

Next, I wait for an opening and then politely thank the person for his or her contributions, moving things along to the next contributor. Those who are skilled filibusterers usually ignore these subtle cues; some of them don't ever seem to take a breath so there is no easy place to interrupt.

Eventually, I know I must do something. I take a deep breath. I use my most soft, gentle, sensitive voice. "Excuse me," I say, "I'm sorry to interrupt," although I'm clearly delighted to do so, "but we seem to be running out of time and have others who want to say something. I wonder if we might get back to you a bit later after others have had a chance."

Then, I hold my breath and wait. I review in my mind if there is any way possible that the person could have taken offense by this gentle reminder. Nope, I tell myself with confidence. I'm home free. I even delude myself that the person will be grateful for my feedback. I should be so lucky.

For Reflection

Think of a time when you were speaking in a group and got a clear message from the leader or teacher that what you were saying was not what he or she wanted to hear. How did you feel inside? How did you feel towards the leader, even if you knew that what he or she was doing was for the good of the group?

Inevitably (or so it seems to me during this moment of self-pity), that intervention will come back to haunt me. Even though I could see clearly that others were getting impatient, frustrated, and bored, as grateful as I was that the runaway train could be derailed, there will be some repercussions in which others will resent the heck out of the authority figure cutting off one of their brethren. Many might feel humiliated vicariously, reluctant to speak for fear that perhaps I will cut them off at the knees as well. If the offender feels spiteful or resentful, then he or she may work behind the scenes to sabotage things.

For a Field Study

Ask a number of experienced group leaders, faculty, or teachers how they handle a situation when someone is talking too much, or taking up more than his or her fair share of time. When the situation can't wait until the session is over, how do they intervene in a way that gets the point across, but in a way that is not offensive? (By all means, let me know if you find out some good options.)

Obviously, this is a tough situation. If possible, the preferred solution is confront the person privately. This is especially the case when working with members of cultures (such as Asian) in which a public censure, no matter how well intended, is experienced as deeply humiliating. The problem, however, is that you can't often wait for the group to be over in order to say something. You must intervene to stop behavior that is patently inappropriate and selfish. The challenge you will face is to do this in a way that does not stir up more trouble.

Distractions and Diversions

There are so many variations of this behavior that it is hard to catalogue all of them. What they have in common is a desire to side-track what is going on to remain in safe territory. Members will do this through a filibuster—a long-winded story that can easily fill up a whole session. They will ramble a lot, create crises on cue, or do anything in their power to divert discussion away from what they feel is most threatening (and what you believe is most useful).

The preferred intervention is to label what you observe going on; better yet, cue others in the group to do so, as illustrated in this interaction.

> **FRANK:** ". . . It was a tough time . . . Maybe the toughest thing I've ever faced . . . I don't know . . ."
>
> **CANDY:** "Well, if you're done, I certainly have something I would like to talk about."
>
> **LEADER:** "Wait a second, Candy. I noticed that Flynn flinched a second ago, and I wonder what he's thinking."

The leader obviously knows why Flynn is startled, for the same reason that everyone else is appalled at Candy's interruption during a time when Frank was trying to talk about something very difficult to share. Consistent with what you have learned earlier, rather than confronting the distracting behavior directly, the leader cues Flynn to do so. You are essentially training everyone in the group to think like a leader, to monitor progress, to protect everyone else's rights, to make sure that everyone gets their fair share of attention.

Argumentative and Abusive Behavior

Some people enjoy verbal combat. They like intimidating others. It may be especially fun to take on the leader or create as much havoc as possible in a group. If you think about it, this would make someone feel very powerful.

That is why acting out, especially by those who feel powerless, is such a common occurrence in groups, as it is in life (Silverstein, 1997). In its most overt form, acting out involves some sort of dramatic attention-seeking scene such as initiating an argument. This behavior can play itself out in other ways as well—the member who comes late or misses sessions, the person who refuses to talk or otherwise refuses to be pinned down.

It is unlikely that you would be able to screen out this person in your interviews. In some cases, you could have seen this person for years in individual therapy and never realized that he or she had such potential to act out in group settings. More likely, however, you viewed this person as feisty and spirited but had no idea that he or she could wreak such havoc.

Under any and all circumstances, you must stop the abusive behavior. If the person does not respond to confrontations in the group or feedback during a private conference, then you must get this person out of there and recommend an alternative treatment setting.

Why People Create Difficulties and What Can Be Done

It is important to understand that in almost all these cases, people are not acting uncooperatively in order to make your life miserable. They are doing the best they can to protect themselves from a situation that feels very threatening. Perhaps the person doesn't want to be in the group in the first place but is being forced/coerced/blackmailed into participating; this would put anyone in a bad mood and predispose them toward belligerence. It is also likely that the environment does not feel very safe and entirely possible that your expectations for their behavior may be beyond what they are willing or able to satisfy. In such circumstances, acting out is some way is actually the "sensible" solution to protect oneself against perceived threats.

For a Class Activity

In small groups, talk to one another about a time you were forced to participate in a group situation that did not feel comfortable or safe. Share examples of what you did to protect yourself and ways that you acted out in the group.

The first step in working with challenging group members is to stop yourself from taking things personally. Their behavior represents an attempt to help themselves in some way, even if this strategy has some annoying side effects. Look for ways that the behavior is functional and adaptive. What benefits and payoffs is it serving?

Generally speaking, people tend to act out because it serves one of the following purposes:

1. It allows the group member to procrastinate, put off action, or avoid taking risks.
    "I distract you from my issues."
    "I prevent others from getting close."
2. It maintains the status quo.
    "I may be miserable but at least there are no surprises."
    "I don't have to grow up."
3. It aids the person in avoiding responsibility.
    "It's not my fault."
    "I can't help it."

4. People revel in their power.
   "*I am destroying things on my own terms.*"
   "*I get lots of sympathy.*"

Whether the time is right to confront the difficult behavior and help the group member to look at payoffs and secondary gains from the acting out, it is important that you realize what is going on so you don't take things personally. In summary, people act in ornery, difficult, obnoxious ways not because they are cruel, heartless folks who want to ruin your group (although it may feel that way) but because they are just trying to protect themselves against something that is perceived as terrifying. They are also engaging in behavior inside your group that has consistently gotten them in trouble outside the group. But then, that's why they are getting help in the first place: It is their job to act in the same annoying ways that have created problems for them in their lives. But then, it is your job to help them to learn alternative ways of getting their needs met, without disrupting your group.

Try Screening First

Almost every group manual (including this text) will warn you about the importance of screening out group members who are poor candidates for the setting. Generally, it is acknowledged that those who have severe personality disorders, especially those who are narcissistic (self-centered), borderline (manipulative), sociopathic (controlling), and hysterical (overly dramatic) should be weeded out. In addition, you would want to screen out those who are unusually hostile, aggressive, fragmented, psychotic, suicidal, anxious, depressed, or paranoid (Corey & Corey, 1997; Yalom, 1995). You might wonder who is left.

You are actually ethically bound to protect the welfare of your group participants against unsuitable or unstable peers who could do severe damage. Remember that groups have potential to do more good, but also more harm, than other forms of treatment.

As has been mentioned previously, it is considered sound practice to schedule screening interviews with prospective group participants, explaining what will be expected, providing informed consent, but also examining their suitability for the group experience. The problem, however, is that often screening does not work very well. Any self-respecting troublemaker is not going to be stupid enough to reveal his or her problematic behavior just because you ask for it. In fact, most people will be on their best behavior. They will appear charming and cooperative, at least until they get into the group or until something triggers an explosion.

Why Screening Does Not Often Work

1. The accuracy of diagnostic initial interviews is not great.
2. Manipulative people know how to make a good impression.
3. Some people do not become difficult until they enter the group.
4. Difficult members may need groups the most.

So, by all means, conduct screening interviews. Do your homework on your clients. Use all your clinical assessment skills to identify potential problems. But keep in mind that although you may keep out the most obvious challenges, you will still end up with more than your fair share of difficult members.

For a Class Activity

In groups of six, decide on some common point of discussion that involves making a decision. Pretend that you have been given the choice of inventing an alternative way for you to be graded in the class or to devise other assignments you could complete.

During this conversation, each of you is to role play your anticipated most difficult group member, whether that person is a whiner and complainer, a screamer, a controller, a manipulator, a distractor, a compulsive talker, or whomever. Really get into the role of *being* that person, talking and acting just as you imagine that he or she would.

After the chaos is over and the laughter has died down, talk about what it felt like to be that person.

Set Boundaries and Limits

Under no circumstances can you risk losing control of your group. People will get hurt. Chaos will result. Manipulative and controlling members will be reinforced for their behavior. You must, therefore, intervene decisively whenever someone acts out in ways that are dysfunctional or destructive. This doesn't mean that you have to be the one to say something, but you must cue others to take responsibility for reining someone in who is out of line.

In previous chapters we have discussed the sorts of circumstances that require intervention, such as when someone is being distracting, disoriented, provocative, abusive, disrespectful, and so on. You must be the one to jump in when things show signs of getting out of hand, keeping challenging members in line. This might look something like the following.

CONNIE: "I've tried so hard to do something about this, but . . ."

RUTH: "God, this is just so boring. I've heard this shit before."

CONNIE: "Excuse me?"

RUTH: "I said . . ."

LEADER: "Wait a minute. Let's stop for a minute. Steve, I can see by the look on your face that you're pretty stunned by what just happened. Perhaps you'd be willing to tell Ruth what you are feeling."

The leader could have confronted Ruth directly, or gone to Connie and invited her to confront Ruth with her inappropriate behavior. It may very well be that Connie *is* being just as difficult as Ruth is. Maybe Connie does ramble and repeat herself a lot. Perhaps Ruth is just expressing the exasperation that many others feel, but just chose a particularly harsh way of getting her point across. It is likely that there are multiple factors operating.

What you will do in your groups is establish clear norms about what is considered appropriate behavior. You will also set boundaries for each group member who has trouble complying with consensual rules. You have already decided, for example, that Ruth is impulsive and must be restrained at times. You also have limits in mind for Connie and her repetitive storytelling, but didn't get a chance to cut her off before Ruth jumped in. Another member in the group hardly ever talks at all, so you have a point at which you would intervene to draw her out. In each case, you do what you can to help members learn appropriate ways of expressing themselves. In the best case, they will generalize what they are learning outside the group, which may be the greatest therapeutic benefit of all.

Some Management Principles

Some general principles to keep in mind when addressing problematic behavior in groups include the following:

1. Keep yourself calm. Address your own countertransference or exaggerated personal reactions to what is going on.
   "Who does this person remind me of? How am I overreacting to what is going on? How is my sense of control being threatened?"
2. Label what you see, or better yet, help others to do so.
   "I notice that as Fred is talking that a number of you are looking frustrated. Perhaps you could tell him what you see is happening."
3. Ask yourself, or the group, what is really going on.
   "What is the meaning of this behavior? What is this person really saying at this moment in time?"
4. Model the kinds of behaviors that you would like others to employ. Encourage others when they follow your lead.
   "I'm having trouble hearing you right now when you appear so angry and out of control. I agree with Sandy when she was telling you to calm down."
5. Give *immediate* feedback to members who are out of line.
   "Stop for a second. Before you continue, I think it might be helpful for you to hear how others are reacting to what you should said, and how you said it."
6. Schedule individual, private conferences in cases when direct, public confrontation may not be indicated.
   "I know you get embarrassed easily so I didn't want to say something in the group but I'd like to talk with about ways that I can help you get more involved."
7. Uncover and confront hidden agendas that are at work.
   "I'm confused by what is happening right now. It appears as if several of you have talked about this outside of group. One of our agreed-upon rules is that such discussions would be disclosed openly in front of everyone."
8. Reframe challenging or provocative behavior as an opportunity for learning and growth, rather than merely as an obstacle to be overcome. Some of the best stuff that happens in groups occurs as a result of some critical or disruptive incident.

"I can see that many of you are upset by what just took place. It is uncomfortable to resolve conflicts like this and I certainly wish we could have prevented it. I'm also aware, however, how much thought and growth this incident has sparked. Let's talk about what you learned from this."

9. Get some help, either in the form of supervision, a co-leader, or a recruited assistant in the group.

"I'm not sure what this is about. I'd like to ask for some help from those of you who might have something to add."

Mediating and Resolving Conflicts

Conflicts are not only inevitable in groups, but highly useful. If you do not have a group in which people are disagreeing and arguing with one another, then you do not have an atmosphere in which it is safe for people to speak their minds. Conflicts actually serve a number of constructive purposes (Kottler, 1994b):

1. They bring attention to important issues that may have been ignored.
2. They underscore underlying issues of power and control.
3. They prevent stagnation.
4. They regulate distance between people.
5. They ease tension.
6. They promote reflection and growth.
7. They can lead to greater intimacy.

For Reflection

Think of a recent time in your life in which you were involved in some sort of conflict. This could have been with a family member, friend, co-worker, or acquaintance. Although this situation may have been tense and uncomfortable and may even have ended on a negative note, consider what good may have emerged from the disagreement. What did you learn from the experience?

During confrontations and conflicts, it is your job to facilitate the interaction in such a way that the participants (and the audience) leave the encounter feeling good about the experience.

Mediating conflicts is not really one skill, but rather a combination of things that you might do:

1. Directing the people in conflict to speak to one another directly rather than about one another
2. Blocking insensitive or inappropriate attacks
3. Reflecting the feelings of what is expressed

4. Clarifying the content of the communications
5. Linking common points of agreement
6. Cuing others to get involved

There are basically several different courses of action you can take when faced with a conflict in the group (Gladding, 1997; Kormanski, 1982).

1. *Beating a hasty retreat.* If in your judgment, the conflict is not a constructive engagement at that moment in time, then you can work to divert the negative energy in other directions. Perhaps the timing is not good at that moment because someone is in the middle of something important. Another possibility is that this has been a recurrent source of struggle between combatants that has not led anywhere useful. Or maybe you just want to wait a while, observe the situation more closely, and collect more information, before you attempt to work things through.

   In this case, you are not necessarily avoiding the conflict altogether, which may not be a good thing. You are merely postponing its resolution until a more opportune time. When the issues are relatively minor, such as a skirmish over who sits where, you may elect to ignore it altogether. It all depends on what the conflict means in the context of the interaction. If you do not know (which often you will not), you can always ask the group to sort it out:

   "I'm puzzled by something I'd like to understand better. I notice that every time that you, Nate and Michelle, talk to one another you usually resort to teasing and ridiculing. I can't tell if this good-natured fun on your part, or whether there is something else going on between you. What's going on?"

2. *Finding a consensus.* In this case, you have decided to mediate the disagreement by helping the participants to develop a solution that meets both their needs. This means that each person is going to have to compromise in order to attain peace.

   Mediation efforts usually involve helping both parties to express their points of view and acknowledge to one another that they have heard what is said. They are then encouraged to find some common ground that each can live with.

3. *Using a power position.* From your position of authority, you can intervene decisively to stop an altercation if someone is getting hurt. This has the advantage of ending the conflict quickly. The disadvantages, however, is that you may not address the source of the problem and that you have taken over the group instead of allowing members to resolve their own issues.

Look at Your Own Contributions to the Problem

Most group leaders prefer to blame their difficult members as being the problem. We call them "resistant" or other names that are less than flattering. Indeed, there *are* individuals who are a gigantic pain to deal with; after all, that's why they are in our groups in the first place.

Some members become difficult because we have made them that way. We are as much a problem as they are because of things we do that are insensitive, inflexible, misguided, inappropriate, or provocative. It would be downright negligent, therefore, not to examine your own contributions to the difficulty.

I know earlier I said that you should not take things personally, but you would not wish to take this to the extreme where you refuse to examine what you might be doing to make group members more difficult than they need to be. It might be useful to ask yourself a series of questions such as:

- What am I doing to create or exacerbate the problems?
- How am I being unusually inflexible in my style or manner?
- What personal issues of mine are being triggered by this incident?
- Who does this group member remind me of whom I have encountered previously?
- How am I acting out my impatience with member's (or group's) progress?
- What expectations am I demanding of this individual that he or she is unwilling or unable to meet?
- What needs of mine are not being met?

Challenges of Group Leadership

This chapter was named "challenges" because the preceding critical incidents are seen as opportunities for significant growth, not only in your leadership skills rising to the occasion, but also in the development of the group. After all, most people have trouble with difficult people in their lives. They need practice dealing with these individuals effectively. If everyone gets along beautifully, if all proceeds according to plan, then you will have little to work with in the group. You actually *need* provocation and challenges in order to help members to learn and grow.

In one sense, difficult members are taking risks, making themselves vulnerable, putting themselves on the line, volunteering themselves as targets of opportunity. They are actually doing more work than anyone else, especially those who are being polite and compliant (Gans & Alonso, 1998).

That is not to say that you want to do everything you can to make problems arise or provoke difficult behavior. Obviously, you've got enough to do in the group without creating more work for yourself. This is a reminder not to complain incessantly about difficult members or challenging situations. I promise that you will hear such complaints a lot: Leaders spend an inordinate amount of time whining about how ornery and uncooperative and resistant their clients are. Resist the impulse to join in on these sessions, which only encourage feelings of victimization and powerlessness. If you really feel stuck, work with a co-leader or supervisor to work through the struggle. Examine not only what is happening in this particular struggle, but it what it means in the larger context of your work and life. That is one of the benefits of this type of work, no extra charge. After each challenge you face, you have the opportunity to learn from the struggle in such a way that you become more effective in facing similar situations in the future.

Confront Failures and Reframe Them

Inevitably, you are going to encounter a number of people you can't help, no matter what you try. Similarly, no matter how much experience you accumulate, how many workshops you attend and training your receive, how many books you read, and how much supervision you get, you are still going to lead groups that just don't work well. This could be because of a variety of reasons, some of them related to the members, some to the environment and context, and some to you as well.

After teaching group work for so long, with a variety of different populations from middle-class suburban counselors to Filipino and Singaporean teachers, Australian Aboriginal social workers, New Zealand Maori psychologists, and Icelandic school counselors, I thought I'd seen and done it all. Yet recently, I had one of my worst classes ever in all the years I have been doing this. As I looked at the situation, I couldn't help but feel that I had somehow failed miserably. Clearly, I had lost my magic.

I know what I say to students and supervisees about this sort of thing—that failures represent an opportunity to learn and grow from mistakes—but this time I had difficulty drawing comfort from this advice. Maybe, I thought to myself, this was the group that saw me most clearly and I was just fooling everyone else until this point. Such are the depressing ruminations of a group leader who encounters failure.

It doesn't have to be this way, of course: Failures can indeed provide excellent opportunities to reflect on your leadership skills, consider ways you could handle things differently in the future, and help yourself to grow to new levels of flexibility (Conyne, 1999; Kottler & Blau, 1989). In order for this to happen, however, you must be brutally honest with yourself about mistakes and misjudgments you have made. This means that rather than blaming certain group members as uncooperative or certain groups as being resistant, you must own your share of the responsibility for things you could do differently.

For Reflection

Think of a time recently when you attempted to serve in some leadership role. It is likely that you did some things that were quite effective, and other that were less than inspired, if not obvious failures. In a balanced way, review what you did best and worst. Ask yourself what you learned from the mistakes that you intend to do differently in the future.

Review of What You Learned

- The most honest resistant clients will display their dissatisfaction overtly; the really tough ones will pretend they are enjoying themselves while they play games and attempt to sabotage things.
- A dozen or so critical incidents are common and predictable, meaning that you can prepare yourself for handling them ahead of time.
- Group members don't necessarily start out difficult and resistant. They may become that way in response to things that you are doing that appear confusing or threatening.
- Whenever possible, cue group members to do the work when a distracting person needs to be confronted or limits must be set.

CHAPTER

14 Ethical Issues Unique to Group Work

In every class you will take, there will likely be some treatment of ethical, legal, and moral issues that must be considered in professional practice. Group work is no exception; in fact, it has some unique challenges that make it among the most difficult helping endeavors. Interestingly, although all the major professional organizations to which group leaders belong—American Psychological Association, National Association of Social Workers, American Counseling Association, American Association of Marital and Family Therapy, and others—have their own ethical codes that cover basically the same areas, there has still been a need for group specialists to develop their own ethical and training guidelines (American Group Psychotherapy Association, 1978; Association for Specialists in Group Work, 1989, 1990).

For Reflection

Based on what you already understand about group work and its unique challenges and hazards, what are some areas where you need the most guidance and direction?

Special Challenges

Throughout this text, it has become evident that group work has potential to be far more potent, and also more dangerous, than other helping modalities. This situation exists for a number of reasons that have been mentioned: (1) Leaders have less control over proceedings, (2) confidentiality can't be guaranteed, (3) peer pressure and coercion create undue influence, and (4) clients receive less attention. For these reasons, and others that have been highlighted, you must familiarize yourself with the unique ethical problems you will face.

Like so many of the subjects we have covered in this beginning text, there are whole books devoted to the subject of ethical issues in helping professions (see Cohen & Cohen, 1999; Corey & Corey, 1997; Cottone & Tarvydas, 1998; Pope & Vasquez, 1998; Welfel, 1998). While there is a risk of redundancy in reviewing ethical issues you may have considered before in a broader context, it is always useful to examine the ways that these dilemmas manifest themselves uniquely in special circumstances.

Major Ethical Issues in Group Leadership

We will review only those ethical challenges that are part of group leadership practice. I will assume that the more general ethical principles that apply to all helping professionals will have been covered in other classes. If not, you will want to familiarize yourself thoroughly with ethical conduct related to concepts like informed consent, privileged communication, dual relationships, and scope of practice.

For Reflection and a Class Activity

Among all the issues that have been raised in this text and class, there are a few that strike terror in your heart. Write down several ethical or moral dilemmas that you are going to face in your work as a group leader.

To get you thinking about possibilities you might overlook, or conveniently push out of your mind, consider these realistic scenarios:

- A group member confides to you secretly that she knows something awful about another member, but warns you not to say anything.
- It comes out in group that someone may be suicidal, but you aren't sure if the person is serious or not.
- A group member tells you that he or she is very attracted to you and wants to have a relationship after the group ends.
- Someone in the group is very toxic to others, constantly disruptive, but refuses to leave; this person threatens to sue you for negligence or abandonment if you force him or her out.
- A number of group members conspire to impose values on others in the group that you find distasteful, if not immoral.
- You find out from a secret source that confidentiality has been breached in group.

In small groups, talk to one another about the ethical dilemmas you fear the most. After each person has had a chance to talk, look for common themes in your disclosures.

Confidentiality Cannot Be Guaranteed

Just imagine the problems associated with a situation in which you are the only one who is ethically bound to maintain the privacy and sanctity of disclosures. As much as you can urge group members to respect the right to privacy, as much as you can stress that this safeguard is the key to any trust that develops in the experience, you can't guarantee that this promise is honored. It might be unfair, even immoral, for people to betray confidences, but you are the one that is ultimately responsible for the outcome.

Imagine that someone in your group discloses she has been sexually abused, or someone else that he is gay, or a third that he is contemplating suicide, and that these secrets slip out so that others find out. Although there is little that you can actually do to prevent such circumstances from happening with 100 percent certainty, you can take steps to protect members as best you can.

The first step is to stress how important confidentiality is in the group. Discuss the problem frankly. Address concerns that come up. Role play how to handle tempting situations that will inevitably arise, such as when a group member is asked directly by a best friend as to what was talked about. Explain how to handle the situation: "While you are permitted, even encouraged, to talk about what happens in this group with respect to your own behavior and issues—in fact, I would hope you would be proud of the work you are doing—you are not allowed to mention anyone else, either by name or identifying features."

Group members must be informed accurately and realistically about the risks they are taking as a member of the group. This includes the possibility that someone else present might not honor their commitments and promises.

Many group leaders follow the guidelines of professional organizations devoted to group work (Association for Specialists in Group Work and American Group Psychotherapy Association) that advocate providing participants with written disclosure statements including:

- Purpose and goals of the group
- Scope and parameters of the sessions
- Expectations for members' participation
- Roles and responsibilities of the leader
- Policies regarding attendance, fees, scheduling
- Discussion of norms and ground rules
- Risks associated with the experience
- Limits of confidentiality
- Respect for cultural and individual differences of members
- Protection against coercion
- Notification of any recording of sessions that might take place and what will happen to those tapes

For a Class Activity

Either in a "fishbowl" in front of the class, or in a private area, role play a group of some very concerned, fearful members who feel reluctance to reveal very much about themselves. Take turns as co-leaders explaining confidentiality and then helping members talk about their concerns.

Give feedback to each set of leaders on things they might do differently to operate more effectively in the future when they talk about confidentiality in groups.

Process what it felt like to be part of a group in which safety is such a deep concern. What are some steps that could be taken to alleviate these fears?

Coercion and Peer Pressure

You have heard this one several times before. It bears repeating because it is so critical. When group members take the risk of jumping into the cold water, they want others to join them. If someone balks, intense pressure will be leveraged to force this person to join the crowd. There is a feeling that goes something like this:

"I paid my dues. I spilled my guts and told you my secrets. You sat there and took it all in. You have me in a vulnerable position because you could use what you now know against me in some way. Now it's *your* turn. Now you have to pay your dues by working on your stuff, or at least telling us something really juicy. That way we will both have something on each other."

Ultimately, peer pressure can have its positive functions in that it does create risk-taking norms. The problem, however, is a matter of timing, since individuals have different readiness levels for taking such risks. It is your job to protect the safety and rights of each group member, to make certain that nobody is coerced or forced to comply with norms that are not consistent with their best interests.

In society at large there is also tremendous pressure for members of minority groups to conform to majority norms. Individual and cultural differences are often seen as a threat to stability. Knowing this, you can expect that a similar phenomenon will develop in your groups in which minority members are coerced into abandoning their core values and beliefs in favor of the dominant culture (Pack-Brown, Whittington-Clark, & Parker, 1998).

Imagine the pressure that would be felt by a Mormon in a group of atheists, an African American woman in a group of white males, a rebellious, creative teenager in a group of overly compliant peers, or a happily adjusted housewife in a group of feminists. Unless you intervene decisively in such situations, individuals can be scapegoated, marginalized, or coerced, causing great harm.

For a Class Activity

Conyne (1998) recommends the following activity for sensitizing students to multicultural issues in group that might lead to coercion or peer pressure. Organize yourselves in groups of eight. Choose two members to sit outside the group and act as observers of the process. Their job will be to take notes on the process that develops. Group members are to take a half hour to talk to one another about the following questions:

1. What are the cultural similarities and differences in your group that are most influential?
2. What norms have developed (or could develop) that lead to oppression or empowerment of some cultures over others?
3. How could you better sensitize yourselves to the various multicultural influences in groups, responding more effectively to members of minority cultures?

After the discussion, observers will report on what they noticed, paying special attention to the various processes that were being talked about in the group. What are the cultures represented in this group? What cultural norms evolved? In ways were members of minority cultures forced to comply with the dominant culture?

Multiple Relationships Become More Complex

It is highly likely there are multiple relationship issues in your participation in this experientially oriented course. Here you are, sitting in a class to learn about group work, being evaluated and graded based on your performance, yet you are also asked to reveal very personal aspects of yourself. Most of these concerns can be addressed through certain safeguards, but you can nevertheless feel the confusion of relating to your instructor and peers in a multitude of roles.

To add to the complexity of relationships, group work is often supplemented by conjoint sessions in which a participant might see the therapist or counselor for individual consultations. This has some distinct advantages in that participants have the opportunity to process what happened in group during their individual sessions, personalizing the material. Likewise, during these consultations they can plan new behaviors that may be practiced in group. For members who are unusually timid, anxious, or in crisis, this structure can be invaluable.

Unfortunately, this also means that some people will have a "special" relationship with the leader that others do not. There is a common fantasy, imagined or real, that members will gossip or talk about others from the group, thereby exacerbating potential resentment. Other problems mentioned include greater risks of compromising confidentiality, overdependence on the leader, and possible financial gain for the leader (Lakin, 1994; Welfel, 1998).

Finally, group members may have other relationships with one another outside the sessions. Coalitions and alliances are formed in the parking lot. Cliques can develop when some members are included in coffees or meals when others are deliberately kept out (often because they are the subject of discussion). Romantic liaisons may develop, and then efforts can be made to hide what has occurred. Phone calls and email messages race back and forth between members, potentially undermining the group. Plots are hatched. Plans are made. As you can easily imagine, these extracurricular relationships can turn out to be a real mess.

For all of these reasons, you must closely monitor what goes on outside the group. Some leaders attempt to forbid such contacts, usually unsuccessfully. One rule that can be helpful is that anything said to anyone outside the group (to the leader or other members) is fair game to be brought up to everyone else. Otherwise, you may find yourself in a situation where people confide things to you, or others, resulting in secrets and hidden agendas that compromise the group trust.

Training Is Often Insufficient

You should by now be convinced that leading groups is quite unlike other forms of helping. It requires additional skills and expertise, greater flexibility, the ability to juggle multiple tasks, and a different sort of mindset. In the Training Standards of the Association for Specialists in Group Work (1990) there are listed fifteen core knowledge competencies, including familiarization with the unique ethical issues, and sixteen skill competencies. While many of these areas are suitable for all kinds of helping, many of them must be adapted to the specific requirements of a group situation.

Ask yourself the question whether a single course in group leadership is nearly enough to prepare you for what you are likely to face. Would even a second course be enough? What would it take for you to be properly trained? I expect your answer would be something along the lines that there is never enough preparation.

There are more than a few professionals out there leading groups who do not know what they are doing. Either they were poorly trained, they did not receive adequate supervision, or they are not well-suited to this type of work. In some cases, group leaders are impacting hundreds of people without any systematic training at all.

Among the professionals who have taken a group course or two, many still do not feel comfortable leading groups because of the added burdens. Visit your local high school and check out how many counselors are actually leading groups. Survey therapists and counselors in any setting and you are likely to find that the majority are not doing groups because they do not feel adequately prepared.

I don't mean to tell you all this to be discouraging, just to be realistic with you. If you are serious about doing this type of work, and you want to get very good at it, then you are going to have to make a major commitment to your training beyond this course. This is not an option but mandatory if you wish to practice in an ethical manner that is consistent with the highest standards.

How can you get the additional training you will need? Continuing education and workshops are one viable alternative, an option that is actually required by most licensing boards. I have mentioned previously about the kind of peer supervision that is possible with a co-leader. You can also take additional courses, participate in training groups, and recruit mentors who have skills that you admire. Other suggestions are offered in the next chapter.

Deception and Moral Conundrums

In addition to the issues that clearly present ethical problems in group, there are also several "little white lies" that you must also wrestle with. There are, after all, several assurances often offered in group that are really not quite true (Kottler, 1994a).

- "You don't have to say or do anything in here unless you want to." This, of course, is bunk. Lots of pressure will come to bear on those who try to hide or pass.
- "This is a safe place for you to work on yourself." We have discussed earlier all the reasons why groups are much less safe than individual sessions: Confidentiality can't be guaranteed, toxic members can be abusive or hurtful, things can get out of control with little warning.
- "I will treat you all the same in here." Obviously, group leaders have their favorites, as well as members who push their buttons, cause them grief, or just appear annoying.
- "I'm sure we can help you with that." It follows sound therapeutic principles to promote positive expectations (the placebo effect), but sometimes we exaggerate in order to give the person hope.
- "What I think doesn't matter." We pretend as if we are value neutral, that we will not take sides, nor impose our beliefs on others. More truthfully, we have some rather strong convictions about what is best for others.

I don't wish to alarm you unnecessarily (see, that's another little white lie because I *do* want to disturb you with the awesome responsibility of being a group leader), but you will never be able to resolve fully the ethical challenges you must face. The best you can hope for is to remain vigilant and cautious, to follow the ethical guidelines as closely as possible, to work hard in supervision, and to be honest with yourself about the impact of your behavior.

Making Sound Ethical Decisions

You will be relieved to know that models for making ethical decisions have been developed to help you (1) identify the problem, (2) reason through which ethical standards might be involved in the dilemma, (3) discover what traps might be waiting, (4) formulate a preliminary response, (5) predict the likely consequences of this choice, and (6) how you might follow through on the best plan of action, (7) process feedback with peers and supervisors along the way (Forester-Miller & Davis, 1995; Kitchener, 1984; Steinman, Richardson, & McEnroe, 1998; Van Hoose & Kottler, 1985; Welfel, 1998).

At least one advantage of ethical challenges in groups is that you are not alone in your struggle. Even if you do not have a co-leader with whom to share the dilemma, you do have the group to consult with. If you have empowered the group to be mutually responsible for all its proceedings, then group members are also involved in the process. You may be the one who is held legally liable and ethically responsible, but the group members are also part of the community that makes decisions.

Ethics does not only involve professional conduct but also the behavior of all participants in the experience, especially one that involves such mutual trust. For this reason, Edelwich and Brodsky (1992) stress the importance of making ethical standards part of the established group climate. Such an ethical atmosphere would include:

- Privilege—belief that it is an honor to share in the experience
- Caring—essential compassion and respect for others
- Responsibility—commitment to protect the safety of others
- Confidentiality—holding what is said sacred and private
- Honesty—being truthful with oneself and others
- Dependability—honoring commitments
- Cooperation—honoring established norms
- Integrity—being true to convictions
- Proactive—opposing injustice or abuse

If such a group climate could be established, then ethical issues that arise could be handled as a group responsibility. When I have been faced with dilemmas similar to the ones we have been examining, I have been inclined to bring them to the group for discussion. "Look," I will confide, "I've got a problem. I am aware of something that has occurred that must be dealt with. I have certain professional and ethical obligations that must be considered. But you are also involved in this process. Let's talk about what we need to do."

The operative word in the preceding invitation is the plural pronoun, "we," meaning that this is a shared problem. Sometimes I don't agree with what many group members decide to do. Occasionally, I can't live with the consensus that has been reached. Yet even if the outcome is not ultimately decided by member contributions, they have at least been a part of the process. This is what happens in good organizations, businesses, and families, in which the person in charge says:

1. "What do you all think about this?"
2. "Thank you for your input."
3. "This is what I heard you say."
4. "This is what I've decided to do."

In high-functioning groups, members will often come to the same conclusion that you would, but that is not always the case. Depending on the particular problem and what it means for others, they may decide to take a very different course of action. Since during your announcement of informed consent at the beginning of group, you explained your role and responsibility and your professional obligations, you must then do what your ethical codes, laws, and conscience dictate. The hard part is living with your decisions.

For a Field Study

Talk to practicing group leaders about the most difficult ethical challenges they have faced as part of their jobs. Beyond the specific issues involved, and even what they did to resolve the dilemma, find out how they handled things internally. What advice do they offer you as to how you can best prepare yourself for the inevitable problems you will face?

Review of What You Learned

- Group leaders face unique ethical challenges balancing the need to protect members' welfare with the need to promote risk-taking behaviors.
- The risk of casualties in groups is far worse than individual sessions because the leader has less control over the proceedings.
- Special ethical challenges you will face involve the enforcement of confidentiality, multiple relationships, and protecting members against coercion.
- One of your jobs is help everyone in the group to feel ethically and morally responsible for everyone else's welfare.

CHAPTER

15

Group Leadership Applied to Social Action

Ordinarily, we are concerned about promoting constructive changes among our designated client populations. When you consider the unique training and expertise that group leaders possess, it may seem entirely possible that we have within our power the ability to facilitate positive social changes on a far grander scale. If, for example, we know how to influence people in such a way that they are willing to do good things for themselves that they feel reluctant to do, why could we not apply these skills to further needs of the community?

What if you had within you the powers to impact people beyond the small groups you lead? What if you could do your part to make the world a better place, to help people get along better, to address issues of racism, oppression, poverty, injustice, and world peace? Sound like the ravings of idealistic pipedream? Wait and see.

This final chapter talks about the responsibility group leaders have not only to promote constructive changes with their clients but in society at large. Many of the most prolific writers in the group work field, beginning with Carl Rogers' commitment to promoting world peace, are devoted to promoting social change (Kottler & Forester-Miller, 1998).

For Reflection

It is likely that you are training to become a group leader because, in some way, you want to change the world, to make it a better place. If you could use your new training and skills to promote special causes that you feel are important for improving the quality of life for all the planet's inhabitants, what would you most like to do?

A Point and Counterpoint

There are some who feel that group leaders have no place being involved in social action movements. "There is a danger here," one reviewer of this book wrote, "of political editorializing." The reviewer is referring, of course, to the supposed credo of the helping professions to remain value neutral.

Whereas, in theory, it is certainly important that the group leaders honor, respect, and value the different lifestyles and moral choices that people make, I side with Doherty (1995) and others who believe that our profession is suffering a crisis of confidence because of our reluctance to take moral stands for positions we know to be right (Kottler & Hazler, 1997).

It is one thing to avoid imposing our particular values on clients with regard to our personal preferences about lifestyle issues; it is quite another to avoid taking a stand on issues related to social injustice, poverty, racism, oppression, and discrimination. I would submit that with our unique training and qualifications, we not only have a responsibility to make things better for the clients in our groups but also for the larger community (Kottler, 2001). Indeed, the ethical codes of our professions share this belief when they include sections on "public responsibility" (American Counseling Association, 1995), "respect for people's rights" and "concern for others' welfare" (American Psychological Association, 1995), "promoting social justice and change" (National Association of Social Workers, 1996), and "community service" (American Association for Marriage and Family Therapy, 1991).

In their book on ethical practice, Cohen and Cohen (1999) advocate that helpers must be more than moral and ethical in their work; they must also be virtuous in the sense that they hold altruism and compassion as their highest values. This means that the choice to be a group leader involves not only doing our best to help the clients in our charge, but also using our skills to make the world a better place (Kottler, 2001).

For a Group Activity

In small teams, brainstorm all the ways that group leadership training prepares you for promoting social action. Make a list of specific things that could be done to address those social issues that you feel are most significant.

How could you possibly change the world, you might justifiably wonder? Just consider the ways that training as a group leader prepares you for social action:

1. *As an expert in conflict resolution, helping diverse people to respect different points of view, you can play a role in mediating conflicts between others.*

    "We can begin to hear what's behind the struggles we encounter," write Ram Das and Gorman (1985, p. 167). "We're more skillful tacticians, nimbler on our toes, ready for conflict if necessary, but always alert to possibilities for reconciliation—not just an end to conflict but a greater harmony than when it all began."

2. *With skills in effective confrontation, you can effectively challenge people who engage in racist, discriminatory, oppressive, or insensitive language without sparking defensiveness.*

    You hear a racist joke. Rather than just letting it go, or offending others by giving a lecture, you attempt to lead a discussion about the deeper meaning of such ridicule. You follow guidelines that have been described as "diversity competent" for group leaders, "to eliminate biases, prejudices, oppression, and discriminatory practices" (Haley-Banez, Brown, & Molina, 1999).

3. *With group process and leadership skills, you can coordinate the activities of many people toward some common good.*

Whether part of a community organization to help the homeless, collect food for the starving, or work within your local parent-teacher organization, nobody is better qualified than a group leader to harness human resources.

4. *As a professional with personal power and status, you can model for others a lifestyle devoted to service and doing good for others.*

Make no mistake: People are watching you very closely. The public is justifiably skeptical whether helping professionals really mean what they say, really practice what they preach in their lives. The media takes glee in drawing attention to hypocrites among us. As but one example, *Newsweek* (August 2, 1999) reports in its most prominent column the case of psychologist Michael Brooks, author of *Instant Rapport*, who screamed at a flight attendant: "Who the fuck do you think you are?" Brooks was so out of control that the pilot had to make an emergency landing.

This is an anomaly, of course. Most group leaders and other helping professionals are able to model in their lives what they ask others to do. I would insist that it is our responsibility to be what we expect of those we wish to help.

5. *With leadership skills, you are an excellent communicator and influencer of others. These verbal abilities can be used to persuade others to become more involved in altruistic causes.*

It is not only through leading by example that we can make the most significant difference. We are good talkers. We are highly skilled at convincing people to do things that they know are good for them, but they are nevertheless reluctant to do. All our persuasive abilities can be employed to recruit the assistance of others to help us fight injustices, bigotry, and other social causes.

Shoot for Bigger Goals

The more people you can reach with the good stuff you offer, the more impact you can have. Consider the professional who does individual counseling, seeing thirty people per week, versus the group leader who runs two groups per day, reaching two or three times as many folks. Now consider that someday you attain a position of leadership as a supervisor, administrator, or instructor. Imagine now that every professional you help not only improves the quality of their lives, but also that of all their clients.

Now imagine that you can organize the efforts of a whole organization or community toward some common good. Using your knowledge about the ways groups operate, your leadership skills, and persistence, you may be able to practice what Galston (1993) calls "cosmopolitan altruism," the kind of compassionate spirit that reaches out to the disadvantaged people who need help the most.

For a Field Study

Identify in your community a half dozen individuals who have been most successful in promoting social action causes, or who have been engaged in altruistic pursuits that have impacted a large group of people. Consider those who volunteer their time to help the needy, as well as philanthropists, heads of charitable organizations, and social activists who address problems of poverty, racism, discrimination, child abuse, and similar causes.

Remember that as a student, you have access to a wide assortment of people when you introduce yourself as, "I'm a student doing research for a class and I'd like to interview you for a few minutes." You may find some people difficult to reach, but you will be surprised at how many will make themselves available. Furthermore, many of them will be very *open* about their motives and activities.

Interview several people who are actively involved in social action causes. Find out how they see their roles as activists and what skills they see as most crucial to promoting their efforts. Talk to them about your own training as a group leader and discuss ways that you could adapt your preparation to include making a difference on a larger scale.

Where to Go Next

Here we are at the end of our journey together. Throughout this semester you have fully entered the world of groups, not only readying and studying about the basic theory, but applying the concepts to your life and work.

This was only an introduction to the subject of group leadership. You were certainly exposed to all the basics you will need to get started, but in order to truly master the skills, you will need lots of good practice and supervision. I would, therefore, like to close by offering you some final advice.

1. Read the good books in the field. Ask instructors and supervisors you respect to recommend those books they feel are most significant and impactful.
2. Go to the library (or internet) and familiarize yourself with the major journals in group work. An extensive list was provided in Chapter 3. As a beginner you may initially feel overwhelmed by the jargon, statistics, and style of scholarly writing. As you gain more experience and training, you will find these journals to be an invaluable resource for finding answers to your questions.
3. There is no substitute for getting experience in a group as a participant. If you have not yet experienced a variety of groups as a member, it will be that much more difficult for you to understand what your clients are going through. Join a support group. Volunteer to be part of as many other groups as you can.
4. Go to professional conferences and watch the masters in action. All the various professional groups sponsor annual conventions in which you can attend demonstrations

and programs in which master practitioners show what they can do. If you are feeling very courageous, you can even volunteer to be a participant in the demonstration groups.

5. Start keeping a journal, if you haven't already, in which you get in the habit of thinking and writing critically about your own behavior in groups. Be forgiving of your mistakes but learn from them.

6. Get as much feedback as you can from peers and supervisors. Whenever you find yourself in group situations in which you experimented with new behaviors, discover the impact you made. People will be polite and lie, so do your best to get them to tell you things they liked least as well as best.

7. Recruit mentors into your life. Identify those individuals who have skills and knowledge that you want most. Study with them. Volunteer to do research with them or lead a group.

8. Co-lead groups with as many different experts as you can. Make sure you take the time to debrief sessions so you have the opportunity to learn from the experience.

9. Take more courses and attend group workshops. Most universities have advanced group courses, or even several of them. Professional organizations, both locally and nationally, sponsor advanced training opportunities as well. Once you join these groups, you will get lots of mail.

10. Have fun with this stuff. In my humble opinion, there really is no other professional work that is as fulfilling and fun as leading groups. Even with your initial apprehensions, fears of failure, and self-doubts, surely you can already see that.

Review of What You Learned

- Group leadership skills can be useful in promoting social action movements for the larger community.
- Although all professional organizations strongly encourage their members to become involved in social action, there is also a danger of imposing your values on others.
- This text and course are just the beginning of your training as a group leader. Expertise will follow continued study, practice, and supervision.

REFERENCES

Abernethy, A. D. (1998). Working with racial themes in group psychotherapy. *Group, 22*(1), 1–13.

Agazarian, Y. M., & Peters, R. (1981). *The visible and invisible group: Two perspectives on group psychotherapy and group process.* London: Rutledge.

Alfonso, C. A., & Cohen, M. A. (1997). The role of group therapy in the care of persons with AIDS. *Journal of the American Academy of Psychoanalysis, 25*(4), 623–638.

Alfred, A. R. (1992). Members' perceptions of co-leaders' influence and effectiveness in group psychotherapy. *Journal for Specialists in Group Work, 17,* 42–53.

Altfeld, D. A. (1999). An experiential group model for psychotherapy supervision. *International Journal of Group Psychotherapy, 49*(2), 237–254.

American Counseling Association. (1995). *Code of Ethics and Standards of Practice.* Alexandra, VA: Author.

American Association for Marriage and Family Therapy. (1991). AAMFT *Code of Ethics.* Washington, DC: Author.

American Psychological Association. (1995). *Ethical Principles of Psychologists and Code of Conduct.* Washington, DC: Author.

American Group Psychotherapy Association. (1978). *Guidelines for Training Group Psychotherapists.* New York: Author.

Anderson, C. M., & Stewart, S. (1983). *Mastering resistance: A practical guide to family therapy.* New York: Guilford.

Association for Specialists in Group Work. (1989). *Ethical guidelines for training group counselors.* Alexandria, VA.: Author.

Association for Specialists in Group Work. (1990). *Professional standards for training of group work generalists and group work specialists.* Alexandria, VA: Author.

Avery, L. (1998). A feminist perspective on group work with severely mentally ill women. *Women and Therapy, 21*(4), 1–14.

Bandura, A. (1969). *Principles of behavior modification.* New York: Holt, Rinehart, and Winston.

Barlow, C. A., Blythe, J. A., & Edmonds, M. (1999). *A handbook of interactive exercises for groups.* Boston: Allyn & Bacon

Beck, A. T., & Haaga, D. A. (1992). The future of cognitive therapy. *Psychotherapy, 29*(1), 34–38.

Becvar, R. J., Canfield, B. S., & Becvar, D. S. (1997). *Group work: Cybernetic, constructivist, and social constructionist perspectives.* Denver: Love Publishing.

Bennis, W. G., & Shepard, H. A. (1956). A theory of group development. *Human Relations, 9,* 415–437

Berg, R. C., Landreth, G. L., & Fall, K. A. (1998). *Group counseling: Concepts and procedures.* Philadelphia: Accelerated Development.

Berman, A., & Weinberg, H. (1998). The advanced-stage therapy group. *International Journal of Group Psychotherapy, 48*(4), 499–518.

Bertalanffy, L. von (1968). *General systems theory: Foundations, development, application.* New York: Braziller.

Bilu, Y., & Witzum, E. (1993). Working with Jewish ultra-orthodox patients: Guidelines for a culturally sensitive therapy. *Cultural Medicine and Psychiatry, 17,* 197–233.

Bloch, S., Browning, S., & McGrath, G. (1983). Humour in group psychotherapy. *British Journal of Medical Psychology, 56,* 89–97.

Bloom, B. L. (1997). *Planned short-term psychotherapy* (2nd ed.). Boston: Allyn & Bacon.

Borgers, S. B., & Koening, R. W. (1983). Uses and effects of modeling by the therapist in group therapy. *Journal for Specialists in Group Work, 8,* 133–138.

Bowman, R. P. (1987). Small-group guidance and counseling in schools: A national survey of school counselors. *The School Counselor, 34,* 256–262.

Brabender, V., & Fallon, A. (1993). *Models of inpatient group psychotherapy.* Washington, DC: American Psychological Association.

Bradley, L., & Jarchow, E. (1997). Group leadership: Learning from the macro to improve the micro. In H. Forester-Miller & J. Kottler (eds.), *Issues and challenges for group practitioners.* Denver: Love Publishing.

Brammer, L. M., & MacDonald, G. (1999). *The helping relationship.* Boston: Allyn & Bacon.

Brinson, J., & Kottler, J. (1995). International students in counseling: Some alternative models. *Journal of College Student Psychotherapy, 9* (3), 57–70.

Brinson, J., & Lee, C. (1997). Culturally responsive group leadership. In H. Forester-Miller & J. Kottler (Eds.), *Issues and challenges for group practitioners.* Denver: Love Publishing.

Brock, S. E. (1998). Helping classrooms cope with traumatic events. *Professional School Counseling, 2*(2), 110–116.

Brok, A. J. (1997). A modified cognitive-behavioral approach to group therapy with the elderly. *Group, 21*(2), 115–134.

Brower, A. M. (1996). Group development as constructed social reality revisited: The constructivism of small groups. *Families in Society, 77*(6), 336–344.

Brown, N. W. (1998). *Psycho-educational groups.* Philadelphia: Accelerated Development.

Budman, S. H., & Gurman, A. S. (1988). *Theory and practice of brief therapy.* New York: Guilford.

Bugental, J. F. T. (1978). *Psychotherapy and process: The fundamentals of an existential-humanistic approach.* Reading, MA: Addison-Wesley.

Bugental, J. F. T. (1990). *Intimate journeys: Stories from life-changing therapy.* San Francisco: Jossey-Bass.

Burnside, I. M. (1993). Themes in reminiscence groups with older women. *International Journal of Aging and Human Development, 37,* 177–189.

Burstow, B. (1992). *Radical feminist therapy.* Thousand Oaks, CA: Sage.

Capuzzi, D., & Gross, D. R. (1998). *Introduction to group counseling* (2nd ed.). Denver: Love Publishing.

Carroll, M., Bates, M., & Johnson, C. (1997). *Group leadership* (3rd ed.). Denver: Love Publishing.

Cathcart, R. S., Samovar, L. A., & Henman, L. (1996). *Small group communication.* New York: McGraw Hill.

Chen, M. W., Noosbond, J. P., & Bruce, M. A. (1998). Therapeutic document in group counseling: An active change agent. *Journal of Counseling and Development, 76*(4), 404–411.

Chen, W. D., Chai, M., & Gunn, R. W. (1998). Splitting and projective identification in multicultural group counseling. *Journal for Specialists in Group Work, 23,*(4), 372–387.

Cho, C., & Cassidy, D. E. (1994). Parallel processes for workers and their clients in chronic bereavement resulting from HIV. *Death Studies, 18,* 273–292.

Clark, A. J. (1998). Reframing: A therapeutic technique in group counseling. *Journal for Specialists in Group Work, 23*(1), 66–73.

Clark, C. F. (1998). Transpersonal group psychotherapy. *Journal for Specialists in Group Work, 23*(4), 350–371.

Clifford, M. W. (1998). Teaching social group work skills: What makes an effective group work teacher? *Psychotherapy in Private Practice, 17*(3), 1–19.

Cohen, E. D., & Cohen, G. S. (1999). *The virtuous therapist: Ethical practice of counseling and psychotherapy.* Pacific Grove, CA: Brooks/Cole.

Colmant, S. A., & Merta, R. J. (1999). Using the sweat lodge ceremony as group therapy for Navajo youth. *Journal for Specialists in Group Work, 24*(1), 55–73.

Conyne, R. K. (1998). What to look for in groups: Helping trainees become more sensitive to multicultural issues. *Journal For Specialists in Group Work, 23*(1), 22–32.

Conyne, R. K. (1999). *Failures in group work.* Thousand Oaks, CA: Sage.

Conyne, R. K., Rapin, L. S., & Rand, J. M. (1997). A model for leading task groups. In H. Forester-Miller & J. Kottler (Eds.), *Issues and challenges for group practitioners.* Denver: Love Publishing.

Corey, G. (2000). *Theory and practice of group counseling* (5th ed.). Pacific Grove, CA: Brooks/Cole.

Corey, G., Corey, M. S., & Callanan, P. (1998). *Issues and ethics in the helping professions* (5th ed.). Pacific Grove, CA: Brooks/Cole.

Corey, G., Corey, M. S., Callanan, P., & Russell, J. (1992). *Group techniques* (2nd ed.). Pacific Grove, CA: Brooks/Cole.

Corey, G., Corey, M. S., & Haynes, R. (2000). *Evolution of a group: Student video and workbook.* Pacific Grove, CA: Wadsworth.

Corey, M. S., Corey, G., (1997). *Groups: Process and practice* (5th ed.). Pacific Grove, CA: Brooks/Cole.

Cottone, R., & Tarvydas, V.M. (1998). *Ethical and professional issues in counseling.* Columbus, OH: Merrill.

Csikszentmihalyi, M. (1990). *Flow: The psychology of optimal experience.* New York: Harper and Row.

Dazzo, B. B. (1998). Non-traditional women's group. *Group, 22*(3), 159–176.

DeChant, B. (Ed.).(1996). *Women and group psychotherapy.* New York: Guilford.

DeLucia-Waack, J. L. (1996). Multiculturalism is inherent in all group work. *Journal for Specialists in Group Work, 21*, 218–223.

DePree, M. (1992). *Leadership jazz.* New York: Dell.

Derlega, V. J., Hendrick, S. S., Winstead, B. A., & Berg, J. H. (1991). *Psychotherapy as a personal relationship.* New York: Guilford Press.

Dies, R. (1980). Current practice in the training of group therapists, International *Journal of Group Psychotherapy, 30*, 273.

Dinkmeyer, D. C. (1975). Adlerian group psychotherapy. International *Journal of Group Psychotherapy, 25*(2), 219–226.

Dinkmeyer, D. C., Dinkmeyer, D. C., & Sperry, L. (1987). *Adlerian counseling and psychotherapy.* Columbus, OH.: Merrill.

Doherty, W. J. (1995). *Soul searching.* New York: Basic Books.

Donigian, J., & Malnati, R. (1997). *Systemic group therapy.* Pacific Grove, CA: Brooks/Cole.

Donigian, J., & Malnati, R. (1999). *Critical incidents in group therapy* (2nd ed.). Pacific Grove, CA: Brooks/Cole.

Dreikurs, R. (1969). Group psychotherapy from the point of view of Adlerian psychology. In H. M. Ruitenbeek (Ed.), *Group therapy today.* Chicago: Aldine-Atherton.

Dufrene, P. M., & Coleman, V. D. (1992). Counseling Native Americans: Guidelines for group process. *Journal for Specialists in Group Work, 17*, 229–234.

Dugatkin, L. (1999). *Cheating monkeys and citizen bees: The nature of cooperation in animals and humans.* New York: The Free Press.

Durkin, H. E. (1981). *Living groups: Group psychotherapy and general systems theory.* New York: Brunner/Mazel.

Dushman, R., & Sutherland, J. (1997). An Adlerian perspective on dreamwork and creative arts therapies. *Individual Psychology, 53*(4), 461–475.

Dye, A. (1980). Thoughts on training. *Journal for Specialists in Group Work, 5*, 5–7.

Dye, A., & Norsworthy, K. (1997). Becoming an effective group counselor: The journey. In H. Forester-Miller & J. Kottler (Eds.), *Issues and challenges for group practitioners.* Denver: Love Publishing.

Dyer, W. W., & Vriend, J. (1975). *Counseling techniques that work.* Alexandria, VA: American Counseling Association.

Dyer, W. W., & Vriend, J. (1980). *Group counseling for personal mastery.* New York: Sovereign.

Dyregrov, A. (1997). The process of psychological debriefings. *Journal of Traumatic Stress, 10*(4), 589–605.

Edelwich, J., & Brodsky, A. (1992). *Group counseling for the resistant client.* New York: Lexington.

Egan, G. (1997). *The skilled helper* (6th ed.). Pacific Grove, CA: Brooks/Cole.

Ellis, A. (1992). Group rational-emotive and cognitive behavioral therapy. *International Journal of Group Psychotherapy, 4*(1), 63–80.

Essandoh, P. K. (1996). Multicultural counseling as the "fourth force": A call to arms. *Counseling Psychologist, 24*, 126–137.

Evans, D. R., Hearn, M. T., Uhlemann, M. R., & Ivey, A. E. (1998). *Essential Interviewing: A programmed approach to effective communication* (5th ed.). Pacific Grove, CA: Brooks/Cole.

Fennel, D. L., & Weinhold, B. K. (1997). *Counseling families* (2nd ed.). Denver: Love Publishing.

Fish, M. C. (1998). Groups for parents of school-aged children with disabilities. In K. Stoiber, T. Kratochwill, et al. (Eds.), *Handbook of group intervention for children and families.* Boston: Allyn & Bacon.

Forester-Miller, H., & Davis, T. E. (1995). *A practitioner's guide to ethical decision making.* Alexandria, VA: American Counseling Association.

Forsyth, D. R. (1999). *Group dynamics* (3rd ed.), Pacific Grove, CA: Brooks/Cole.

Frank, J., & Ascher, E. (1951). The corrective emotional experience in group therapy. *American Journal of Psychiatry, 108*, 126–131.

Frank, J. (1991). *Persuasion and healing* (3rd ed.). Baltimore: Johns Hopkins Press.

Frankl, V. (1963). *Man's search for meaning.* New York: Washington Square.

Fuller, G. B., & Fuller, D. L. (1999). Reality therapy approaches. In H. Prout, D. Brown, et al. (Eds.), *Counseling and psychotherapy with children and adolescents.* New York: Wiley.

Gainer, K. A. (1992). Internalized oppression as a barrier to effective group work with Black women. *The Journal for Specialists in Group Work, 17*(4), 235–242.

Galston, W. A. (1993). Cosmopolitan altruism. In E. Paul, F. Miller, & J. Paul (Eds.), *Altruism.* New York: Cambridge University Press.

Gans, J. S., & Alonso, A. (1998). Difficult patients: Their construction in group therapy. *International Journal of Group Psychotherapy, 48*(3), 311–326.

Garrett, M. W., & Myers, J. E. (1996). The rule of opposites: A paradigm for counseling Native Americans. *Journal of Multicultural Counseling and Development, 24*, 89–104.

Gazda, G. (1989). *Group counseling: A developmental approach.* Boston: Allyn & Bacon.

Gergen, K. J. (1985). *The saturated self.* New York: Basic Books.

Gibbs, J. C., Goldstein, A. P., & Potter, G. B. (1995). *The Equip Program: Teaching youth to think and act responsibly through a peer helping approach.* Champaign, IL: Research Press.

Gilbert, L. A., & Scher, M. (1999). *Gender and sex in counseling and psychotherapy.* Boston: Allyn & Bacon.

Ginott, H. G. (1982). Group play therapy with children. In G. L. Landreth (Ed.), *Play therapy: Dynamics of the process of counseling with children.* Springfield, IL: Charles C. Thomas.

Gladding, S. (1997). The creative arts in groups. In H. Forester-Miller & J. Kottler (Eds.), *Issues and challenges for group practitioners*. Denver: Love Publishing.

Gladding, S. (1999). *Group work: A counseling specialty* (3rd ed.). Englewood Cliffs, NJ: Prentice-Hall.

Glantz, K., & Pearce, J. K. (1989). *Exiles from eden: Psychotherapy from an evolutionary perspective*. New York: W.W. Norton.

Glasser, W. (1965). *Reality therapy: A new approach to psychiatry*. New York: Harper and Row.

Glasser, W. (1985). *Control theory: A new explanation of how we control our lives*. New York: Harper and Row.

Glasser, W. (1998). *Choice theory*. New York: HarperCollins.

Glodich, A., & Allen, J. G. (1998). Adolescents exposed to violence and abuse: A review of the group therapy literature with an emphasis on preventing trauma reenactment. *Journal of Child and Adolescent Group Therapy, 8,* 135–154.

Gloria, A. M. (1999). Apoyando estudiantes Chicanas: Therapeutic factors in Chicana college student support groups. *Journal for Specialists in Group Work, 24,* 260–273.

Goldenberg, I., & Goldenberg, H. (1999). *Family therapy: An overview* (5th ed.). Pacific Grove, CA: Brooks/Cole.

Goldstein, E. G., & Ehrenkranz, S. M. (1999). *Short-term treatment and social work practice: An integrative perspective*. New York: The Free Press.

Gore-Felton, C., & Spiegel, D. (1999). Enhancing women's lives: The role of support groups among breast cancer patients. *Journal for Specialists in Group Work, 24,* 274–287.

Haley-Banez, L., Brown, S., & Molina, B. (1999). Association for Specialists in Group Work principles for diversity-competent group workers. *Journal for Specialists in Group Work, 24,* 7–14.

Halton, M. (1998). The group and the oedipal situation. *Psychoanalytic Psychotherapy, 12*(3), 241–258.

Hansen, J. C., Warner, R. W., & Smith, E. J. (1980). *Group counseling: Theory and practice*. Chicago: Rand McNally.

Harre, R. (1984). *Personal being: A theory for individual psychology*. Cambridge, MA: Harvard University Press.

Hawkins, D. M. (1998). An invitation to join in difficulty: Realizing the deeper promise of group psychotherapy. *International Journal of Group Psychotherapy, 48*(4), 423–438.

Hazler, R. J., Stanard, R. P., Conkey, V., & Granello, P. (1997). Mentoring group leaders. In H. Forester-Miller & J. Kottler (Eds.), *Issues and challenges for group practitioners*. Denver: Love Publishing.

Henry, C., & Cashwell, C. S. (1998). Using reality therapy in the treatment of adolescent sex offenders. *International Journal of Reality Therapy, 18*(1), 8–11.

Hepworth, D. H., & Rooney, R. H., & Larsen, J. A. (1997). *Direct social work practice*. Pacific Grove, CA: Brooks/Cole.

Holkup, P. A. (1998). Our parents, our children, ourselves: A therapy group to facilitate understanding of intergenerational behavior patterns and to promote family healing. *Journal of Psychosocial Nursing, 36*(2), 20–26.

Hopps, J. G., & Pinderhughes, E. (1999). *Group work with overwhelmed clients*. New York: The Free Press.

Horne, A., & Campbell, L. F. (1997). Round pegs in square holes. In H. Forester-Miller & J. Kottler (Eds.), *Issues and challenges for group practitioners*. Denver: Love Publishing.

Hulse-Killacky, D., Kraus, K. L., & Schumacher, R. A. (1999). Visual conceptualizations of meetings: A group work design. *Journal for Specialists in Group Work, 24,* 113–124.

Imber-Black, E. (1988). *Families and larger systems*. New York: Guilford.

Jacobs, E. E., Masson, R. L., & Harvill, R. L. (1998). *Group counseling: Strategies and skills* (3rd ed.). Pacific Grove, CA: Brooks/Cole.

Jacobson, B. (1997). Working with existential groups. In S. Du Plock, et al., *Case studies in existential psychotherapy and counseling.* Chichester, UK: Wiley.

Jennings, M. L., & Anderson, K. J. (1997). Process groups: A survey of small counseling center issues and solutions. *Journal of College Student Psychotherapy, 12*(2), 65–74.

Jennings, M. L., & Skovholt, T. M. (1999). The cognitive, emotional, and relational characteristics of master therapists. *Journal of Counseling Psychology, 46*(1), 3–11.

Johnson, D. W., & Johnson, F. (2000). *Joining together: Group theory and group skills* (7th ed.). Boston: Allyn & Bacon.

Johnson, R. D. (1997). An existential model of group therapy for chronic mental conditions. *International Journal of Group Psychotherapy, 47*(2), 227–250.

Kahn, M. (1997). *Between therapist and client: The new relationship* (rev. ed.). New York: W.H. Freeman.

Kees, N. L. (1999). Women together again: A phenomenological study of leaderless women's groups. *Journal for Specialists in Group Work, 24,* 288–305.

Kelsey, B. L. (1998). The dynamics of multicultural groups: Ethnicity as a determinant of leadership. *Small Group Research, 29*(5), 602–623.

Kernberg, O. (1975). *Borderline conditions and pathological narcissism.* New York: Jason Aronson.

Kitchener, K. S. (1984). Intuition, critical evaluation and ethical principles: The foundation for ethical decisions in counseling psychology. *The Counseling Psychologist, 12,* 43–55.

Kleinberg, J. L. (1997). How does the analytic supervisor teach group therapy? *Group, 21*(4), 313–329.

Kleinberg, J. L. (1999). The supervisory alliance and the training of psychodynamic group psychotherapists. *International Journal of Group Psychotherapy, 49*(2), 159–180.

Knight, B. G. (1996). *Psychotherapy with older adults* (2nd ed.). Thousand Oaks, CA: Sage.

Kohut, H. (1971). *The analysis of the self.* Madison, CT: International Universities Press.

Kormanski, C. (1982). Leadership strategies for managing conflict. *Journal for Specialists in Group Work, 7,* 112–118.

Kormanski, C. (1988). Using group development theory in business and industry. *Journal for Specialists in Group Work, 13,* 30–41.

Kormanski, C. (1999). *The team: Explorations in group process.* Denver: Love Publishing.

Kormanski, C., & Eschbach, L. (1997). From group leader to process consultant. In H. Forester-Miller & J. Kottler (Eds.), *Issues and challenges for group practitioners.* Denver: Love Publishing.

Kottler, J. A. (1992). *Compassionate therapy: Working with difficult clients.* San Francisco: Jossey-Bass.

Kottler, J. A. (1993). *On being a therapist* (2nd ed.). San Francisco: Jossey-Bass.

Kottler, J. A. (1994a). *Advanced group leadership.* Pacific Grove, CA: Brooks/Cole.

Kottler, J. A. (1994b). *Beyond blame: A new way of resolving conflicts in relationships.* San Francisco: Jossey-Bass.

Kottler, J. A. (1999). *The therapist's workbook: self-assessment, self-care, and self-improvement exercises for mental health professionals.* San Francisco: Jossey-Bass.

Kottler, J. A. (2000). *Nuts and bolts of helping.* Boston: Allyn & Bacon.

Kottler, J. A. (2001). *Doing good: Passion and commitment helping others.* Philadelphia: Accelerated Development.

Kottler, J. A., & Blau, D. (1989). *The imperfect therapist: Learning from failure in therapeutic practice.* San Francisco: Jossey-Bass.

Kottler, J. A., & Brown, R. W. (2000). *Introduction to therapeutic counseling: Voices from the field.* Pacific Grove, CA: Brooks/Cole.

Kottler, J. A., & Forester-Miller, H. (1998). Personal and social change in the lives of group leaders. *Journal for Specialists in Group Work, 23*, 338–349.

Kottler, J. A., & Hazler, R. (1997). *What you never learned in graduate school.* New York: W.W. Norton.

Kottler, J. A., & Kottler, E. (2000). *Counseling skills for teachers.* Thousand Oaks, CA: Corwin Press.

Kottler, J. A., & Markos, P. (1997). The group leader's uses of self. In H. Forester-Miller & J. Kottler (Eds.), *Issues and challenges for group practitioners.* Denver: Love Publishing.

La Coursiere, R. (1980). *The life-cycle of groups: Group development and stage theory.* New York: Human Sciences.

Lakin, M. (1994). Morality in group and family therapies: Multiperson therapies and the 1992 ethics code. *Professional Psychology, 25*, 344–348.

Landreth, G. L., & Sweeney, D. S. (1997). Child-centered play therapy. In K. J. O'Connor & L. M. Braverman (Eds.), *Play therapy theory and practice.* New York: Wiley.

Lee, C. (1982). Black support group. *Journal of College Personnel, 23*, 217–223.

Leeman, L. W., Gibbs, J. C., & Fuller, D. (1993). Evaluation of multi-component group treatment program for juvenile delinquents. *Aggressive Behavior, 19*, 281–292.

Leong, F. T. (1992). Guidelines for minimizing premature termination among Asian American clients to group counseling. *Journal for Specialists in Group Work, 17*(4), 218–228.

Leszcz, M. (1989). Group psychotherapy of the characterologically difficult client. *International Journal of Psychotherapy, 39*(3), 311–334.

Liebling, H., & Chipchase, H. (1996). Feminist group therapy for women who self-harm: An initial evaluation. *Issues in Criminological and Legal Psychology, 25*, 24–29.

Lipincot, J. A., & Robinson, G. (1994). Group counseling for socially disenfranchised college students. *Journal of College Student Development, 35*(3), 227–228.

Livingston, M. S. (1999). Vulnerability, tenderness, and the experience of the self object relationship. *International Journal of Group Psychotherapy, 49*(1), 19–40.

Mackewn, J. (1997). *Developing gestalt counseling.* London: Sage.

McBride, N. F. (1997). *How to have great small-group meetings.* Colorado Springs, CO: Navpress.

McBride, N. F. (1998). *Real small groups don't just happen.* Colorado Springs, CO: Navpress.

McDuff, A. C., & Dryden, W. (1998). REBT and emotion: A roleplay experiment. *Journal of Rational-Emotive and Cognitive Behavior Therapy, 16*(4), 235–254.

McFarland, W., & Tollerud, T. (1999). Counseling children and adolescents with special issues. In A. Vernon (Ed.), *Counseling children and adolescents* (2nd ed.). Denver: Love Publishing.

McGee, M., & Burton, R. (1998). The use of co-therapy with a reflecting mirror as a supervisory tool. *Journal of Family Psychotherapy, 9*(4), 45–60.

McGoldrick, M. & Gerson, R. (1999). *Genograms in family assessment* (2nd ed.). New York: W. W. Norton.

McWhirter, B. T, McWhirter, E. H., & McWhirter, J. J. (1988). Groups in Latin America. *Journal for Specialists in Group Work, 13*, 70–76.

McWhirter, E. H. (1994). *Counseling for empowerment.* Alexandria, VA: American Counseling Association.

Meissan, G., Warren, M. L., & Kendall, M. (1996). An assessment of college student willingness to use self-help groups. *Journal of College Student Development, 37*(4), 448–456.

Mitchell, J. T., & Everly, G. S. (1993). *Critical incident stress debriefing: An operations manual for the prevention of traumatic stress among emergency services and disaster workers.* Ellicott City, MD: Chevron.

Molinari, V. (1994). Current approaches to psychotherapy with elderly adults. *Directions in Mental Health Counseling, 4*, 3–13.

Monk, G., Drewery, W., & Winslade, J. (1997). Using narrative ideas in group work: A new perspective. In H. Forester-Miller & J. Kottler (Eds.), Issues and challenges for group practitioners. Denver: Love Publishing.

Moreno, J. K. (1998). Long-term psychodynamic group psychotherapy for eating disorders. *Journal for Specialists in Group Work, 23* (3), 269–284.

Moreno, J. L. (1964). *Psychodrama.* Bacon, NY: Beacon House.

Morgan, B., & Hensley, L. (1998). Supporting working mothers through group work. *Journal for Specialists in Group Work, 23*(3), 298–311.

Myers, J., Poidevant, J., & Dean, L. (1991). Groups for older persons and their caregivers: A review of the literature. *Journal for Specialists in Group Work, 16*(3), 197–205.

Nadler, R. S., & Luckner, J. L. (1992). *Processing the adventure experience: Theory and practice.* Dubuque, IA: Kendall/Hunt.

Nakkab, S., & Hernandez, M. (1998). Group psychotherapy in the context of cultural diversity. *Group, 22*(2), 95–103.

Napier, R. W., & Gershenfeld, M. K. (1993). *Group theory and practice* (5th ed.). Boston: Houghton Mifflin.

National Association of Social Workers (1996). *Code of ethics.* Washington, DC: Author.

Nichol, B. (1997). Emotional pain in learning: Applying group-analytic experience in non-clinical fields. *Group Analysis, 30,* 93–105.

Nolan, E. J. (1978). Leadership interventions for promoting personal mastery. *Journal for Specialists In Group Work, 3*(3), 132–138.

Pack-Brown, S. P., Whittington-Clark, L. E., & Parker, W. M. (1998). *Images of me: A guide to group work with African-American women.* Boston: Allyn & Bacon.

Patterson, C. H. (1986). *Theories of counseling and psychotherapy* (4th ed.). New York: Harper and Row.

Pedersen, P. (1996). Multicultural counseling: From diversity to universality. *Journal of Counseling and Development, 74,* 227–231.

Pedersen, P. (1997). *Culture-centered counseling interventions: Striving for accuracy.* Thousand Oaks, CA: Sage Publications, Inc.

Peterson, J. V., & Nisenholz, B. (1999). *Orientation to counseling* (4th ed.). Boston: Allyn & Bacon.

Ponterotto, J. G., Casas, J. M., Suzuki, L. A., & Alexander, C. M. (1995). Handbook of multicultural counseling. Thousand Oaks, CA: Sage.

Pope, K., & Vasquez, M. (1998). *Ethics in psychotherapy and counseling: A practical guide for psychologists.* San Francisco: Jossey-Bass.

Pope, M. (1999). Applications of group career counseling techniques in Asian cultures. *Journal of Multicultural Counseling and Development, 27,* 18–30.

Rainer, T. (1978). *The new diary.* New York: Tarcher.

Ram Das, & Gorman, P. (1985). *How can I help?* New York: Knopf.

Rank, M. G. (1997). Critical incident stress debriefing. In W. S. Hutchinson, et al., *Employee assistance programs: A basic text* (2nd ed.). Springfield, IL: C. C. Thomas.

Ray, R. G. (1999). *The facilitative leader: Behaviors that enable success.* Upper Saddle River, NJ: Prentice-Hall.

Reddy, W. B. (1994). *Intervention skills: Process consultation for small groups and teams.* San Diego: Pfeiffer.

Riordan, R. J., & White, J. (1996). Logs as therapeutic adjuncts in groups. *Journal for Specialists in Group Work, 21,* 94–100.

Rittenhouse, J. (1997). Feminist principles in survivor's groups: Out-of-group contact. *Journal for Specialists in Group Work, 22*(2), 111–119.

Rogers, C. R. (1967). The process of the basic encounter group. In J. F. T. Bugental (Ed.), *Challenges of humanistic psychology*. New York: McGraw-Hill.

Rogers, C. R. (1970). *On encounter groups*. New York: Harper and Row.

Rogers, C. R. (1980). *A way of being*. Boston: Houghton Mifflin.

Rohnke, K. (1989). Cowstails and cobras: *A guide to games, initiatives, ropes courses, and adventure curriculum*. Dubuque, IA: Kendall/Hunt.

Roller, B., & Nelson, V. (1991). *The art of co-therapy: How therapists work together*. New York: Guilford.

Rose, S. R. (1998). *Group work with children and adolescents*. Thousand Oaks, CA: Sage.

Rosenthal, H. G. (1998). *Favorite counseling and therapy techniques*. Philadelphia: Accelerated Development.

Rosenthal, H. (Ed.)(2000). *Favorite counseling and therapy homework assignments: 51 therapists share their most creative strategies*. Philadelphia: Accelerated Development.

Roth, B., Stone, W., & Kibel, H. (1990). *The difficult patient in group*. Madison, CT: International Universities Press.

Rutan, J. S., & Stone, W. N. (1993). *Psychodynamic group psychotherapy*. New York: Guilford.

Saiger, G. M. (1996). Some thoughts on the existential lens in group psychotherapy. *Group, 20*(2), 113–130.

Sandu, D. S., & Brown, S. P. (1996). Empowering ethnically and racially diverse clients through prejudice reduction: Suggestions and strategies for counselors. *Journal of Multicultural Counseling and Development, 24*, 202–217.

Satir, V. (1972). *Peoplemaking*. Palo Alto, CA: Science and Behavior Books.

Schmidt, J. J. (1999). *Counseling in schools: Essential services and comprehensive programs* (3rd ed.). Boston: Allyn & Bacon.

Schoenwolf, G. (1998). The scapegoat and the holy cow in group therapy. *Journal of Contemporary Psychotherapy, 28*(3), 277–287.

Schutz, W. C. (1958). *FIRO: A three dimensional theory of interpersonal behavior*. New York: Rinehart.

Scott, M. J., & Stradling, S. G. (1998). *Brief group counseling: Integrating individual and group cognitive-behavioural approaches*. Chichester, GB: Wiley.

Shapiro, J. L., Peltz, L. S., & Bernadett-Shapiro, S. (1998). *Brief group treatment: Practical training for therapists and counselors*. Pacific Grove, CA: Brooks/Cole.

Silverstein, J. L. (1997). Acting out in group therapy: Avoiding authority struggles. *International Journal of Group Psychotherapy, 47*(1), 31–45.

Silvester, G. (1997). Appreciating indigenous knowledge in groups. In G. Monk, J. Winslade, K. Crocket, & D. Epston (Eds.), *Narrative therapy in practice: The archaeology of hope*. San Francisco: Jossey-Bass.

Smith, K. K., & Berg, D. N. (1995). A paradoxical approach to teaching group dynamics: First thoughts, first findings. *Journal of Applied Behavioral Science, 31*(4), 398–414.

Smith, R. J., & Steindler, E. M. (1983). The impact of difficult patients upon treaters. *Bulletin of the Menninger Clinic, 47*, 107–116.

Spiegler, M. D., & Guevremont, D. C. (1998). *Contemporary behavior therapy* (3rd ed.). Pacific Grove, CA: Brooks/Cole.

Steinman, S. O., Richardson, N. F., & McEnroe, T. (1998). *The ethical decision making manual for helping professionals*. Pacific Grove, CA: Brooks/Cole.

Stewart, G. L., Manz, C. C., & Sims, H. P. (1998). *Teamwork and group dynamics*. New York: Wiley.

Struder, J. R., & Allton, J. A. (1996). When parents divorce: Assisting teens to adjust through a group approach. *Guidance and Counseling, 11*, 33–36.

Strupp, H. H. (1992). The future of psychodynamic psychotherapy. *Psychotherapy, 9*(1), 21–27.

Sue, D. W., Ivey, M. B., & Pedersen, P. B. (1996). *A theory of multicultural counseling and therapy.* Pacific Grove, CA: Brooks/ Cole.

Sue, S., & Zane, N. (1987). The role of culture and cultural techniques in psychotherapy: A critique and reformation. *American Psychologist, 42*(1), 37–45.

Tomasulo, D. J. (1998). *Action methods in group psychotherapy.* Philadelphia: Accelerated Development.

Toner, B. B., Segal, Z. V., Emmott, S., Myran, D., Ali, A., DiGasbarro, I., & Stuckless, N. (1998). Cognitive-behavioral group therapy for patients with irritable bowel syndrome. *International Journal of Group Psychotherapy, 48*(2), 215–241.

Trotzer, J. P. (1999). *The counselor and the group: Integrating theory, training, and practice* (3rd. ed.). Philadelphia: Accelerated Development.

Tuckman, B. W. (1965). Developmental sequence in small groups. *Psychological Bulletin, 63,* 384–399.

Tuckman, B. W., & Jensen, M. A. (1977). Stages of small-group development revisited. *Group and Organizational Studies, 2*(4), 419–427.

Turner, N. W. (1996). *Leading small groups: Basic skills for church and community organizations.* Valley Forge, PA: Judson Press.

Vander Kolk, C. J. (1985). *Introduction to group counseling and psychotherapy.* Columbus, OH: Merrill.

Van Hoose, W. H., & Kottler, J. A. (1985). *Ethical and legal issues in counseling and psychotherapy* (2nd ed.). San Francisco: Jossey-Bass.

Vassallo, T. (1998). Narrative group therapy with the seriously mentally ill: A case study. *Australian and New Zealand Journal of Family Therapy, 19*(1), 15–26.

Walters, R. P. (1989). Nonverbal communication in group counseling. In G. Gazda, *Group counseling: A developmental approach.* Boston: Allyn & Bacon.

Wastell, C. A. (1997). Description of an experiential course in group processes incorporating community-based practitioners. *Journal of Group Psychotherapy, Psychodrama, and Sociometry, 48*(1), 21–29.

Welfel, E. R. (1998). *Ethics in counseling and psychotherapy: Standards, research, and emerging issues.* Pacific Grove, CA: Brooks/Cole.

Wheelan, S. A. (1994). Group processes: A developmental perspective. Boston: Allyn & Bacon.

Whitaker, D. S., & Lieberman, M. (1964). *Psychotherapy through the group process.* New York: Atherton Press.

White, M., & Epston, D. (1990). *Narrative means to therapeutic ends.* New York: W. W. Norton.

Williams, C. B., Frame, M. W., & Green, E. (1999). Counseling groups for African American women: A focus on spirituality. *Journal for Specialists in Group Work, 24,* 260–273.

Wright, R. (1994). *The moral animal: The new science of evolutionary psychology.* New York: Pantheon.

Wubbolding, R. E. (1990). *Expanding reality therapy: Group counseling and multicultural dimensions.* Cincinnati: Real World Publications.

Yalom, I. D. (1980). *Existential psychotherapy.* New York: Basic Books.

Yalom, I. D. (1995). *Theory and practice of group psychotherapy* (4th ed.). New York: Basic Books.

INDEX